U.S. LEGAL WRITING FOR INTERNATIONAL LAWYERS AND LAW STUDENTS

■ ■ ■

Ann M. Piccard
Professor of Legal Skills
Stetson University College of Law

AMERICAN CASEBOOK SERIES®

WEST
ACADEMIC
PUBLISHING

American Casebook Series is a trademark registered in the U.S. Patent and Trademark Office.

© 2017 LEG, Inc. d/b/a West Academic
    444 Cedar Street, Suite 700
    St. Paul, MN 55101
    1-877-888-1330

West, West Academic Publishing, and West Academic are trademarks of West Publishing Corporation, used under license.

Printed in the United States of America

ISBN: 978-1-63459-472-1

ACKNOWLEDGMENTS

This book was written with the support of a research grant from Stetson University College of Law, but the seed for it was sown during a casual conversation in my office with one of West Academic Publishing's Acquisitions Editors. After using Jill Ramsfield's excellent *Culture to Culture* in the mid-2000s, I had been unable to find a more current textbook devoted to teaching U.S. legal writing to international lawyers and law students. The international lawyers who join my class every Fall semester are among my favorite students, and it was with great pleasure that I accepted the challenge of writing a textbook to help me, as well as other teachers, and these very exceptional students. If this book fulfills those goals, I will count it as a success. I wrote it on behalf of all the hardworking international students who are studying in U.S. law schools, and I hope it helps.

Special thanks are due to Julie Ann Embler, who spent countless hours over several semesters as my teaching assistant and so much more. While I sat in the chair and wrote, in the peace and quiet of my family's cabin in northern Minnesota, Julie Ann toiled away in steamy Gulfport, Florida, doing the research, checking the facts, and cleaning up after me. After she had graduated from law school and passed the Florida Bar with flying colors, Julie Ann continued to work with and for me. This book would not exist without her incredible commitment and hard work.

In the final stages of pulling together the manuscript, Danielle Breiter stepped up to the plate to whip things into shape. Working with Danielle has been one of the most valuable intellectual exercises of my teaching career, and her willingness and ability to step in at the last minute have been invaluable. Thank you, also, Alyssa Shook Aquaviva, Julius Matusewicz, and Monica Strady for lending me your written products.

Finally, and most importantly, this book could not have been written without the unfailing support and patience of the world's most wonderful husband, daughters, and son. To Charles, Liz, Mary, and Paul: You all are my life.

SUMMARY OF CONTENTS

TABLE OF CONTENTS

―――――――

U.S. Legal Writing for International Lawyers and Law Students

INTRODUCTION

WHY THIS BOOK MATTERS

▪ ▪ ▪

This book is based on my ten years of experience teaching international lawyers and law students to adapt to the methods of effective U.S. legal writing. Every lesson contained in this book is based on a question or a misconception or simply an area of significant confusion that I have witnessed among my own students. Added to my students' questions are those that arose during my experience as an international student pursuing an LL.M. in International Human Rights law from a university in a different nation, on a different continent. Aside from the substantive confusion of learning new legal systems, my own experience in adapting to even the relatively simple differences between American English and British English reinforced my understanding of the importance of writing for a particular type of reader. Knowing one's audience is one of the fundamental keys to successful writing.

When I was engaged in pursuit of my LL.M., writing essays that were marked by three different British professors, I had to do more than remember that the substance of my essays needed to differ from essays written for American law professors. Some differences were small. For example, I had to wince every time I left some poor little comma or period all alone, outside the protective arms of quotation marks—in American English, periods and commas are always placed inside quotation marks. In British English, they are placed outside those same quotation marks. But I reminded myself that the professors who graded my essays expected to see those small marks of punctuation left out in the cold to fend for themselves. I did my best to give my readers what they expected and what they wanted Every time I successfully changed my approach to writing to suit my audience, I learned something new to teach my own international students.

I empathize with the need to adapt, and I bring to the classroom, and to this book, my own experiences in doing so. The combination seems to be a winning one, by and large, as my students learn in quantifiable leaps and bounds. Many go on to pass various states' bar exams, including the notoriously difficult New York State Bar Exam, and still more return to their home countries well-equipped to bring added value to their universities, employers, and clients. As a teacher, these are my goals for my students. So far, so good.

1

This book, then, is a practice-oriented guide for internationally trained lawyers and visiting international law students who wish to become proficient in the written communication used by U.S. lawyers. It is a great pleasure to share with you, my readers, those who teach as well as those who study, the benefits of my own experiences, as well as those of my hundreds of students, in learning to think like U.S. lawyers. On behalf of myself and all of my students, past, present, and future, I welcome every reader to the journey.

Every year, law schools in the United States welcome more and more lawyers and law students from other countries. International lawyers, typically experienced and well-educated, generally enroll in one- or two-year Master of Laws (LL.M.) programs. They come for a wide variety of reasons. Some may come to make themselves more valuable to their clients and to their employers; they return home to resume the practice of law, primarily business law, with new professional skills. Others may come from nations where life is hard, even for those who are privileged and well-educated, with the hope of finding jobs in the United States that enable them to use their professional knowledge and education without having to complete an entire J.D. program. Some may hope to sit for a bar exam in one of the handful of states that will allow them to do so without having obtained a J.D. from an ABA-accredited law school. Still other international lawyers come to enroll in one of the many accelerated J.D. programs offered by U.S. law schools to those who are both proficient in English and already lawyers in their home nations. In other words, international LL.M. students come for personal, business, and other reasons; the reasons are as varied as are the lawyers themselves.

In addition to the LL.M. students, more law schools than ever before are welcoming international exchange students. Exchange students come from law schools around the world. Many are significantly younger than U.S. law students because in most parts of the world the law degree is an undergraduate, not a graduate, degree. Exchange students may be dealing with homesickness in addition to the cultural and educational challenges faced by all international students. The language barrier alone can be daunting, a fact well-known by anyone who has ever studied abroad.

This book is written for all of these students. It is a writing textbook. It is not an academic support manual that tries to teach international students how to pass exams in a U.S. law school. It is not a citation manual, like the Bluebook or the ALWD Manual. It is not a research guide. There are plenty of books available for all of those purposes because international students have the same learning needs in those areas as do U.S. law students. Similarly, there are many excellent writing style manuals available for any student who seeks to learn the conventions of legal writing in the United States; most law faculty who teach legal writing to international students will either require or recommend that their students purchase and use one of the many style manuals written specifically for lawyers or law students.

This book, specifically written for international students enrolled in U.S. law schools, illustrates and explains the skills that are commonly addressed in legal writing courses that most law schools require. Throughout the book, the substantive materials will be followed by exercises that provide students the opportunity to practice the skills implicated in those materials. The skills thus acquired by the students are transferrable to every other legal writing context.

The courses taken by international lawyers and law students tend to be as varied as the students themselves, but most students will (or should) be required to study U.S. legal writing. Their legal writing courses will probably have at least one common goal: to introduce and teach the skills— including not just writing but also research, citation, and professional responsibility—that will enable foreign-educated attorneys and exchange students to communicate effectively and ethically with any U.S.-educated attorney or judge.

Recent changes in the way U.S. lawyers work have increased the importance of writing in a lawyer's practice. The skills lawyers must possess have changed as the practice of law in the United States has changed. For example, more clients decline the services of lawyers who charge by the "billable hour," opting instead to retain lawyers who offer their services at flat-rate fees. This requires that practicing lawyers be skilled and adept at identifying legal issues, engaging in legal research, and drafting documents that clearly reflect the analysis of that research. Only criminal defense and prosecuting attorneys are guaranteed courtroom time, much less jury trial experience; only in a work of fiction is courtroom-style law practice still the norm. The courts are crowded, and while criminal defendants have certain speedy-trial rights under the U.S. Constitution, civil litigants do not.[1] Civil cases that go to trial may wait years to get to a courtroom, resulting in more and more cases being resolved outside the courtroom via settlement agreements or other types of dispute resolution.

In the United States lawyers spend more of their time in front of a computer screen than in front of a judge or jury. They must be able to resolve clients' problems by dealing with many types of people in many different situations, most often through written documents. To be effective advocates in today's legal system, U.S. lawyers must be able to communicate in easily-understood words, they must write well, and they

---

[1]   Chapter One explains that "civil" cases in the United States are those cases that do not involve a criminal prosecution. This is likely to be a very foreign concept to most students, but it is just one of many.

must have the skill to say what needs to be said concisely, clearly, and correctly. To be a lawyer, then, is to be a writer.

This textbook uses examples drawn from actual laws, cases, and legal opinions, but focuses in particular on case law because the common law[2], in particular, is most unfamiliar to people who study or practice law outside of the United States and the United Kingdom. The cases used in this book will show students what to look for in effectively written documents over the lifespan of administrative and civil cases and criminal prosecutions, in both the state and federal systems, from the initial client contact through the appeal of an adverse decision. This book does not use hypotheticals (fictional legal disputes) as examples because, frankly, there are more than enough real and fascinating cases in the U.S. system. As readers will come to see, probably quite early in the book, you really cannot make this stuff up.

As you read this book, bear in mind its two primary goals: 1) This book aims to serve as a tool that law professors may use to help international law students learn what effective legal writing looks like in the United States, and 2) This book endeavors to enable students to understand and acquire the skills needed to make their own legal writing effective in the United States. Whether the students are here for a year or for a lifetime, the writing principles that form the core of this book will position them to be successful legal writers in the United States.

And so we begin.

---

[2]   The generally accepted definition of common law is the law of the U.S. that derives from cases rather than statutes or regulations. For more explanations, see Martha A. Field, *Sources of Law: The Scope of Federal Common Law*, 99 Harv. L. Rev. 881, 890 (1986). Professor Field began her analysis by clarifying that she would "use 'federal common law' to refer to any rule of federal law created by a court (usually but not invariably a federal court) *when the substance of that rule is not clearly suggested by federal enactments*—constitutional or congressional."

CHAPTER 1

THE ART OF LEGAL WRITING IN THE UNITED STATES

■ ■ ■

> We'll always be able to find something or someone that says, "Yes, you're right." But our goal should be to understand the opposite of what we believe, put it into context with what we think is true, and then see where we stand. Otherwise, what we "think" we know will someday be trumped by what we don't.[1]

> [T]here are known knowns: there are things we know we know. We also know there are known unknowns. That is to say, there are some things [we know] we do not know. But there are also unknown unknowns—the ones we don't know we don't know.[2]

These two quotes illustrate the good, the bad, and the ugly of written American English. Both say essentially the same thing: everyone has something to learn. As legal writers, we must put aside any preconceived notions of what is true. Written legal analysis involves identifying issues, researching for answers, and then demonstrating what happens when the law, the research result, is applied to a new set of facts. Even persuasive writing must apply the law as it stands. Thus, the results of research dictate what is written, rather than vice versa.

For lawyers and law students who come to the United States to study U.S. law, the prospect of having to adapt both thinking and writing processes to a new system can be intimidating. But a piece of good news for international students is that they face the same analytical and writing hurdles as do the law students who were born in the United States. Almost no students sitting in law school classrooms around the world have been taught the types of analytical thinking and writing that are introduced in a U.S. law school. This puts the international students on the same footing as their U.S. classmates.

---

[1] Carl Richards, New York Times (May 20, 2013), http://bucks.blogs.nytimes.com/2013/05/20/challenge-what-you-think-you-know/?_r=0.

[2] Donald Rumsfeld, Known and Unknown: A Memoir (Sentinel 2010). Donald Rumsfeld served the United States in many ways, including as Ambassador to Iraq in 1983, as President Ronald Reagan's envoy to Saddam Hussein. Despite his career of service, Mr. Rumsfeld is probably best known for malapropisms and incomprehensibly convoluted sentence structure. Students might be well advised to use Mr. Rumsfeld as an example of what not to do.

The primary goal of any course designed to teach students the skills needed for U.S. legal research, reasoning, or writing is to introduce to students the requirements of thinking like a lawyer. This is just as difficult for a U.S. student as it is for an international student: it is hard, and it takes a lot of time and practice, but it is equally hard for every single law student.

Furthermore, the goal for the international student is the same as it is for the J.D. student born and educated in the United States: to adapt to the way U.S.-trained lawyers and judges approach any legal question. We might call it legal analysis, or critical thinking, or we might refer to various forms of logic. Whatever we call it, this is what makes law school so challenging for every law student.

Another piece of good news is that if the international student has studied English grammar rules relatively recently, that student may be pleasantly surprised to learn that he or she has a distinct advantage over many law students who were educated in the United States. Students in the United States come to law school with a wide variety of educational backgrounds, having pursued a broad range of areas of study. Depending on the type of university or college[3] they attended or their undergraduate major, they may have completed their Bachelor's degrees without having written more than one or two research papers of relatively short length. Some undergraduate students write doctoral-level theses as a prerequisite to graduation, but this is an exception rather than the rule. Many U.S. university degrees require students to undertake almost no re-writing based on substantive critiques from their professors. In this regard, internationally educated students may be better prepared than their U.S. classmates.

On the other hand, language and cultural barriers can make the tasks of international law students more challenging than those of U.S. born students. International students' English proficiency is as varied as are the students themselves, and some will struggle with the language more than others.

When all of the good and the bad news is totaled, international students should see that the outlook is good. To the international law student: You are now reading a book written for the sole purpose of guiding you as you acquire the skills needed for effective written legal communication in the United States. The challenges presented by learning to think and write like a U.S. lawyer are both manageable and rewarding. Putting in the hours of work required to meet those challenges is never

---

[3] In the United States, a college is a post-secondary institution that offers undergraduate degrees. A University is also a post-secondary institution, but it offers both undergraduate and graduate degrees. Colleges may exist within universities, as Stetson University's College of Law does. In the U.S., a law degree is a graduate degree, not an undergraduate degree; the youngest U.S. law students are typically twenty-two years old.

boring. It might, in fact, be entertaining at times. The cases discussed in the following sections of this book are examples of case law that might defy imagination. Again, as we say in the United States, you cannot make up this stuff.

A. AN OVERVIEW OF THE U.S. LEGAL AND LEGAL EDUCATION SYSTEMS

In the U.S., our approach to legal education is largely shaped by the fact that there is no such thing as a single body of "U.S. law." Instead, there is a vast, multi-part body of constitutional, statutory, administrative, and common law, from local, state, and federal sources, covering criminal as well as civil law. All of these laws have the potential to interact in a system that defies memorization. In addition, case law plays a very significant role, both as the source of law in some areas (common law) and as the guide—sometimes mandatory, sometimes persuasive—for interpreting statutory and other types of law.

A Note to International Students

In the United States, any legal action that does not involve a government prosecuting an alleged criminal is referred to as a "civil" case. Unlike non-common law jurisdictions, the U.S. does not use the term "civil law" in reference to a Code or statute. Civil cases are simply all cases that are not criminal cases.

As a result of the unique role case law plays, legal education, especially in its early stages, focuses extensively on case law. The format for U.S. legal education usually follows some basic principles established in the late 1800s by a man named Christopher Columbus Langdell, whose given names (Christopher Columbus) might strike readers as ironic if they are familiar with the "discovery" of this continent by the Spanish explorer Christopher Columbus. Professor Langdell served as Dean of the Harvard Law School from 1870 until 1895. He created the system of studying and analyzing cases that is still the norm in U.S. law schools today. This "case method" is designed to change the way students think, to change the way they approach legal questions: the way they learn, as a mythical and fictional Professor Kingsfield droned in the book and movie *The Paper Chase*,[4] to "think like a lawyer."

Many student readers have no doubt been forewarned about the Socratic Method of instruction traditionally used in U.S. law schools. The Socratic Method creates a classroom dynamic that is the polar opposite of most students' previous classroom experiences. When a law professor uses

---

[4]   John Jay Osborne, THE PAPER CHASE (Whitston Publishing Company 2004); *The Paper Chase*, 20th Century Fox 1973.

the Socratic Method, students are called upon, traditionally at random and with no warning, to answer rather than to ask questions about the materials assigned for that day's lesson. Most law students are intimidated by the Socratic Method, and would much rather be asking than answering questions—especially when called upon to do so before a room full of their peers. It may be frustrating when a student is finally able to ask a question, only to be met with yet another question from the professor. However, generations of lawyers and thousands of former law students can attest to the effectiveness of the Socratic Method, whether in spite of or because of the fear and loathing its use inspires in the hearts and minds of law students across the United States.

Learning how to "think like a lawyer" carries over from the classroom to the written documents that law students and lawyers are required to produce. Every document that becomes a part of every proceeding in the U.S. legal system must be organized in a recognizable form of logic. Recognizable logic is required from the first written communication with a client or opposing counsel, through pre-trial and trial documents, and on into post-trial proceedings, if any, perhaps going as far as an appeal to the United States Supreme Court. Whether a court case will eventually be filed is often determined by the effectiveness of a lawyer's initial written communications, which might be letters or even emails. In the U.S. legal system, cases are more likely to be resolved before trial than to proceed to full courtroom proceedings.

> This part of the discussion refers to trials and courtrooms, where both civil and criminal cases are heard, in the local, state, and federal systems. Some trials are heard by juries, whose decisions must then be approved by presiding judges, while most are simply heard by a judge. But students should remember that there is a vast network of sources of law in the U.S., at the local, state, and federal levels. If you have studied the three branches of government established by the U.S. Constitution and by most state Constitutions, you may remember that those three branches are the judicial, the legislative, and the executive. The judicial branch is the source of case law; the legislative branch enacts the codified laws; and the executive branch creates and enforces the regulations that comprise administrative law. The balance and separation of these three branches of government are at the very heart of the U.S. legal system, so students must keep these things in mind at all times.

A well-written letter or email that positions the parties to resolve their legal dispute without the need for any formal proceedings saves time, money, and stress for everyone involved. Obviously, with so much at stake it is important to do it well. When the problem cannot be resolved amicably and the case goes forward, more written documents are required. Trials may be followed by appeals, which proceed from the trial court to an intermediate appellate court and ultimately to the highest court in the jurisdiction. Being a lawyer in the United States means being a writer.

All law students, including those who have come from very different legal and educational systems, are expected to acquire the skills needed to engage in the process of critical thinking promoted by the Socratic method and to then express analysis and persuasive arguments in writing in ways that U.S. lawyers, professors, and judges will recognize as demonstrating the writer's ability to "think like a lawyer." The sections below describe various writing tools for organizational, style, and editing approaches that are used widely in legal writing in the United States, although some writers may call them by slightly different names.

Students should remember that the most successful U.S. lawyers are those who communicate most effectively in writing. When using this book, students should remain aware that the exercises are derived from real cases, not hypothetical ones, and thus the skills students gain by successfully completing the exercises are real-life, not hypothetical, skills.

B. SOME BASIC TOOLS OF THE LEGAL WRITING TRADE

1. CREAC, IRAC, TREAT, AND ALL THEIR VARIATIONS

Law students and lawyers need to write with some expected and recognizable structure. Whether the student is answering an essay question during an exam, writing a seminar paper for an upper-level course, or writing a memorandum that analyzes a client's situation, the quality of the written product usually dictates the student's successes (or lack thereof).

The first tool used to teach any law student how to organize legal analysis might be called IRAC or CREAC, or some similar acronym. This organizational structure can be used effectively in virtually any legal writing context. The core concept is that the writer begins with a sentence that articulates the essence of the analysis—a thesis sentence, a prediction, or anything that answers the question the writer was asked to answer. For CREAC purposes, we call this the Conclusion; in using IRAC, the thesis sentence identifies the Issue—the legal question that needs to be answered. The next sentence is an articulation of the Rule of law that is applicable to the issue; this requires a citation to the legal authority from which it came. The Rule is usually then Explained by describing its origin or context. The Application of that Rule to the new facts that present the underlying issue is the most important part because it demonstrates the writer's ability to apply established law to new facts. All of this ends by returning to the initial Conclusion.

IRAC, CREAC, CRAC, TREAT: whatever the acronym, all involve some form of identifying an issue or predicting a conclusion (I or C), either of which might be a thesis sentence at the beginning of a paragraph (T). When added to rule explanation plus analysis (application of the cited rule to new facts), leading explicitly back to the conclusion, this equals CREAC. It might seem odd to start with a conclusion, because a conclusion is, by definition, the end—and we do not normally start at the end. However, many good writers believe, and some reliable research shows, that it is most effective for you, the writer, to tell the reader what you intend to write, then write it, and then tell the reader what you just wrote. It might feel repetitive to the writer, but if it helps the reader it is a good thing to do.

> If IRAC is not included in your law school's orientation program, or if you are unclear about the purpose or meaning of using a logical framework, keep reading; if things do not clear up soon, do not hesitate to make an appointment with a professor, a Teaching Assistant, or the school's Academic Support personnel. In the U.S., law students are expected to ask for help when they need it. If your background has not prepared you to ask for help, it may take some adjustment. However, remember that knowing when to ask for help is never a sign of weakness; it is instead a sign that the student has been working hard and questions naturally arise, for which the student is expected to seek answers. Law school is a new culture for everyone, not just for international students.

By the end of your first semester in a U.S. law school, this organizational method should be second nature to you, even if you are learning of it for the first time as you read this book. Only law students and lawyers think this way; other fields of study might find it strange and unfamiliar, but on some level, every legal reader in the United States expects to see analytical legal documents organized along the lines of CREAC or IRAC. It may help to look at each piece of this acronym separately; remember that every aspect of this is transferrable to fit the context of analytical legal writing in the United States.

a.   Conclusion or Issue

U.S. legal analysis is largely dependent on "issue spotting." **The issue in a case is the precise legal question that needs to be answered;** there may be multiple issues in any case. Spotting the issue, in an exam or in a client interview or in a conversation with opposing counsel or a professor, is absolutely necessary in order to produce anything that might be of value to anyone. Lawyers look for the issues, or the questions, in the way other professionals look for answers. Issue spotting is crucial to success on a law school exam, and it is absolutely the most important thing to do when writing essays for any state's bar exam. Ultimately, this first part of IRAC states the question to be addressed.

In many forms of legal writing, the Issue is replaced by a **conclusion** or a **thesis** sentence. Each has the same function: they identify the precise legal issue under discussion. An Issue is framed as a question, while a Conclusion or Thesis sentence is framed as a statement of what the writer believes the answer to the issue is (in a predictive document) or should be (in a persuasive document).

> Remember the possible acronyms: IRAC is just one form of CREAC or CRAC or TREAT. Don't be distracted by the label; focus on the purpose. Writing in a predictable, logical way is the most important skill any law student can hope to master in a first-year U.S. law school curriculum. International students whose time in a U.S. law school is limited to one or two years should expect to master this skill as quickly as possible.

b. Rule

The rule is the law that will, could, or should be applied to any new case that involves the same issue as the rule. The "rule" in this context might be a statute (local, state or federal); it might be one part of a court's written decision (any kind of court); it might be a constitutional protection; or it might be an administrative regulation or an order from an administrative law judge. When identifying the rule in case law, students are well-advised to bear in mind that the rule of law from the court is always more important than the facts. The rule from a case is that part of the court's decision that becomes precedent: the legal principle that can be applied to future cases. It is not the holding, which is applicable only to that case. Identifying the applicable rule is dependent upon identifying the relevant issue. These pieces are inseparable.

Many legal writers also include an **explanation** of the rule by describing the source of that rule. If a cited rule comes from case law, the writer might provide a one paragraph **case description**, describing the key components of that precedent case, such as the most legally relevant facts, the court's holding, and an explanation of the court's reasoning. This helps any reader understand the context in which the rule was created. Explanations of codified rules (local, state, or federal ordinances or statutes) might, instead, include legislative history to establish context.

Example of a Case Description/Explanation of a Case	
Rule	Any action by the employee that is "detrimental to the [employer's] business interest, his reputation, [or] violate[s] the [employee's] duty to [reasonably] advance the interest of the business," constitutes good cause for termination. *Curtis v. Reeves*, 736 S.W.2d 108, 112 (Tenn. Ct. App. 1987).
Facts	In *Curtis*, the employer testified that terminating the employee was necessary because the employee had negatively affected the employer/landlord's reputation among his tenants "by discussing his marital problems and making derogatory remarks about him." *Id.* at 110. Specifically, the employee asked one tenant how she could stay in a "building when her landlord, the [employer], was of such low moral character." *Id.*
Holding	The court determined there was good cause for termination, reversed the trial court's decision, and dismissed the employee's suit for wrongful termination. *Id.*
Reasoning	The court reasoned that though "actual loss is not essential," by "poisoning the tenants" against her employer the employee had disregarded her duty to put the "best interest" of the business first, and consequently injured the employer's reputation and business interest. *Id.* at 112.

c.   Analysis

In any form of legal writing, the analysis is the bit that makes the difference between good, bad, and mediocre work product, between effective and ineffective writing. This is where the writer demonstrates the **application** of the cited rule to the real or hypothetical client's situation. The "A" in IRAC or CREAC can stand for Analysis and it can stand for Application. It may not be the longest part of a document, but it is always the most important. And again, if the issue has been misidentified, or if the rule that is applied does not actually address the issue that must be answered, the written product has no value. It is especially important that the Analysis actually demonstrates application of cited rules rather than just describe it.

> *Do This:*   Just as in the precedent case, in our client's case the employee may not have caused actual damage to the employer, but by saying untrue things about the employer and driving away potential customers, the employee failed in his "duty to put the

'best interest' of the business first," and consequently injured the employer's reputation and business interest. *Id.*

Not This: Because the facts of the precedent case are similar to the facts of our client's case, the outcome will probably be the same.

d. Conclusion

The conclusion is where the writer sums up the three preceding parts. In persuasive writing, the conclusion tells the reader how the question posed in the issue should be answered. In predictive or objective writing, or in the answer to an essay question on an exam, the conclusion tells the reader how the question posed in the issue is most likely to be answered. In many types of legal writing the conclusion is no more than one sentence; in some contexts it requires more elaboration and recommendations. As with the analysis, it may be short but its presence is essential: without a conclusion, the reader is left to wonder what the point of the writing was supposed to have been.

CREAC Example in Predictive/Objective Memorandum	
C	Mr. Fears appears to have had good cause to terminate Ms. French's employment.
R	Good cause for termination exists when an employee fails in his or her "duty to [reasonably] advance the interest of the business," even when the employer can show no "actual monetary loss." *Curtis v. Reeves*, 736 S.W.2d 108, 112 (Tenn. Ct. App. 1987).
E	In *Curtis*, the court explained that the employee had negatively affected the employer/landlord's reputation among his tenants "by discussing his marital problems and making derogatory remarks about him." *Id.* at 110. Specifically, the employee asked one tenant how she could stay in a "building when her landlord, the [employer], was of such low moral character." *Id.* The court determined there was good cause for termination, reversed the trial court's decision, and dismissed the employee's suit. *Id.* The court reasoned that though "actual loss is not essential," by "poisoning the tenants" against her employer the employee had disregarded her duty to put the "best interest" of the business first, and consequently injured the employer's reputation and business interest. *Id.* at 112.

A	Similarly, Ms. French "negatively affected" Mr. Fears' reputation with potential customers by claiming, untruthfully, that Mr. Fears substituted an inferior grade of shrimp for the Key West shrimp customers sought. *Id.* at 110. Even though Mr. Fears cannot show how much money, if any, he lost as a result of his employee's false accusations, the employee had a duty to advance the interests of Mr. Fears' business, and telling lies about the quality of Mr. Fears' products, or about his moral character, would violate that duty.
C	A court would likely find that Mr. Fears had good cause to terminate her employment, and Mr. Fears should not be held responsible for any wrongful termination alleged by Ms. French.

Using IRAC, CREAC, or any variation thereof will put your writing into an organized framework that makes it easier for any reader to understand the point of the written document. As writers, we usually think we have written what we intended to write; using this structure as a checklist will help ensure that your reader will agree with your perception that you've written what you intended to write.

> *Writing Tip:* Remember, it is always easier to edit than it is to write; do not wait until you think you have the material mastered and organized before you begin to write. Start writing sooner rather than later, and then be sure to go back through your own writing and identify the pieces of IRAC or CREAC. It can feel tedious and burdensome, but it can also make the difference between writing something that accomplishes its purpose and writing something that seems to have no purpose. Using CREAC or IRAC is the best way for you, as a writer, to invest your time.

> Most lawyers in private practice in the U.S. still operate primarily on a "billable hour" system. This means the lawyer records how he or she spends every working hour, in six-minute increments, and the client is billed accordingly. The more billable hours, the more money for the lawyer. Time is, literally, money. If a lawyer spends two hours writing something that has no value, the lawyer cannot ask the client to pay for that time. Wasted time is wasted money, so learning to write effectively and efficiently is money in the bank.

Now that you have been introduced to organization of analysis, try this: In the paragraphs below you should be able to identify a form of IRAC or CREAC. Begin by looking for the sentence that identifies the *issue* the court was faced with deciding. You should then see the *rule(s)* identifying the law that is applicable to this issue. Note the citations that tell a reader the source of the rule; citations are as much a part of the rule as anything else. Next, look at the way the court *applies* the rule to the facts of the case under consideration. This is one sign of clear and complete analysis, because it demonstrates—it does not just describe—application of the rule to the facts of the new case. And finally, the court's *conclusion* should be apparent because it tells you how the court decided this case. To verify your understanding of IRAC, take apart the excerpt below and put each sentence in its proper place in a list as follows:

a.   Issue or Conclusion

b.   Rule (with citations) and Explanation

c.   Analysis

d.   Conclusion

Defendant assigns as error certain portions of the charge relating to first degree burglary and to the sufficiency of the evidence to sustain a conviction for first degree burglary.

To justify submission of felonious breaking or entering as a permissible verdict there must be evidence tending to show that defendant could have gained entry to victim's motel room by means other than a burglarious breaking, *i.e.*, a forcible entry. *State v. Bell*, supra; *State v. Chambers*, 218 N.C. 442, 11 S.E.2d 280 (1940). Here, all the evidence tends to show a burglarious breaking. A breaking in the law of burglary constitutes any act of force, however slight, "employed to effect an entrance through any usual or unusual place of ingress, whether open, partly open, or closed." *State v. Wilson*, 289 N.C. 531, 223 S.E.2d 311 (1976). A breaking may be actual or constructive. *Id.* A constructive breaking occurs where entrance is obtained in consequence of violence commenced or threatened by defendant. *Id.* The evidence in this case tends to show that defendant gained entry into victim's motel room by pushing victim into the room as he opened the door. This clearly constitutes a constructive breaking. Accordingly, it was not error for the trial court to exclude felonious breaking or entering as a permissible verdict. This portion of defendant's fifth assignment of error is overruled.[5]

For more practice: Assume that you have been retained to represent a client who was convicted of burglary in North Carolina and who now wishes to appeal that conviction. The essential issue of the case involves the method by which your client admittedly entered the apartment that was burglarized: Your client simply followed his co-defendants into the apartment; he did not, himself, force open the door, he simply walked through a door that had already been forced open. Analyze his chances of succeeding in appealing his conviction for burglary under the North Carolina law applied in the above excerpts. Write objectively, as if you are

---

[5]   This sample is taken from *State v. Jolly*, 254 S.E. 2d 1, 5 (N.C. 1979).

still evaluating the potential merits of the client's case. Use CREAC. When you have completed this exercise, you may check the substance of your response by reading *State v. McCoy*, 207 N.C. App. 378, 699 S.E. 2d 685 (2010).

2.   PASS

Having an organizational framework for your document is the first step toward effective legal writing. Now that you have an understanding of IRAC/CREAC, it is time to turn to the skills that are required to write appropriately in any context. All legal writing is written for a particular purpose and a particular audience; U.S. lawyers never write just for the sake of writing (unless they write fiction as a hobby[6]). Legal writing is the law student's, or lawyer's, work product.

As work product, legal writing is the visible result of the lawyer's research, analysis, and writing. If it does not demonstrate that the lawyer has earned his or her fee, the lawyer should not expect to be paid. Not many of us can afford, or even want, to work for free; therefore, legal writing must accomplish its goals. To ensure that your legal writing will serve its purposes, and to be effective, remember this straightforward mechanism: always write with an eye on your **PASS**—Purpose, Audience, Scope, and Stance.

a.   Purpose

Some legal writing is designed to persuade its reader, whether the reader is a client, an opposing counsel, or a court. Some legal writing is designed to inform its reader: here is the law, here is its source, and here is how it is likely to be applied to this client's case. Overall, law students write in a variety of contexts, and with a different purpose in each, whether it be in their Legal Writing classes, in response to exam questions, in lengthy seminar papers, for publication in a law review, and sometimes in response to assignments from supervising or employing attorneys. Before you begin to write, think about the purpose of your document, and make sure the finished product fulfills that purpose.

b.   Audience

Most lawyers and law students in the United States write all day, every day. Students write case briefs for their own study guides and in preparation for class. Those case briefs should look quite different from a case description that might be included in an objective, internal office memorandum written for a supervising attorney, which would in turn look different from a case explanation used to support an argument in a trial or

---

[6] Practicing law apparently provides good fodder for crafting popular fiction, as demonstrated by the best-selling author John Grisham. Fiction is fun, and it has its place, but it is not legal writing.

appellate brief written for a judge. Writers in every discipline succeed best when they write to their intended audience. As just one example, a client letter might not include any citations to authority because many clients have no understanding of the meaning or significance of citations. But in a document intended for another lawyer or a judge to read, citations are essential because they demonstrate the law's support of the writer's position. Citations, as you will see, show that the lawyer has done the research necessary to support any conclusions or predictions. Knowing your audience will always make you a better writer.

c.   Scope

Remember when we addressed the importance of identifying the issue? The issue defines the scope of every kind of legal writing. The issue is the question that must be answered. If the issue is misidentified, the writing has no value. The issue might be correctly identified but the written product might not actually answer the question posed by the issue or the document might analyze things other than the issue. The document fails to accomplish its purpose if the issue is not correctly identified and answered, and if the focus does not remain on the issue. There is no point in writing at all if the writing does not address the issue that needs to be addressed. Legal writing requires focus and precision: everything a lawyer or law student writes must fulfill, but not exceed, its scope.

d.   Stance

Think about whether your document is intended to persuade or inform. Are you writing to predict an outcome or to demonstrate why your reader(s) should agree with your conclusion(s)? These are the things that define the stance from which your document must be written. If a legal writer misinterprets the required stance, the written product will be, at best, pointless; at worst, it will be offensive. If a seminar paper requires that the student pose a previously unanswered question, the student could write ten thousand pages of interesting ideas without fulfilling the assignment, and the student's grade would reflect that deficiency. If a lawyer writes a brief to the United States Supreme Court but uses a tone that would be appropriate for a client advice letter, that lawyer's future is dim indeed. Understanding stance requires understanding the nuances of the U.S. legal system, including jurisdiction and procedure. You should not expect it to be easy the first time you write, or even the tenth time. It takes practice.

All of this takes practice, and it can become discouraging for students who must cope with the difficulty of trying to write like lawyers. But every legal writer uses a variety of tools to write more effectively, and every time those tools are used the writer's skills are honed. PASS, like IRAC or CREAC, is an invaluable tool in every type of legal writing. These tools will always make your writing better, and they should always be used to your advantage.

Now that you know about PASS, try this: Read the passage below, which is a portion of a legal document, and try to identify the document's Purpose, Audience, Scope, and Stance. You may need to guess to a certain extent, but you should be able to determine why this document was written, who its intended audience may have been, what its scope was, and the stance from which it was written. To verify your understanding of PASS, create a list as follows:

a.   Purpose

b.   Audience

c.   Scope

d.   Stance

Insufficient Evidence of Nighttime

"The offense of first-degree burglary consists of six elements: (1) the breaking, (2) and entering, (3) in the nighttime, (4) into a dwelling house or sleeping apartment of another, (5) which is actually occupied at the time of the offense, and (6) with the intent to commit a felony therein. . . . If, however, the breaking and entering into a dwelling house or sleeping apartment of another with the intent to commit a felony therein occurs during the daytime, the offense committed is felonious breaking and entering, and not burglary." *State v. Cox*, 281 N.C. 131, 187 S.E.2d 785 (1972). In North Carolina, there is no statutory definition of nighttime; however, our courts adhere to the common law definition of nighttime as that time after sunset and before sunrise "when it is so dark that a man's face cannot be identified except by artificial light or moonlight." *State v. Frank*, 284 N.C. 137, 145, 200 S.E.2d 169, 175 (1973). Therefore, to survive the motion to dismiss, the State must have produced substantial evidence of nighttime. *State v. Barnett*, 113 N.C.App. 69, 74, 437 S.E.2d 711, 714–715 (1993).

Here, there is no substantial evidence to infer the breaking and entering of the Andrews' residence was at "nighttime." The Andrews were not awakened during the night (T. p. 16). When they awoke, saw their home had been entered, called police, and saw the car was gone, it was light outside (T. pp. 16–18). All of the times given—Sandra Andrews "about 7:00, 7:30" (T. p. 16) and Officer Khan "a little after 7:00" (T. p. 28)—are after the 6:57 a.m. time of sunrise on 14 November 2012 in Winston-Salem reported by the U.S. Naval Observatory (R. pp. 17–21; T. pp. 70, 72–73). Moses was only a block away when police caught him in the

Andrews' car about an hour after the Andrews awoke (T. pp. 27–30).

Even considered in the light most favorable to the State, the evidence establishes a breaking and entering of the Andrews residence only at some point in a time frame from night to after sunrise. Accordingly, this case is indistinguishable from *State v. Barnett*, 113 N.C.App. 69, 437 S.E.2d 711, above, where the Court of Appeals reversed a conviction of first degree burglary and remanded for judgment on a conviction of felony breaking or entering because: "The evidence, in the light most favorable to the State . . . shows someone broke into the . . . home between 10:00 p.m. on 3 April 1992 and around 6:30 a.m. on 4 April 1992 when [the homeowner] awoke to find her purse gone and her back door open. . . . The State did not present any evidence as to the condition of light outside when [the homeowner] arose . . . but we take judicial notice that on 4 April 1992 in Gaston County, civil twilight began at 5:41 a.m., and the sun rose at 6:07 a.m." 113 N.C. App. at 75, 437 S.E.2d at 715. Here, the State did present evidence as to the condition of light when Mr. and Mrs. Andrews arose—Sandra Andrews' testimony it was light outside (T. p. 16).

Absent any evidence from which to infer Moses did not get up after spending the night in the Little house (T. pp. 57–59, 65), then wake up the Andrews by breaking and entering their home after sunrise and leaving with the keys to Andrews' car (T. pp. 16–18), the evidence does nothing more than raise a suspicion of guilt of burglary. The Superior Court should have granted Moses' motion at the conclusion of the evidence to dismiss the burglary charge (T. pp. 74–77) and should have submitted to the jury only the lesser included offense of felony breaking and entering for the breaking and entering of the Andrews home.[7]

3. THE THREE C'S

Many U.S. law students, and many U.S. residents who are not trained or educated in the law, think that writing like a lawyer means using lots of fancy words—the longer, the better. Nothing could be further from the truth. The best legal writing is that which is clear, concise, and correct.

---

[7] To see this document in its entirety, look up the briefs that were filed in this case: *State v. Moses*, 768 S.E. 2d 63, 2014 WL 3382021 (N.C. App.). Many jurisdictions in the United States have traditionally distinguished burglary as a crime that may only be committed at night by breaking and entering another's home, without consent, and with the intent to commit some sort of felony therein. Other jurisdictions have removed the "at night" element, but burglary is still a unique crime in the United States due to the sanctity and expectations of privacy and safety in one's own home.

a.   Clear

Legal writing in the United States is not creative or fancy or even, necessarily, pretty. But it must be clear. The writer who tries to hide things from the reader is a failure. The best writing is the clearest writing. For example, read the following passage written recently by the U.S. Supreme Court:

> These considerations lead to the conclusion that the right to marry is a fundamental right inherent in the liberty of the person, and under the Due Process and Equal Protection Clauses of the Fourteenth Amendment couples of the same-sex may not be deprived of that right and that liberty. The Court now holds that same-sex couples may exercise the fundamental right to marry.[8]

The clarity of these two sentences should leave no doubt about the Court's decision, regardless of whether the reader is a trained, experienced U.S. lawyer or an international law student reading U.S. case law for the very first time.

b.   Concise

Concise writing is always preferable to verbose writing. Think about efficient use of the reader's time, and you will recognize that fewer words are better than more so long as the essential purpose of the writing is not sacrificed. Concise writing does not mean incomplete writing; it will not work to simply take out some words here and there to keep your word count low. Instead, concise writing is that which makes the best use of the words it does include, without adding any that are unnecessary. Write what needs to be written, and move on. Notice in the passage below that the U.S. Supreme Court did not feel compelled to enumerate every right protected under the Bill of Rights.[9] The following is an example of concise, clear writing:

> Under the Due Process Clause of the Fourteenth Amendment, no State shall "deprive any person of life, liberty, or property, without due process of law." The fundamental liberties protected by this Clause include most of the rights enumerated in the Bill of Rights.

---

[8] *Obergefell v. Hodges*, ___ U.S. ___, 135S. Ct. 2584 (2015). In this landmark ruling, the Supreme Court analyzed the Constitution's applicability to the institution of marriage between members of the same sex. Whether one agrees or disagrees with the Court's decision, the clarity of the writing cannot be denied.

[9] The "common wisdom" is that the Bill of Rights, contained in Amendments One through Ten, were added to the original Constitution to protect "individual rights" such as: the rights to freedom of speech, press, religion, and assembly; the right to privacy; the rights to be free from unreasonable searches and seizures; and the right to due process under the law. *See generally* Akhil Reed Amar, *The Bill of Rights as a Constitution*, 100 Yale L.J. 1131 (1991). Professor Amar points out that an entire law school course is often devoted to studying just one of the rights enumerated in the Bill of Rights. But that should not prevent you from seeing the Court's concise, clear writing.

See *Duncan v. Louisiana*, 391 U.S. 145, 147–149, 88 S.Ct. 1444, 20 L.Ed.2d 491 (1968). In addition these liberties extend to certain personal choices central to individual dignity and autonomy, including intimate choices that define personal identity and beliefs. See, e.g., *Eisenstadt v. Baird*, 405 U.S. 438, 453, 92 S.Ct. 1029, 31 L.Ed.2d 349 (1972); *Griswold v. Connecticut*, 381 U.S. 479, 484–486, 85 S.Ct. 1678, 14 L.Ed.2d 510 (1965).[10]

In terms of concise writing, note the role the citations play in the above passage. Each citation supports the correctness of the Court's assertion. The citations speak for themselves, and no explanation is needed. Remember to let citations do their jobs, so words are not wasted.

c.   Correct

No amount of clear, concise writing, however well organized and brilliant it might be, can overcome a lack of correctness. If legal writing is inaccurate, it has no value, and its author has no credibility. This observation should bring you full circle, back to the importance of correctly identifying the issue, the question that must be answered. If the issue is whether the Constitution's guarantee of due process extends to marriage between two people of the same sex, it could never be correct to analyze, for example, a dog's right to marry a cat. It would simply be wrong (not to mention silly) to do so.

There is no such thing as writing well enough to compensate for incorrect analysis. The issue must be correctly identified, and the writing must demonstrate credible application of primary, binding authority to new facts. One of the most common complaints lawyers have about their law clerks or new associates is that the inexperienced person will research and respond to a question that differs from the question posed by the supervising lawyer. Clients will not pay for incorrect work, and lawyers will not pay their underlings for it. There is almost always room for disagreement, but in the end, legal analysis requires correct application of law to facts. An example appears below, taken from the dissenting opinion issued by Justices Roberts, Scalia, and Thomas regarding same-sex marriages:

Although the policy arguments for extending marriage to same-sex couples may be compelling, the legal arguments for requiring such an extension are not. The fundamental right to marry does not include a right to make a State change its definition of marriage. And a State's decision to maintain the meaning of marriage that has persisted in every culture throughout human history can hardly be called irrational. In short, our Constitution does not enact any one theory of marriage.

---

[10]   This passage also comes from *Obergefell*, 135 S. Ct. at 2589.

The people of a State are free to expand marriage to include same-sex couples, or to retain the historic definition.[11]

The dissenting Justices wrote an opinion grounded in their interpretation of states' rights under the U.S. Constitution. It is a solid legal argument, albeit an unsuccessful one.

C. BRINGING IT ALL TOGETHER

IRAC, CREAC, PASS, and the three C's: many acronyms that require much practice in order to produce effective legal writing. Having seen some examples and deconstructed others, try the following exercise.

YOUR ASSIGNMENT: WRITING TOOLS

Below you will find a portion of a legal document. Your assignment is to identify the issue, rule, application, and conclusion, as well as the purpose, audience, scope, and stance. In the process, evaluate the degree to which this passage is clear, concise, and correct. If you find it lacking in any respect, be assured that your assessment may be valid; articulate and identify the deficiencies, if any, in terms of CREAC, PASS, and the three C's.

> No union is more profound than marriage, for it embodies the highest ideals of love, fidelity, devotion, sacrifice, and family. In forming a marital union, two people become something greater than once they were. As some of the petitioners in these cases demonstrate, marriage embodies a love that may endure even past death. It would misunderstand these men and women to say they disrespect the idea of marriage. Their plea is that they do respect it, respect it so deeply that they seek to find its fulfillment for themselves. Their hope is not to be condemned to live in loneliness, excluded from one of civilization's oldest institutions. They ask for equal dignity in the eyes of the law. The Constitution grants them that right.

> The judgment of the Court of Appeals for the Sixth Circuit is reversed.

Complete your assessment in the following list to verify your understanding of CREAC, PASS, and the three C's:

a.   Conclusion or Issue

b.   Rule of Law

c.   Application or Analysis

d.   Conclusion

e.   Purpose

f.   Audience

---

[11] *Id.* at 2611.

     g.   Scope

     h.   Stance

     i.   Clear?

     j.   Concise?

     k.   Correct?

If you find it difficult to identify or evaluate the qualities listed above, now is the time to explore the difficulties inherent in legal writing. There is no such thing as a question that is not worth asking. Instead, the reluctance to ask questions is a sign of weakness. This may be quite different from the academic culture in which you were educated, but in the Unites States it is a sign of intellectual strength to ask questions. Remember that U.S. legal education is based on asking, rather than answering, questions.

D. DRAFTING, REWRITING, AND TIME MANAGEMENT

The concept of rewriting is generally a new one for all U.S. law students, regardless of their place of origin or the quality of their university education. However, students must accept rewriting as a necessary part of the writing process. Lawyers across this country routinely write three or more drafts, or versions, of the same document. Every writer develops methods for rewriting. Determining what works best for you as a writer will take time, practice, and experience. At this early stage in the process of learning to write like a U.S. lawyer, the most important thing to remember about rewriting is that it is absolutely necessary. Turning in a first draft, whether in school or in an office or in a courtroom, is never a good idea. The writer almost always knows what he or she intends to say, but unless the reader shares the writer's understanding of the written words, the document has no value to either party.

Lots of people write in their daily journals, for personal reasons; this works quite well because the writer is the only intended reader. Such a writer has complete freedom. But when one's writing becomes one's work product, the reader takes priority over the writer. It is notoriously hard for writers to see our own mistakes, omissions, gaps in logic, or flaws in sentence structure; if we write it, we see what we want to see. But a reader will spot these errors immediately, and with every error the writer's credibility slips lower and lower until it becomes nonexistent. If the writer has no credibility, the document has no value. The only way to identify and correct these problems is by writing, rewriting, reading, revising, and rewriting again as many times as possible in order to get as close as possible to a flawless document. It takes a lot of time, but without investing that time there is generally no point in writing at all.

Almost every law student in the United States struggles with what we call "time management." For most students, law school is the busiest, most challenging, and most stressful endeavor they have yet to undertake. International students who come to U.S. law schools with professional experience are likely to be better prepared to deal with the workload and pressure that every law student faces, and so the international students may be in a much better position than their domestic peers to handle "time management." Very few of us will ever have the luxury of the elite writers who may devote full days at a time to crafting a single, stellar sentence. Most of us write when and where we can, in bits and pieces. Students who wait until they have "enough" time to write will find that the deadline passes before that mythical "enough time" is in sight. We must all write, in some form or another, every day.

A Note About Academic Writing in the U.S.

Most law professors are not simultaneously law practitioners. As a consequence, their academic writing differs from the writing of legal practitioners and law students. Law students may engage in academic writing as part of a seminar course or through membership on the staff of one of the many law journals found in most U.S. law schools. Academic writing is different from practice-oriented writing, but the basic concepts for effective legal writing will work in every context encountered by the student during his or her law school education, and indeed beyond. While context will always matter, there will never be a time when some form of CREAC will not serve the writer well, or when the writer can afford to lose track of the document's PASS, and never is it appropriate to write without regard for the Three Cs. These skills are transferable; the benefits of their use cannot be overstated.

The best writing tip for any writer is this: Do not wait to start writing until you feel ready, have completed all of your research, and have enough time to sit down and write the entire document. I first heard this tip a dozen or more years ago during a one-day seminar for academic writers. The tip was, and still is, quite simple, and indeed I have since seen it introduced many times in many settings. You will never have what you think is enough time. If you wait to start writing, you will find yourself rushing to meet a deadline. You will submit work that reflects your hurry. Nobody will devote time to reading your work if you have not devoted the time necessary to properly write it.

Effective writers adapt to writing in small blocks of time. In ten minutes, you can write a paragraph. If you do that a few times a day, you will have written a page. Do it for a week, and you may have a first draft. Remember, it is always easier to rewrite than it is to write—but there has to be something written before it can be rewritten. Ten minutes, half an hour, little bits of time here and there can add up to "enough" time. Postponing, waiting, or trying to find hours to devote to a writing project is not realistic for most of us, and it turns into just another type of procrastination. Deadlines and daunting tasks call for productivity, not procrastination. "Writer's block" is a term used to describe a frustrated writer who cannot put words to paper. In the realm of legal writing, there is no place for writer's block: a "blocked" legal writer will be an unemployed legal writer.

When you are faced with a daunting writing assignment, whether in an office or in a classroom, approach it in manageable pieces. Make an outline. Put words on paper (or on the computer). Don't worry about grammar, sentence structure, punctuation or spelling at this stage. Think about what needs to be said and try various organizational schemes until you find one that will be logical and easy for a reader to understand. Start with the larger concepts and write your way through to the smaller ones. Do keep track of the sources on which you base any legal proposition or conclusion because eventually you will need to include adequate citations to authorities; it will make your life much easier, and the writing process will be much more efficient, if you do not have to stop and track down everything that will require a citation. It is expected and normal for a lawyer's document to include a citation to authority after almost every sentence, and that can add up to hundreds of citations. During the writing process, keep track of those sources, but save the citation formatting for the end of the writing process because citations will change based on where, when, and how they are used.

A Note on Writer's Block

Only writers claim to be "blocked." Imagine if you were in need of surgery and when you went to the hospital you were told to come back in a day or two because the surgeon was "blocked" that day. On a less life-or-death level, if I stood in front of a classroom full of students and said I couldn't teach that day because I was having teacher's block, those students would be justified in going directly to the dean's office to complain about my failure to do my job. I don't believe in writer's block any more than I believe in surgeon's block or teacher's block. It's just a description of an inability or unwillingness to do the hard work that needs to be done. I can empathize with that feeling but I cannot succumb to it if I want to earn my paycheck.

The important thing is to write. "Put yourself in the chair and stay there," as a good friend once advised me, and just write. Do not strive for perfection, but do strive for productivity. Early drafts may eventually be so changed that they are unrecognizable in the final product, and that is a good thing. Some professional writers set up internal deadlines to keep themselves moving forward. Others hold themselves to some minimum required daily output. I've known writers who reward themselves with chocolate or wine when they've met their internal deadlines. Find a system that motivates you to start writing, to keep writing, to rewrite, to polish, and to produce the best possible document well before the deadline. You may not think of yourself as "a writer," but as long as you are studying legal writing, you are, in fact, a writer. Start thinking like a writer and soon you will be writing like a writer. Everyone can do it.

Legal writing in the United States is as far from creative writing as it can possibly be. Legal writers need not be born storytellers, nor must they be particularly imaginative or innovative (but such qualities can come in handy). Legal writing is more like a mathematics equation than it is like a novel. In math, one misplaced number or decimal point may mean the difference between success and failure. Legal writing works the same way. Law + Facts = Conclusion, every time; nothing more and nothing less. If the pieces of that equation are taken out of order, or if one piece is in the wrong spot, or if the wrong information is plugged into the right spot, that writing cannot succeed. Formulas or equations are easier for most people to work with than some nebulous notion of "writing." This is why it takes time and practice to produce effective legal writing, and that is why rewriting, proofreading, revising, and polishing are all part of the process. With these concepts in the forefront of your mind, the writing process will get easier every time you practice it. We all have to start somewhere, so let's start with one more exercise.

YOUR ASSIGNMENT: EDITING FOR EFFECTIVENESS

Below you will find various excerpts from one bit of legal analysis (CREAC), written by the Supreme Court of the state of Vermont. *First,* arrange the sentences below in a clear and logical way. *Then* polish the sentences. The result should be a series of logically related sentences and paragraphs that, when taken as a whole, demonstrate a very tidy, clear, and correct example of substantive legal analysis. You may assume that all of the internal citations are accurate and correctly formatted, so focus on the content and its organization first; then look at the writing style, taking care to look at the organization of sentences and paragraphs. This case involved an employer, Bradford's Trucking, appealing findings that it owed the State more money for unemployment taxes because some workers who were claimed by Bradford's as independent contractors were, in fact, employees.

> This is not uncommon in U.S. administrative, state, and federal law. Unemployment taxes are paid by employers in order to fund the programs that provide some financial support to workers who are unemployed through no fault of their own. Such employees should receive unemployment compensation benefits. Employers are not responsible for unemployment benefits for their independent contractors. For your purposes, be aware that the issue in this case was whether the complaining workers were employees or independent contractors.

Because unemployment taxes are a function of the Executive Branch of government, the case was first heard by an Administrative Law Judge (an ALJ) and then by the Vermont Employment Security Board; from the Board, the appeal was taken directly to the Vermont Supreme Court because Vermont, a small, sparsely populated state, is one of only ten states, of fifty, with no intermediate courts of appeal.

The record demonstrates that none of the individuals in question met other elements of the statutory test. See *Fleece on Earth,* 2007 VT 29, ¶ 7 (noting that "failure of any one part of the test compels the conclusion that an employer-employee relationship exists"). Thus, as summarized earlier, the record evidence here supports the Board's conclusion that neither Swenor nor Reed was "customarily engaged in an independently established" business, as required by third part, or Part C of the statutory test. 21 V.S.A. § 1301(6)(B)(iii). This standard requires that employer show that the business in question was "established, independently of the employer or the rendering of the personal service forming the basis of the claim"; that the individual was engaged in the independent business "at the time of rendering the service"; that the individual was "customarily" or "regularly" so engaged; and that the business was "established," meaning "one that is permanent, fixed, stable and lasting." *Vt. Secs., Inc. v. Vt. Unemployment Comp. Comm'n,* 118 Vt. 196, 201, 104 A.2d 915, 917 (1954); *accord In re Bargain Busters, Inc.,* 130 Vt. 112, 119, 287 A.2d 554, 559 (1972).

All workers who receive wages are presumed to be employees, and the burden is on the employer to rebut this presumption by showing that the workers "meet all three elements of the statutory exception commonly known at the ABC test." *Fleece on Earth v. Dep't of Emp't & Training,* 2007 VT 29, ¶ 7, 181 Vt. 458, 923 A.2d 594. "The failure of any one part of the test compels the conclusion that an employer-employee relationship exists." *Id.* The three elements of the exception are: (1) the worker "has been and will continue to be free from control or direction over the performance of such services"; (2) "[s]uch service is either outside the usual course of the business for which such service is performed, or . . . such service is performed outside of all the places of business of the enterprise for which such service is performed"; and (3) "[s]uch individual is customarily engaged in an independently established trade, occupation, profession or business." 21 V.S.A. § 1301(6)(B)(i), (ii), (iii).

The Board affirmed the ALJ's finding that Bradford's Trucking, hereinafter referred to as employer (employer) had met its burden as to the first part of the test, noting that Ms. Bradford, Secretary of the employer's Board of Directors as well as employer's bookkeeper, was a corporate officer and therefore generally free from control and that employer exercised only "limited control" over Swenor's and Reed's [the bookkeepers hired by Ms. Bradford when she became too busy to do handle all of the employer's bookkeeping] payroll work.

The Board also agreed with the ALJ's finding that employer had not met either of the independent elements of the second part of the test with respect to Bradford, Swenor or Reed. They concluded, in this regard, that bookkeeping was "integral" to and a "necessary part of doing business" for employer, and therefore was not "outside the usual course" of employer's business, and further concluded that the work was not performed "outside of all the places of business" of employer.

The Board affirmed the ALJ's finding that, while Ms. Bradford establishes that she met the third part of the test because she was "providing bookkeeping services" for at least a couple of years, neither Swenor nor Reed is engaged in such a business when they worked for employer. Thus, because employer had failed to demonstrate that Ms. Bradford, Swenor, or Reed met all three of the statutory criteria, the assessments were sustained. This appeal followed.

Employer has not carried their evidentiary burden under the relevant applicable binding standard. As noted, the ALJ found, and the undisputed record evidence showed, that Reed "did have an independently established trade, but it was not bookkeeping, but daycare." Furthermore, while was it was clear that Swenor had worked as a bookkeeper, it was equally clear that his service was as an employee, not as the proprietor of an independently established business, accordingly and consequently in the instant case at bar employer failed to satisfy the third prong of the ABC test as to these individuals.

Our review is deferential. We will affirm the Board's findings of fact unless they are clearly erroneous, and its conclusion of law if they are fairly and reasonably supported by the findings. *Bouchard v. Dep't of Emp't & Training,* 174 Vt. 588, 589, 816 A.2d 508, 510 (2002) (mem.).[12]

---

[12] *Bradford's Trucking, Inc., v. Department of Labor,* ___ A.3d ___, 2015 WL 3795950, 2015 Vt. 85. NOTE: Some parts of the redacted material have been altered in order to fit the purposes

of this exercise, but no substantive alterations have been made. If a student looks up this case and reads the court's opinion, there is no point in engaging in this exercise. Students should re-organize and polish this material *on their own* and then check their own work by referring to the Court's opinion as it is reported. All errors in style have been created solely for the purposes of this exercise, and should not be attributed to the Vermont Supreme Court.

CHAPTER 2

READING CASES

■ ■ ■

U.S. law comes in several forms, some of which may be more familiar to international lawyers than others. Codes—statutes, ordinances, and any other legislatively enacted law—are familiar to lawyers around the world. Similarly, in the United States, administrative rules and regulations look and act like codes. These should not be too challenging for international students, but case law—the source of common law—is often completely new for international students. Again, this should not be cause for undue concern because most U.S. law students are in the same boat, having never read or studied case law in their lives. Understanding how to read case law is a necessary part of producing effective legal writing, so this chapter will deconstruct a judicial opinion for students. This, like all of the other skills addressed in this book, is a transferrable skill: understanding how one case should be read will enable students to take the right approach to reading any other case. And you will read many, many cases during your time in a U.S. legal environment.

Sources of Law

An "ordinance" is usually a local law enacted by elected officials. It comes from the legislative branch of a city or town, sometimes referred to as "municipalities." Understanding the source of law is a necessary part of understanding its effect because not all laws are "binding" in every jurisdiction in the United States. Binding law is mandatory: it must be followed within that jurisdiction. Binding or mandatory laws are always primary, not secondary, sources. But not all primary sources contain binding or mandatory law. It gets confusing, which is why students should not rely on their memories: look up the binding sources of law for any jurisdiction you are assigned to research. If you are using the ALWD Citation Manual, Appendix One contains every jurisdiction in the United States, arranged alphabetically, and shows the sources of binding authority and their correct citation format.

A. READING BLACKIE THE TALKING CAT: APPEARANCES CAN BE DECEIVING

Reading case law in the United States is a goal-oriented endeavor. We read cases to learn the common law and to learn how courts have interpreted and applied statutory, constitutional, and administrative law. Not all case law is binding, nor is it all relevant. Lawyers and law students spend years learning and practicing how to identify primary, binding authority; how to choose the best authority to cite in the context in which it will be cited; and then how to organize and analyze the selected authorities in a way that best accomplishes the lawyer's goal.

Writing about cases depends on the context of course, as does every other type of legal writing. Formal transactions are always put in writing, but even less formal conversations may find themselves reduced to writing in a court or client file. Virtually every piece of a lawyers' communications should expect to be reduced to writing, even if for the sole (and very important) purpose of memorializing a verbal conversation. From a telephone call with a potential new client to an argument before the U.S. Supreme Court, the lawyers' work is not completed without a written record of that work. Effective legal writing is thus one of, if not the single, most important skills for a U.S. lawyer.

It is impossible to separate the writing process from the research process[1] because without accurate research and identification of the best legal authorities, the lawyer's written work has no credibility. A legal document is only as good as the sources it cites. The lawyer's personal opinions or experiences are generally not of any interest to anyone. U.S. lawyers need to identify the legal issue, or issues, in any case or controversy, conduct research to find the best primary, binding authority to address that issue, or those issues, and then demonstrate in a logically organized manner how the existing law could, should, or would be applied to the new case or controversy. Nowhere in this scenario is there room for the lawyer's opinion, gut instinct, personal life experiences, or the notion that "everybody knows this." We will cite to the death in order to give our analysis credibility.

All of this explains why lawyers never read the law in a vacuum. Learning to focus on the legal issue at hand, while keeping in mind the Purpose, Audience, Scope, and Stance of any legal analysis, takes years of practice. In U.S. law school curricula, that learning process usually begins with reading a case. If the class is Contracts, the textbook will contain carefully selected and edited legal opinions from the courts of any

---

[1]   As a reminder, this book is not a research or citation manual. The many excellent books on the market in these areas serve the needs of the international law student as well as those of the domestic law students. If they are not required to do so, students are advised to purchase and retain one good research guide and one good citation manual.

jurisdiction, state or federal, that the textbook's author(s) believe illustrate a specific point of contracts law. Thus, in a textbook (sometimes called a case book), the authors or editors have done a lot of the students' work for them: the cases have been located, the best opinions have been selected, and any part of the opinion that is not pertinent has been conveniently deleted. The student need not worry about the jurisdiction (unless that is part of the legal issue itself), nor does the student need to worry about whether the case is still "good law," because it would not have been selected for inclusion in the case book if it had been reversed, overruled, superseded, or specifically criticized by a higher court. The student need not plow through copious amounts of words that really have nothing to do with the point the student is trying to learn, because that job has already been done by the book's editor(s). Of course, this does not make it easy for law students, especially new law students, to understand what they are reading or why it might matter. It simply means that the hardest aspects of reading case law have been taken out of the equation by whoever chose to include that case in the case book.

Researching and then reading entire court opinions, in order to be able to construct a written document that thoughtfully analyzes a specific legal question, is, as we say for some reason, a different kettle of fish. Not, of course, literally a kettle of fish; this is a saying, or an idiom; you probably know many of these, whether in English or in some other language(s). Idioms help all non-native speakers speak in the vernacular.

> ***Idioms*** are a part of every language. Some idioms that are common in U.S. English are baffling to those for whom English is not a first language. It would be highly unusual to employ idioms in formal written documents in the United States, although courts are allowed to do so. The idiom's role in conversations and explanations should not be under-estimated. When I teach a class in which all of the students are from countries other than the United States, I try to introduce an Idiom of the Day in every class session. You can expect to see such idioms throughout this book. If the origin is knowable, it will be included, but some idioms, such as "a different kettle of fish," defy explanation.

In the legal field, "research" means more than just locating sources. Legal research requires both locating and understanding the found sources, and evaluating their relative worth in some future analysis. Writers must take the time and care to research in order to know that their jobs have been performed professionally—but also because if they skimp on or rush through the research they run the risk of missing the rare legal opinions that are fun to read. The following is one of the most famous examples of such a case.

In 1981, in the small town of Augusta, Georgia, Mr. Carl Miles was assessed a fine by the city for failure to obtain a business license.[2] In the United States, each state has the inherent power to require its residents, or those who conduct business within the state, to pay taxes. Most states delegate that power to smaller governmental entities: states are divided into counties, and counties are further divided into towns or townships, cities, or villages. These towns and cities are collectively called "municipalities." In most states, some taxes are assessed by the state, some by the county, and some by the municipality. Traditionally, a person or company that wanted to conduct business within a municipality was required to pay a fee, or tax, to that municipality.

You may, and should, read the entire opinion, probably several times, after reading this chapter. Here, with a brief citation lesson, is where the case may be found: The case name consists of the plaintiff's surname, or family name (Miles) versus the entity he sued, the City Council of Augusta, Georgia. With abbreviations, that case name looks like this: *Miles v. City Council of Augusta, GA.* Case names are always italicized, but the remainder of the citation is not. Note also that Mr. Miles' first name is not included in the case name—only his family name is included. The trial court's opinion was published in West's Federal Supplement, Volume 551, beginning on page 349. The Reporter volume, name, and initial page number are abbreviated to look like this: 551 F. Supp. 349. The last part of the citation is in parentheses and indicates the court that decided the case as well as the year in which it was decided. Here, that looks like this: (S.D. Ga. 1982); it signifies to the reader that the case was decided in 1982 by the United States District Court for the Southern District of Georgia—a federal court. When the pieces are all put together, the full citation to this case looks like this: *Miles v. City Council of Augusta, GA*, 551 F. Supp. 349 (S.D. Ga. 1982). Do not try to memorize the rules of citation, but do remember that you must use a citation manual to guarantee that your citation accurately includes all of information that is both necessary and expected in a case citation. U.S. courts, lawyers, and law students all follow the citation rules contained in either the Blue Book or the ALWD Citation Manual. This way, everyone knows how and where to locate any cited source. Remember, without a citation, a lawyer's statement has no credibility or value. In addition to identifying the location of the cited material, the citation tells a trained reader whether the cited source is primary or secondary, binding or persuasive. Citations communicate so much information that their accuracy is absolutely essential.

---

[2]   *Miles v. City Council of Augusta, Ga.,* 551 F. Supp. 349 (S.D. Ga. 1982).

A Note on the Evolution of Business Licenses

These days, most municipalities are eager (perhaps desperate) to attract new businesses, especially larger ones; it is not unusual for a municipality or even a county or state to offer "incentives" to attract new businesses. Those incentives translate to foregoing the payment of any business license fees. In effect, then, governments pay businesses rather than the other way around. But in 1982, in Augusta, Georgia, the city required a business license.

When Mr. Miles was fined for failure to obtain a business license, he filed a civil lawsuit in federal court against the city.[3] Mr. Miles raised two different federal constitutional claims in his lawsuit. First, he argued that the Georgia law that authorized the city to require a business license was an unconstitutional infringement on his First Amendment right to freedom of association because the cost of the business license would render his business unprofitable. Second, Mr. Miles argued that the same statute (legislatively enacted law) was unconstitutionally broad ("overbroadth") and void for vagueness."[4] The trial was held in the United States District Court for the Southern District of Georgia. That court decided that the statute was constitutional, so Mr. Miles filed an appeal to the United States Court of Appeals for the Eleventh Circuit.[5]

"Void for vagueness" is a term of art generally used in criminal, not civil, cases. The Constitution guarantees that a person should have adequate forewarning, from statutory language, which conduct is permitted or forbidden. Statutes that are too vague or are overly broad may be declared unconstitutional by the federal courts; this was the goal of Mr. Miles' lawsuit.

---

[3]   *Id.*

[4]   *Id.* at 353.

[5]   *Miles v. City Council of Augusta, GA*, 710 F. 2d1542 (11th Cir. 1983). Note that the name of the case did not change: Mr. Miles filed the original lawsuit, so his name came first at the trial court level; he lost at trial, and he initiated the appeal. Therefore, his name is still first. The West Reporter in which federal intermediate appellate court decisions are published is called the Federal Reporter (and there are now Second and Third Series). And no, it is not unusual for a case that arose in 1981 to still be weaving its way through the courts in 1983. Today, it would take much, much longer because the courts are so crowded.

Federal trial courts are always called District Courts; federal intermediate appellate courts are always called Circuit Courts of Appeal; and the highest federal court is, of course, the United States Supreme Court (which you may see referred to as SCOTUS). States call their courts differing names, but at this point every state in the United States has the same three levels of courts, whatever they may be called: trial courts, intermediate appellate courts, and the highest court of the state (which is usually, but not always, referred to as the state's Supreme Court; New York, for example, calls its highest court its Court of Appeals). The names need not be memorized, but the basic court structures do.

In his appeal to the Eleventh Circuit, Mr. Miles again argued that the city's business license statute was too vague and overly broad to be constitutional. The Eleventh Circuit was having none of that argument[6], and agreed with the District Court that the local ordinance (the statute) was perfectly fine as written. The Eleventh Circuit further agreed with the District Court that Mr. Miles was, indeed, engaged in a business for which a license was required. Mr. Miles had unsuccessfully argued that even if the city had the right kind of ordinance, it should not apply to him because he was not actually engaged in any business listed in that ordinance.

This is where the case gets interesting (for those of us who are not particularly riveted by arguments about municipal licensing and taxing authorities). Mr. Miles' argument that he was not engaged in a business was related to yet another (unsuccessful) argument he raised in the Eleventh Circuit. Mr. Miles said he was not carrying on any business activity, but was instead only requesting donations from passersby as he stood on the street with his cat, whose name was Blackie. But Mr. Miles was no ordinary panhandler[7] and Blackie was no ordinary cat. Blackie, as the trial judge himself observed on a city street one day, was a talking cat. With some encouragement from Mr. Miles, which came upon receipt of an appropriate "donation," Blackie would entertain passersby with his impressive, if limited, repertoire of words and phrases: "I love you" and "I want my Mama." The Eleventh Circuit ultimately decided that Mr. Miles' solicitation of "donations" was, in fact, a business activity as defined in the city ordinance, and therefore the city did have the authority to require that

---

[6]   This is another idiom: "have none of it," or "have nothing to do with it," means to reject a thing, person, or argument. Here, the court would have nothing to do with the argument that Blackie's constitutional rights were violated.

[7]   This is a slightly nicer way of saying "beggar." It refers to a person who stands on a public street asking for spare change or money from those who pass by. If you live in any U.S. city, you will probably see many of these people. Some of them are in genuine need; others have alcohol or drug problems. Whether to give money or to withhold it is an entirely personal choice, as long as the pan-handler is not threatening you with any physical violence; if you are threatened, the general advice is to hand over any valuables you might have and then immediately run screaming to the nearest police station and/or well-populated, brightly lit location.

Mr. Miles obtain a business license.[8] The Eleventh Circuit specifically held that the ordinance was neither overbroad nor unconstitutionally vague, and that the actions in which Mr. Miles engaged were definitely commercial in nature because the cat would not speak unless and until passersby "donated" money.

Mr. Miles lost on his third and final argument as well when he attempted to argue that Blackie's right to freedom of speech, as guaranteed by the First Amendment to the United States Constitution, was violated when the city required Mr. Miles to obtain a business license prior to collecting "donations" in response the Blackie's talking. In essence, Mr. Miles said that Blackie's right to speak was infringed by the license requirement. The Eleventh Circuit was not impressed.[9] Cats do not have any constitutional rights; only human beings have constitutional rights. In fact, cats have no rights whatsoever, let alone a right to freedom of speech. In the United States, animals are chattel: any objects, including living creatures, that are subject to ownership by people. As talented as Blackie may have been, he was, after all, just a cat. Mr. Miles lost his arguments to the Eleventh Circuit, and apparently did not feel it was incumbent on him to try an appeal to the U.S. Supreme Court. This may have been one of his wiser decisions.

If you have not already done so, now would be a good time to read the opinions of both the District and Circuit courts in Mr. Miles' case. Reading a case with no context is difficult. U.S. lawyers read cases for specific reasons, with specific issues (questions) in mind.

If you attempted to read the Eleventh Circuit's opinion on Mr. Miles' appeal, and you were reading either a physical case reporter (a book) or a commercial legal research service (such as Westlaw or Lexis), you would still see the same information: the case name, a short summary of the case, and then a list (anywhere from one to one hundred, depending on the complexity of the case) of numbered paragraphs, each of which is devoted to a discrete legal point. Similar material appears at the beginning of every case published in a commercial venue. It is always prepared by the publisher and is not part of the court's opinion; it should never be quoted or cited because it was not written by a court and thus cannot be primary or binding authority.

The numbered paragraphs are still called "headnotes" even if the publisher calls them Key Cites; this is a lingering relic from the days before computerized legal research existed. Headnotes are helpful research tools, but that is all they are: they should never be quoted or cited. Instead, the headnote number is useful when the reader needs to locate the material of

---

[8]   Mr. Miles had, in fact, already accepted the need for a license and paid $50.00 to obtain one before he filed his lawsuit.

[9]   *Miles,* 710 F.2d 1542.

interest within any court's opinion. Headnotes are finding tools, not authority.

In the example below, students can compare the headnotes from the trial court's opinion with the headnotes from the appellate court's opinion. The topic names and numbers are consistent but the case-specific headnote numbers are not. For example, in the District Court's decision, Headnote 11 is identified as addressing Constitutional Law, Number 82(4). In the Circuit Court's opinion, that same topic and its numbered subsection are addressed in Headnote 4. The headnote number (here, 11 and then 4) simply indicates the location within that specific opinion of the material that has been classified, by the Reporter's editors rather than by the court, as falling within subsection 82 (4) of the broad topic called Constitutional Law. To find additional sources that discuss this particular legal point, the researcher must pay attention to the topic and subsection, not to its location within any given case.

Note that of the fourteen headnotes prepared by the editors who published the trial court's opinion, not one mentions a talking cat. This alone should motivate students to remember that reading headnotes is no substitute for reading cases.

Every new law student in the U.S. must learn to use the headnotes as finding tools in order to read cases efficiently. In the District Court's opinion denying Mr. Miles' claim that the city's ordinance was unconstitutional because it was written too broadly, Headnote Eleven addresses the question of how courts are to determine whether a statute is overly broad. To find that part of the court's decision, look at the opinion itself, which begins on page 350, and look for the paragraph within the opinion that is identified by the number eleven in brackets: [11]. That paragraph can be found on page 354.

When reading cases, either online or in an actual book in an actual library, lawyers and law students may need to turn, or scroll through, a few pages, but it is easy to find the numbered paragraph and the page number (which would be the pinpoint cite in any written citation to the case). When reading cases on a commercial legal research database, such as Westlaw or Lexis, one click on the number eleven next to the listed headnote will "jump" the computer directly to that part of the opinion. This is easy and efficient, but the reader is still required, when engaged in written analysis, to identify the exact page number on which the cited information may be found. Page numbers are required even when cited authority is found on Westlaw or Lexis because, for citation purposes, U.S. lawyers act as if we all still research using books. Electronic databases currently indicate printed page numbers by a predetermined number of asterisks (*).

MILES v. CITY COUNCIL OF AUGUSTA, GA.   **349**

Cite as 551 F.Supp. 349 (1982)

Carl M. MILES, et al., Plaintiffs,

v.

CITY COUNCIL OF AUGUSTA,
GEORGIA, et al., Defendants.

Civ. A. No. CV181–157.

United States District Court,
S.D. Georgia,
Augusta Division.

Nov. 15, 1982.

Plaintiffs attacked municipal ordinance imposing business license tax. The District Court, Dudley H. Bowen, Jr., J., held that: (1) ordinance is not vague or overbroad, and (2) ordinance does not violate equal protection clause.

Ordered accordingly.

1. Municipal Corporations ⬅956(1)

Taxing power is power of the state that is delegated to municipality it creates.

2. Licenses ⬅7(1, 9)

Licenses, or occupation taxes, placed upon trades and occupations are legitimate methods of taxation even though such tax may render business unprofitable.

3. Licenses ⬅7(2)

Amount of tax levied against different trades and businesses need not be uniform or result of application of precise scientific formula.

4. Licenses ⬅5½

City council in Georgia is authorized to require procurement of business licenses.

5. Constitutional Law ⬅90.1(4), 91

Georgia municipal ordinance levying occupation tax does not violate First Amendment rights of speech or association as ordinance was not designed to regulate speech or association but merely to raise revenue and ordinance did not subject anyone's speech or associational activity to any penalty unless committed within context of one's occupation for which tax has not been paid. Ga. Const. Art. 1, § 1, Par. 1; U.S. C.A. Const.Amends. 1, 14.

6. Criminal Law ⬅13.1(1)

To avoid constitutional vagueness, statute must provide ascertainable standard of guilt sufficient to enable persons of ordinary intelligence to have fair warning of conduct proscribed by law and exacting attention to detail in drafting is not required.

7. Constitutional Law ⬅48(4)

Court may avoid vagueness of statute by means of statutory interpretation.

8. Constitutional Law ⬅48(1)

If statute can be read in constitutional manner, it must be accorded that meaning.

9. Statutes ⬅188

If statute does not define its terms, ordinary and common meanings are applied, unless there is established technical meaning, or legislative body intended otherwise.

10. Licenses ⬅7(1)

Georgia municipal ordinance imposing business license tax was not unconstitutionally vague or overbroad as it contained exhaustive list of businesses, occupations and trades subject to taxation, given exhaustive detailing of wide variety of occupations and businesses covered, it required no great leap in logic to hold that a "catch-all" category was intended for those unique, extraordinary occupations such as plaintiffs' talking cat. U.S.C.A. Const.Amend 1.

11. Constitutional Law ⬅82(4)

Before statute is invalid for overbreadth, overbreadth of statute must not only be real but substantial as well, judged in relation to statute's plainly legitimate sweep.

12. Constitutional Law ⬅91

Georgia municipal ordinance imposing business license tax did not impermissibly infringe upon plaintiffs' right to association since that right does not extend to commercial ventures. U.S.C.A. Const.Amend. 1.

13. Constitutional Law ⬅230.2

Plaintiffs' right to equal protection was not violated by Georgia municipal ordinance imposing business license tax in light of fact that ordinance was not arbitrary and without rational foundation and fact that plaintiffs' tax was in different amount than that required of other businesses did not constitute violation of equal protection. U.S.C.A. Const.Amend. 14.

14. Taxation ⇐42(1)

Revenue laws of states and municipalities do not have to be applied uniformly class to class.

John H. Ruffin, Jr., Augusta, Ga., for plaintiffs.

Stanley G. Jackson, Augusta, Ga., for defendants.

ORDER

BOWEN, District Judge.

This case is before the Court on the cross-motions for summary judgment of plaintiffs Carl and Elaine Miles and defendant City Council of Augusta, Georgia. For the reasons to follow, summary judgment is GRANTED IN FAVOR OF DEFENDANT AND DENIED AS TO THE PLAINTIFFS. The plaintiffs' motion will be discussed first.

I

PLAINTIFFS' MOTION

In this case, the attack upon the power of the City of Augusta to levy an occupation tax arises under somewhat unusual circumstances. The pertinent undisputed facts, as gleaned from the record,[1] are as follows:

A. The Cat

Carl and Elaine Miles are an unemployed, married couple who own "Blackie, The Talking Cat." Trained by Carl Miles, Blackie allegedly is able to speak several words and phrases of the English language. On June 22, 1981, plaintiffs were required by defendant to obtain a business license. From May 15, to June 22, 1981, plaintiffs had accepted contributions from pedestrians in the downtown Augusta area who wanted to hear the cat speak. People would stop the plaintiffs who strolled the streets with the cat. Upon being stopped, plaintiffs would ask for a contribution. There is, however, evidence of the plaintiffs soliciting an off-duty policeman for money in exchange for a performance. Plaintiffs dispute this allegation. It is undisputed that plaintiffs would ask for, and lived off, the contributions received for Blackie's orations. Several complaints were received by the Augusta Police Department regarding the plaintiffs' solicitations. Plaintiffs were warned by the police not to solicit unless they first obtained a business license.

Through their exploit of his talents, Blackie has provided his owners with at

---

1. In ruling on the motions for summary judgment, the Court has considered only the evidence in the file. However, it should be disclosed that I have seen and heard a demonstration of Blackie's abilities. The point in time of the Court's view was late summer, 1982, well after the events contended in this lawsuit. One afternoon when crossing Greene Street in an automobile, I spotted in the median a man accompanied by a cat and a woman. The black cat was draped over his left shoulder. Knowing the matter to be in litigation, and suspecting that the cat was Blackie, I thought twice before stopping. Observing, however, that counsel for neither side was present and that any citizen on the street could have happened by chance upon this scene, I spoke, and the man with the cat eagerly responded to my greeting. I asked him if his cat could talk. He said he could, and if I would pull over on the side street he would show me. I did, and he

did. The cat was wearing a collar, two harnesses and a leash. Held and stroked by the man Blackie said "I love you" and "I want my Mama." The man then explained that the cat was the sole source of income for him and his wife and requested a donation which was provided. I felt that my dollar was well spent. The cat was entertaining as was its owner. Some questions occurred to me about the necessity for the multiple means of restraint and the way in which the man held the cat's paw when the cat was asked to talk. However, these are not matters before the Court and are beyond the purview of a federal judge. I do not know if the man whom I saw with the cat was the plaintiff Mr. Miles.

This sequence has not been considered as evidence or as an uncontroverted fact in the case. It is simply stated for the purpose of a disclosure to the parties of the chance contact.

At Headnote Eleven, on page 354, the trial court's language is significantly different from the language used in the headnote. Legally trained readers in the U.S. recognize headnote language immediately for its lack of articles. The headnotes, again, are not legal authorities, and should never be cited or quoted as if they were. To cite or quote a headnote is a recipe for disaster; do not do it. Note the slight, but significant, difference in language in Headnote Eleven. The headnote begins: "Before statute is invalid for overbreadth, ..." The court actually wrote: "As stated by the Supreme Court . . . , before a statute is invalid for overbreadth. . . ." The only overlap in language is the phrase "invalid for overbreadth." This phrase can be cited because the court wrote it, and yes, it was included in the headnote. Note that any written citation must be to page 354, not to page 349, in order to accurately identify the source of this language as the trial court rather than as the headnote.

Writers are responsible for making their readers' jobs easier, and citations are a key aspect of achieving this goal. Every legal writer must use a citation manual and provide the required citations to every authority mentioned in any written document. One way to make the reader's job easier is to include pinpoint citations. Pinpoint citations identify for the reader the exact location in any cited source at which the cited material can be located.

Parallel cites, on the other hand, do not necessarily make a reader's job easier because a parallel citation simply provides the same citation from more than one publication. If a case, for example, is cited in more than one reporter (as is true with a state appellate court opinion that is published in both a West regional reporter and the state's own reporter), it is not always required or expected that the writer would list multiple publications. Absent local rules to the contrary, with which the writer is always obliged to become familiar, writers are expected to cite the "official" reporter without including parallel citations to un-official reporters.

One notable exception for parallel citations arises when citing U.S. Supreme Court cases: The U.S. reporter is the official reporter, but because it is published by the government rather than by a commercial publisher it may take months longer to appear than the unofficial commercial reporters. While awaiting the official citation, legal writers must indicate its absence as follows: *Miles v. City Council of Augusta, GA.*, ___ U.S. ___, 200 S. Ct. 123 (2015). Note that the parenthetical information includes only the year here: When it is clear from the cited source which court decided a case, that court's abbreviated designation need not be included in the parenthetical with the year of the decision. This means that citations to cases reported in the Federal Supplement, the Federal Reporter, or any of West's Regional reporters must include the abbreviation of the deciding court in the parenthetical with the year in which the case was decided.

1542   **710 FEDERAL REPORTER, 2d SERIES**

accrued since April 18, 1970, the date of the closing of the Bank, should be delivered over to the rightful owner, the FDIC.[18]

The judgment of the trial court is AFFIRMED.

Carl M. MILES, et al.,
Plaintiffs-Appellants,

v.

CITY COUNCIL OF AUGUSTA, GEORGIA, et al., Defendants-Appellees.

No. 82–8766
Non-Argument Calendar.

United States Court of Appeals,
Eleventh Circuit.

Aug. 4, 1983.

Plaintiffs attacked municipal ordinance imposing business license tax. The United States District Court for the Southern District of Georgia, Dudley H. Bowen, Jr., J., 551 F.Supp. 349, granted summary judgment in favor of defendant city council, and plaintiffs appealed. The Court of Appeals held that: (1) promotion of talking cat was "occupation" or "business" within meaning of ordinance requiring payment of $50 license fee by any "Agent or Agency not specifically mentioned;" (2) attack on vagueness of ordinance provision which council did not seek to enforce was not

properly before Court of Appeals; (3) plaintiffs failed to make case of overbreadth with respect to ordinance provision at issue; and (4) plaintiffs' activities in promoting talking cat were within legitimate exercise of city's taxing power.

Affirmed.

1. Licenses ⟜11(1)
Promotion of talking cat was "occupation" or "business" within meaning of city business ordinance provision requiring payment of $50 license fee by any "Agent or Agency not specifically mentioned."
See publication Words and Phrases for other judicial constructions and definitions.

2. Municipal Corporations ⟜121
Attack on vagueness of provision of city business ordinance was not properly before court where city council sought only to enforce other provision of such ordinance.

3. Licenses ⟜7(1)
City business ordinance provision requiring payment of $50 license fee by any "Agent or Agency not specifically mentioned" was not unconstitutionally overbroad. U.S.C.A. Const.Amend. 1.

4. Constitutional Law ⟜82(2)
Talking cat could not be considered a "person" and therefore was not protected by Bill of Rights.

5. Constitutional Law ⟜82(4)
Overbreadth of statute must be judged in relation to statute's plainly legitimate sweep.

6. Municipal Corporations ⟜966(1)
Promotion of talking cat was within legitimate exercise of city's taxing power.

———

N. Kenneth Daniel, Augusta, Ga., for defendants-appellees.

---

18. SFC's argument that it is equitably entitled to the interest accrued on the escrow account must fail since the FDIC had the right of pos-

session and right of ownership to the money in the escrow account at all times subsequent to the Bank's closing.

Now look at how different the headnotes look in the appellate court's decision. In the Eleventh Circuit's opinion on Mr. Miles' appeal, you will see six headnotes on page 1542, the first page of the case. The first page of the reported opinion contains nothing that was actually written by the court in that case. The court's opinion begins on page 1543, following the words "Per Curium," which mean the decision came from all of the judges on the panel. For new lawyers and law students, it can be hard to know exactly where a court's opinion begins, especially when reading a case electronically. If your law school's library no longer carries printed Reporters, Westlaw makes it easy for the reader to click on the link to a PDF of the original printed version of the case; the link is located at the top left of an electronically published case. Most law students find it easier to understand the parts of a reported case by looking at a printed version. But in whatever form a case is read, the legal writer has a responsibility to make sure he or she has not cited or quoted anything that was not written by the court. Even a dissenting or concurring opinion (which appear in some but not all appellate court opinions, when judges on the panel disagree with each other to some extent) must be identified as such in its citation. The rule of thumb is to cite the majority opinion because only that is the actual law of a case. Concurring and dissenting opinions might be persuasive but only a majority opinion becomes binding precedent. And for the legal writer, primary, binding precedent is always the goal.

Looking at the six headnotes in the Eleventh Circuit's opinion on Mr. Miles' appeal, you will see that each numbered paragraph has a topic name, just as the headnotes in the trial court's opinion did; older cases will also have a topic number designated by the picture of a key. In this case, headnote number five is labeled "Constitutional Law" (the topic name) followed by a small key and the number 82(4). This is the same topic and key number that was found in headnote eleven of the trial court's opinion. The topic and key number for that particular point of law do not change, but the location within the opinion, obviously, does. Remember that the headnote number is the finding tool within any opinion, but the topic and key number are finding tools across all U.S. jurisdictions' primary, secondary, binding, or persuasive authorities. Knowing how this system works (it is still commonly referred to as the Digest system despite the fact that the Digest books may or may not ever be seen) will help a researcher find other cases that address this specific legal point.

Just as an interesting example, look at the legal point addressed in headnote four of the Eleventh Circuit's opinion: "Talking cat could not be considered a 'person' and therefore was not protected by Bill of Rights." How many other cases can you imagine in which the personhood of a talking cat is at issue? The answer is, none. But the personhood of various other non-persons can and is at issue in more cases than you might imagine. If a non-person's protections under the Bill of Rights are at issue, that judicial opinion should have a headnote with this same topic) (Constitutional Law) and number (82(4)).

Notice the way the appellate court opinion's headnotes are worded, just as the trial court headnotes were worded: articles are omitted. Headnote four (which is just more interesting than headnote five) uses this language: "Talking cat could not be considered a 'person'. . . ." The court wrote it much more eloquently, in a footnote on page 1544: "[A]lthough Blackie arguably possessed a very unusual ability, he cannot be considered a 'person' and is therefore not protected by the Bill of Rights." The headnote is an accurate summary of the legal point, but it is not part of the court's opinion, and as you now know it should never be cited, quoted, or in any way included in any piece of legal writing.

Any trained legal reader in the United States will immediately recognize a headnote by the style in which it is written. A writer's credibility is ruined, and the document has no value, when a headnote is quoted. Use the headnotes as the finding and research tools they are intended to be, and not for any other reason. Can you tell how serious this is? I assume anyone reading this book hopes to become a good or even better-than-good legal writer, and citing a headnote will sink that ship.[10]

> If the common law system is new to you, this focus on legal points or issues and their place in the search for primary binding authority will seem particularly unfamiliar. Think of it this way: if you have been trained to begin your legal research with a code, in the United States you might begin with a code (statute), a case, a constitutional provision, or even an administrative regulation. The sources are different, but the skills needed to be a good advocate are essentially the same. Despite the way it might feel, you are not, in fact, starting from scratch the way most U.S. J.D. students are when they begin to study law.

Many inexperienced, rushed, and/or careless (sloppy) legal researchers will read the headnotes of a published case, but not the entire opinion. It's certainly true that it is not always necessary to read an entire opinion, including concurring and dissenting opinions. Some higher court opinions can exceed one hundred pages, especially from SCOTUS,[11] and reading every page would probably not be a good use of the researcher's time. But at some point in the process, the legal reader and writer must read what the court actually said. There may be nuances that are not included in a

---

[10] Another idiom: "sink that ship" means to dash all hope, or to ruin any chance, and is not to be confused with "float your boat," a far more casual idiom with an entirely different meaning (as in, whatever makes you happy).

[11] SCOTUS is another popular way to refer to the "Supreme Court Of The United States." It is far too informal for legal writing, but if you see it written in a blog or other electronic medium you should know what it means.

headnote; there are stories, anecdotal but plentiful, of headnotes getting the law wrong. Again, if nothing else, the headnotes are written by the editors who publish the opinions, and as such they are not law, and they must never be treated as if they were the law. Any source that will be cited in a written document or an oral argument must be read with painstaking attention in order to maintain the advocate's credibility.

Besides, if a law student or lawyer reads only the headnotes of, for example, the trial court's opinion in Mr. Miles' case, that reader knows nothing about Blackie, the talking cat. Remember the headnotes for the District Court's opinion? There are fourteen headnotes, not one of which mentions a talking cat. The headnotes, if read alone, would have given the reader information about municipal corporations (cities), licenses, taxes, and various aspects of constitutional law related to freedom of speech, right to association, overly broad or vaguely written statutes . . . but there is no clue within the headnotes that this court's opinion addresses issues raised when a pet cat is indentured to speak for his dinner. A reader who read only the headnotes would have missed one of the most entertaining, and best written judicial opinions ever published. Blackie's is a very well-known case among U.S. lawyers and law students. Blackie the Talking Cat is famous; municipal corporations' rights to require business licenses? Not so much.[12]

And while we are still on the subject of reading case law, please take a close look at the **footnotes** (not to be confused with the headnotes) in the trial court's opinion regarding Blackie, the talking cat. Many readers, legal and otherwise, skip over footnotes, assuming that if information was important enough to bother with, it would be in the main text rather than relegated to the bottom of a page in small print in a footnote.[13] It is in footnote 1, on page 350, that Judge Bowen describes his chance meeting on the street with a talking cat he presumed to be Blackie. Judge Bowen's description of their encounter is a lovely piece of writing: clear, concise, and correct. It also adds depth to the context within which the case was decided. If the reader had skipped the footnote, as most readers do, this entertaining and informative tidbit would have been lost, and the reader's understanding of the case would have been the poorer for it. On the following page, in footnote two, Judge Bowen expounds poetically on the

---

[12] "Not so much" is a casual expression that would not normally have a place in any discussion of legal writing. It is used to signify "no," but with a slightly sarcastic tone. Most English speakers find this a useful phrase in many contexts. For example, at the end of the day my husband might ask me if I had fun teaching six hours of class to U.S. college graduates whose grammar is at approximately a third-grade level; did I have fun? Not so much.

[13] I personally love writing and reading footnotes. In a scholarly article, I use footnotes as often as I can. Footnotes are the "asides" that occur in normal conversations, and I view writing as a conversation with a reader. When writing formal journal articles, I might use footnotes to express a personal, often snarky, opinion that would hit a wrong note if it appeared in the text. Footnotes serve many purposes, and I like to take advantage of them to the fullest extent.

350   **551 FEDERAL SUPPLEMENT**

imposing business license tax in light of fact that ordinance was not arbitrary and without rational foundation and fact that plaintiffs' tax was in different amount than that required of other businesses did not constitute violation of equal protection. U.S.C.A. Const.Amend. 14.

14. Taxation ⬤⟿42(1)

Revenue laws of states and municipalities do not have to be applied uniformly class to class.

John H. Ruffin, Jr., Augusta, Ga., for plaintiffs.

Stanley G. Jackson, Augusta, Ga., for defendants.

ORDER

BOWEN, District Judge.

This case is before the Court on the cross-motions for summary judgment of plaintiffs Carl and Elaine Miles and defendant City Council of Augusta, Georgia. For the reasons to follow, summary judgment is GRANTED IN FAVOR OF DEFENDANT AND DENIED AS TO THE PLAINTIFFS. The plaintiffs' motion will be discussed first.

I

PLAINTIFFS' MOTION

In this case, the attack upon the power of the City of Augusta to levy an occupation tax arises under somewhat unusual circumstances. The pertinent undisputed facts, as gleaned from the record,[1] are as follows:

A. The Cat

Carl and Elaine Miles are an unemployed, married couple who own "Blackie, The Talking Cat." Trained by Carl Miles, Blackie allegedly is able to speak several words and phrases of the English language. On June 22, 1981, plaintiffs were required by defendant to obtain a business license. From May 15, to June 22, 1981, plaintiffs had accepted contributions from pedestrians in the downtown Augusta area who wanted to hear the cat speak. People would stop the plaintiffs who strolled the streets with the cat. Upon being stopped, plaintiffs would ask for a contribution. There is, however, evidence of the plaintiffs soliciting an off-duty policeman for money in exchange for a performance. Plaintiffs dispute this allegation. It is undisputed that plaintiffs would ask for, and lived off, the contributions received for Blackie's orations. Several complaints were received by the Augusta Police Department regarding the plaintiffs' solicitations. Plaintiffs were warned by the police not to solicit unless they first obtained a business license.

Through their exploit of his talents, Blackie has provided his owners with at

---

1. In ruling on the motions for summary judgment, the Court has considered only the evidence in the file. However, it should be disclosed that I have seen and heard a demonstration of Blackie's abilities. The point in time of the Court's view was late summer, 1982, well after the events contended in this lawsuit. One afternoon when crossing Greene Street in an automobile, I spotted in the median a man accompanied by a cat and a woman. The black cat was draped over his left shoulder. Knowing the matter to be in litigation, and suspecting that the cat was Blackie, I thought twice before stopping. Observing, however, that counsel for neither side was present and that any citizen on the street could have happened by chance upon this scene, I spoke, and the man with the cat eagerly responded to my greeting. I asked him if his cat could talk. He said he could, and if I would pull over on the side street he would show me. I did, and he

did. The cat was wearing a collar, two harnesses and a leash. Held and stroked by the man Blackie said "I love you" and "I want my Mama." The man then explained that the cat was the sole source of income for him and his wife and requested a donation which was provided. I felt that my dollar was well spent. The cat was entertaining as was its owner. Some questions occurred to me about the necessity for the multiple means of restraint and the way in which the man held the cat's paw when the cat was asked to talk. However, these are not matters before the Court and are beyond the purview of a federal judge. I do not know if the man whom I saw with the cat was the plaintiff Mr. Miles.

This sequence has not been considered as evidence or as an uncontroverted fact in the case. It is simply stated for the purpose of a disclosure to the parties of the chance contact.

MILES v. CITY COUNCIL OF AUGUSTA, GA.   **351**
Cite as 561 F.Supp. 349 (1982)

least the minimal necessities of life.[2] Plaintiff Carl Miles has entered into several contracts with talent agents in Georgia, South Carolina and North Carolina. These agents have paid, at least in part, the Miles' living expenses over a period of time. The evidence does not clearly show that this support was provided during the relevant time period of May 15th to June 22nd. It does, however, permit the inference that prior to the plaintiffs' arrival in Augusta, they intended to commercially exploit Blackie's ability.

B. The Ordinance

Under its charter the City of Augusta is empowered to impose license taxes. Section 139 of the charter states, in pertinent part:

> The City Council of Augusta, by ordinance, may require any person, firm or corporation to pay a license tax upon any occupation, trade or business followed or carried on within the corporate limits of the City of Augusta. . . .

Pursuant to this enabling provision, the City Council enacted Ordinance No. 5006, the 1981–1982 business license ordinance. The ordinance exhaustively lists the trades, businesses and occupations subject to the ordinance and the amount of tax to be paid. Although the ordinance does not provide for the licensing of a talking cat,[3] section 2 of the ordinance does require any "Agent or Agency not specifically mentioned . . ." to pay a $50.00 tax.

C. The Attack

Plaintiffs attack the ordinance as being unconstitutionally vague and overbroad in contravention of the Due Process clauses of the fourteenth amendment to the United States Constitution and of the Georgia Constitution. Ga.Code Ann. § 2–101.[4] They contend they are not required to obtain a license and that requiring them to do so before they may solicit on the streets violates their first amendment rights of speech and association as well as the right to equal protection secured by the fourteenth amendment. Prefatory to the analysis of plaintiffs' vagueness and overbreadth challenges the nature of the ordinance being challenged and the authority to enact it must be established.

The purpose behind the ordinance questioned in this case is to generate revenue. It is a tax on occupations and businesses.

---

2. That a talking cat could generate interest and income is not surprising. Man's fascination with the domestic feline is perennial. People of western cultures usually fall into two categories. Generally, they are ailurophiles or ailurophobes. Cats are ubiquitous in the literature, lore and fiber of our society and language. The ruthless Garfield commands the comic strips, the Cat in the Hat exasperates even Dr. Seuss, and who hasn't heard of Heathcliff, Felix or Sylvester? Historically, calico cats have eaten gingham dogs, we are taught that "a cat can look at a king" and at least one cat has "been to London to see the Queen."

   It is often said that imitation is the sincerest form of flattery. To the animal world, I am sure that the sincerest form is anthropomorphosis. The ailurophobes contend that anthropomorphosis abounds, and that it is the work of ailurophiles. The ailurophiles say that they do not anthropomorphize cats but, rather, that cats have such human qualities as they may condescend to adopt for their own selfish purposes. Perhaps such was the case with Saki's ill-fated Tobermory, the cat who knew too much and told all, who, when asked if the human language had been difficult to learn, ". . . looked squarely at [Miss Resker] for a

moment and then fixed his gaze serenely on the middle distance. It was obvious that boring questions lay outside his scheme of life."

   For hundreds, perhaps thousands of years, people have carried on conversations with cats. Most often, these are one-sided and range from cloying, mawkish nonsense to topics of science and the liberal arts. Apparently Blackie's pride does not prevent him from making an occasional response to this great gush of human verbiage, much to the satisfaction and benefit of his "owners." Apparently, some cats do talk. Others just grin.

3. It seems doubtful that the city fathers would anticipate the need for a specific category of this sort.

4. Plaintiffs do not address their state constitutional claims in their summary judgment motion, but merely state that the federal constitutional arguments apply to the state claims. Because of the similarity of the two claims and the legal principles applicable to both, only the federal claims will be discussed, inasmuch as the result is the same under the state claim.

long history of humans' relationships with felines. He may have used a footnote because putting all of this in the text of the opinion might have caused some confusion: it really had no direct bearing on the legal issues (the point of footnotes one and two was simply that a talking cat is worth paying a dollar to hear). Placed within a footnote, however, this information adds clarity, not to mention entertainment value, to Judge Bowen's opinion.

Notice that the footnotes contain almost as much information as does the text of the trial court's opinion in Mr. Miles' case. This is typical of academic writing and of judicial opinions, but U.S. lawyers almost never use footnotes in court documents. Instead, citations are imbedded in the text, and any explanatory information that might have been included in a footnote is either omitted (because it is only tangentially related to the substance) or is written into the text itself. There is an ongoing, if intermittent, debate among lawyers in this country about the practice of using imbedded citations rather than footnotes; so far, the footnote advocates have lost that debate. But take another look at the trial judge's opinion in *Miles* and think about the depth that would be missing if Judge Bowen had elected to omit his eloquent descriptive footnotes.

Summarizing the points made in this section, first and foremost, legal writers must be careful and fastidious legal readers. No legal writing can occur, in any form, without someone, ideally the writer, having first researched, located, and read the law that will be binding. Consequently, every legal writer is also a legal reader.

U.S. lawyers and law students rely on case law to establish legal precedent, frequently when courts explain and illustrate the application of statutory, administrative, and/or constitutional law. Cases are never read in a vacuum, but instead are read with an eye toward a particular legal issue, or issues, that poses the question(s) the legal writer will attempt to answer. If, in that process, a little entertainment comes into the picture, that is an added bonus.

Finding the right case law requires identifying the issue(s) correctly, and then knowing what sources of law will be considered primary and binding authority within the writer's jurisdiction. Every legal writer must be familiar with, and constantly cognizant of, the basic structure of the U.S. legal system so that he or she will know how to determine which law is binding and which is merely persuasive. The particulars of the U.S. court structures, state and federal, criminal, civil, and administrative, need not be memorized, but the writer must know enough to look up the jurisdiction for any legal controversy. Similarly, U.S. legal writers need not memorize every rule of legal citation, despite the fact that citations are critically important to every U.S. legal document, but the writer must recognize the need to look up the applicable citation rules in a reliable legal citation manual, generally either the ALWD Manual or the Bluebook. A writer whose research leads him to rely on non-binding authority, or whose sloppy or non-existent citations draw the reader's attention away from the substance to the form of the document, has not done his or her job well enough to keep it.

And finally, having read the relevant case law, the legal writer must quote and cite with accuracy and care, and must never (ever) cite, quote, or rely on any printed information, virtually or physically printed, that is not a part of a court's majority opinion. Reading carefully, and truly understanding the material being read, is a time-consuming process for everyone, but even more so for those who are working with a language that is not their first. The time spent reading, however, is the best investment one can make in one's own writing. If you do not know what you are writing about, you cannot possibly write about it effectively.

In the United States, a lawyer's (or law student's) credibility, effectiveness, and reputation rely more heavily than ever on that person's legal writing. When reading case law, pay attention to every detail, read every footnote, and always keep your focus on the legal issue as much as, if not more than, the facts. When writing, again, pay attention to every detail; check every citation and every punctuation mark. It is the writer's job to make the reader's life easier. A written document that forces a reader to struggle to find its meaning is worthless. And without effective legal writing, a U.S. lawyer or law student cannot, as we say, amount to a hill of beans.[14]

YOUR ASSIGNMENT: OBJECTIVE ANALYSIS

Assume that you are employed by a small law firm in Augusta, Georgia, that has been contacted by one pf its most important clients, Mr. Joseph Banks. Mr. Banks' business is important to your firm, so your supervising attorney has instructed you to address a small question raised by Mr. Banks on behalf of his seven-year-old daughter, Cindy Banks. Cindy, with her parents' knowledge and consent, has begun selling lemonade from the end of the family's driveway. Cindy sells lemonade on Saturday afternoons, and occasionally after school during the week. She has raised almost $100.00 in the past few weeks. Half of her profits have been donated to charity, while Cindy has saved half to spend in the future as she sees fit (she would like to own a pony by the time she is ten). According to Mr. Banks, a representative of the City of Augusta told Cindy yesterday that she muse either procure a business license, for $50.00, or shut down her lemonade stand. Cindy is heartbroken, her father is angry, and your supervising attorney has instructed you to draft an internal office memorandum assessing the legal issue of whether, under the

---

[14] I have no idea where this expression comes from, but it has always evoked, in my mind, an image of a rural farmer wearing a straw hat, with a puzzled look on his face and empty pockets turned out, standing next to a mound of beans that apparently has no monetary value. Whatever its true origin, the expression refers to a person or thing that never reaches its potential.

same ordinance that governed Mr. Miles' case, Cindy Banks may be required to obtain a business license.

Such internal office memoranda are a typical tool for law firms that need to answer client questions and maintain records of the work that supports those answers. Your memorandum should predict, not argue, an answer to this legal question. For the purposes of this assignment, assume that you must write the following: A statement of the Issue(s) to be decided; a Statement of the Facts as we know them thus far; the Analysis, including citations to applicable authorities; and a short Conclusion, including recommended courses of action as appropriate. The memorandum should not exceed 2999 words (but it may certainly contain far fewer words).

B. READING ADMINISTRATIVE LAW CASES

Carl Miles sued to have a city ordinance declared unconstitutional, and the resulting judicial opinions became part of the U.S. common law. This illustrates the interplay between statutory and case law in the U.S.: neither exists in a vacuum without the other. It is this combination of civil and common law that makes the U.S. legal system different from the law that is familiar to most international students.

This same process takes place in the administrative law context. Administrative law is promulgated by the administrative agencies that are part of the Executive Branch of the government. Administrative rules and regulations are promulgated by Administrative agencies, and are then interpreted in judicial-type proceedings that originate in administrative hearings decided by Administrative Law Judges. Administrative agencies promulgate (a nice way of saying "make") administrative rules and regulations that are, for most practical purposes, treated in the same ways as are legislatively created laws. Administrative agencies exist at all levels of the U.S. legal system, from local to state to federal. At each level, the administrative agency must follow the established processes for providing notice and an opportunity to comment on proposed regulations before those regulations take on the force of law. Students may have an opportunity to devote an entire law school course to the principles of administrative law. For now, it is enough to keep in mind that a properly enacted administrative rule or regulation has a function that is equivalent to a code or statute. When a regulation's meaning or interpretation is called into question by parties who have an actual case or controversy arising under that regulation (which cannot be resolved in some alternative manner) the case is decided by an Administrative Law Judge, or ALJ (without a jury). Decisions of Administrative Law Judges look like, and are treated like, the written opinions of trial courts. The ALJ's written decision then becomes part of our common law. Administrative Law Judges write opinions that look and act like the decisions of the judges who serve on courts in the judicial branch of our government. A losing party may have a right to appeal; ALJ decisions are usually appealed to the jurisdiction's intermediate court of appeals and then, perhaps, to its highest court.

Reading administrative law cases involves the same skills as reading cases that were decided by the judicial branch of our government. Reading any case requires context.

In the following case,[15] an Oregon state appellate court was called on to interpret that state's administrative regulations regarding the intersection of an employee's disability benefits and her unemployment insurance. The disability regulations at issue were part of the Oregon Administrative Regulations, while the unemployment laws were part of the Oregon Revised Statutes (the state code). This case, then, mingles statutory, administrative, and case law to illustrate how the U.S. legal system strives to arrive at results that are both fair and just. Most nations utilize no more than one or two sources of law, such as a code and a constitution, so the U.S. hybrid system probably differs from the law in which international students have been educated and trained. Reading cases is challenging but not impossible, as should be apparent as you read and prepare to deconstruct parts of this court's decision.

Employer petitions for judicial review of a Workers' Compensation Board order directing employer to pay claimant temporary partial disability benefits and not reduce those payments by the amount of short-term disability benefit payments that it made to claimant. We review the board's order for errors of law, ORS 656.298(7); ORS 183.482(8), and affirm.

The relevant facts are not in dispute, and we state them consistently with the board's findings. On April 7, 2005, claimant suffered a compensable knee injury that required surgery. Following the operation, claimant's surgeon released claimant to modified work, and claimant returned to modified work the first week of September 2005. Claimant received temporary partial disability benefits based on the difference between her preinjury wages and the wages she earned at modified work. Less than two weeks later, on September 10, 2005, claimant suffered a heart attack. Because of the heart attack, claimant was unable to work until October 31, 2005, when she returned to modified work.

The dispute in this case arises because claimant simultaneously collected temporary disability benefits and short-term disability benefits for her on-the-job knee injury and short-term disability benefits for her off-the-job heart attack. For

---

[15] *Safeway Stores, Inc., v. Martinez*, 243 P. 3d 1203 (Or. App. 2010). The Court's footnotes have been omitted for purposes of this text but they do contain helpful information for students who want to understand more fully how administrative law operates in the U.S.

context, we begin with a description of the benefits claimant received.

Claimant received payments under a short-term disability plan for the wages she lost due to her heart attack between September 2005 and January 2006. The benefits were provided under an income protection plan sponsored by employer without contribution from claimant. The plan provides that, in the event that an off-the-job sickness or injury prevents the worker from working for a period of time, the plan replaces a portion of the worker's income. The plan pays 66 and two-thirds percent of the worker's weekly earnings. It expressly excludes benefits for disabilities due to an occupational sickness or injury. As to sick leave, the plan provides that short-term disability benefits will not be reduced by sick leave payments that a worker receives, and allows a worker to use accumulated sick leave to supplement the short-term disability benefit up to 100 percent of the worker's pay.

Next, we turn to the payment of temporary partial disability payments under the Workers' Compensation Law. In the event that a worker's disability is or becomes partial, the worker is entitled to temporary partial disability benefits proportionate to the worker's lost wages. Those benefits are calculated by subtracting the wages the worker earns, or is able to earn, from the wages used to calculate temporary total disability. ORS 656.212(2); *Stone Forest Industries, Inc. v. Bowler,* 147 Or.App. 81, 84, 934 P.2d 1138 (1997). Thus, calculation of temporary partial disability benefits requires a determination of the wages that the worker earns or is able to earn while partially disabled.

Here, employer concluded that the short-term disability benefits that claimant received reduce the temporary partial disability benefits to which claimant is entitled. Accordingly, employer paid claimant a reduced amount of temporary partial disability. Claimant disagreed and requested a hearing. She argued that employer could not reduce her partial disability benefits by the amount of short-term disability benefits that she received. Employer argued that the reduction was mandated for two reasons: (1) short-term disability benefits are a "similar advantage" to board, rent, housing, or lodging and are therefore "wages" as defined by ORS 656.005(29); or, alternatively, (2) short-term disability benefits are analogous to sick leave payments and are therefore "post-injury wages" under OAR 436–060–0030(10).

The Administrative Law Judge agreed with claimant and ordered employer to pay claimant temporary partial disability benefits without reducing those benefits by the amount of short-term disability benefits claimant received. Employer requested review by the board, and the board affirmed.

The board adopted the ALJ's reasoning that short-term disability benefits are not wages under ORS 656.005(29) because short-term disability benefits are not "the same kind of remuneration as 'board, rent, housing, and lodging,'" as provided by the statute. The board also concluded that short term disability benefits are not post-injury wages under OAR 436–060–0030(10), reasoning that employer distinguished between sick leave payments and short-term disability payments, that employer made short term disability payments even after claimant exhausted her sick leave, and that the short term disability plan distinguished between short-term disability and sick leave by describing accumulated sick leave as a separate supplement to the short-term disability benefit.

On judicial review, the parties repeat their arguments. We begin with employer's argument that short-term disability benefits **1206 are "wages" under ORS 656.005(29). We examine the text of that statute in context and any helpful legislative history offered by the parties. *State v. Gaines,* 346 Or. 160, 171–72, 206 P.3d 1042 (2009); *PGE v. Bureau of Labor and Industries,* 317 Or. 606, 610–12, 859 P.2d 1143 (1993). Our paramount goal in interpreting a statute is to discern the legislature's intent, and the most persuasive evidence of the legislature's intent is the words the legislature used. *Gaines,* 346 Or. at 171, 206 P.3d 1042.

Accordingly, we begin with the statutory definition of "wages":

> "'Wages' means the money rate at which the service rendered is recompensed under the contract of hiring in force at the time of the accident, including reasonable value of board, rent, housing, lodging or similar advantage received from the employer, and includes the amount of tips required to be reported by the employer * * * ."

ORS 656.005(29). Under that definition, wages are the agreed-upon rate of payment for the services a worker provides to the employer. Here, employer does not argue that the short-term disability benefits are paid in exchange for services. Indeed, the money was paid precisely because claimant could not provide services. Nonetheless, employer argues that short-term disability benefits are included in the definition of wages because they are a *similar advantage* to board, rent, housing, and lodging. But that argument ignores the problem that we just described; the short-term disability benefits in this case were paid because claimant could not provide services. Setting that problem aside, we disagree with employer that short-term disability benefits are a similar advantage to board, rent, housing, and lodging.

Although the legislature's use of the term "including" means that the legislature intended that wages are not limited solely to money paid by the employer to the worker in exchange for services, the itemized list following "including" is nonexclusive. Yet the terms "including" and "or similar advantage received" provide boundaries to the items that fall within the list. "Including" identifies items that share characteristics with named items. *See State v. Kurtz,* 233 Or. .App. 573, 577, 228 P.3d 583, *rev den,* 348 Or. 621, 237 P.3d 221 (2010) ("Includes" is a nonexclusive term that "describes in particular those things that are contained in or embraced by the term."). The phrase "or similar advantage received" likewise permits inclusion of some unnamed items, but only those unnamed items that share relevant characteristics with the listed items. Thus, we must determine whether short-term disability benefits are a similar advantage as board, rent, housing, and lodging.

Board, rent, housing, and lodging are all payments for specific benefits or are specific benefits themselves. Housing and lodging are specific benefits of shelter. Similarly, rent and board are payments for specific benefits of shelter or food. In contrast, short-term disability benefits are fungible. Those benefits may be used to pay for meals, rent, housing, or lodging, but the benefits are not limited to those narrow uses. Rather, the payments of short-term disability benefits may be used to pay for any item available for purchase, or saved, or even given away. Thus, we conclude that employer is incorrect. Short-term disability benefits are not a "similar advantage" to board, rent, housing, and lodging. The board did not err in reaching that conclusion.

We next consider whether short-term disability benefits are "post injury wages" under OAR 436–060–0030(10). We **1207 interpret administrative rules so as to give effect to the intent of the body that promulgated the rule. *Abu-Adas v. Employment Dept.,* 325 Or. 480, 485, 940 P.2d 1219 (1997). We do so by utilizing the same methodology that we use to interpret statutes. *Tye v. McFetridge,* 342 Or. 61, 69, 149 P.3d 1111 (2006). That is, we begin by examining the text of the rule in context. Context includes other provisions of the same rule, related rules, the statute pursuant to which the rule was created, and other related statutes. *Abu-Adas,* 325 Or. at 485, 940 P.2d 1219.

OAR 436–060–0030(10) defines "post-injury wages" as "wages a worker could have earned by accepting a job offer, or actual wages earned, whichever is greater, and any unemployment, sick or vacation leave payments received." That is, the rule provides a list of items that are "post-injury wages."

Employer argues that short-term disability benefits are "post-injury wages" because they are sick leave. Sick leave is not defined by the rule, so we give that term its common meaning. Sick leave is a contractual benefit that an employer provides employees. *See, e.g., Funkhouser v. Wells Fargo Corp.,* 224 Or.App. 308, 313, 197 P.3d 592 (2008), *rev. den.,* 346 Or. 115, 205 P.3d 887 (2009) (sick leave is a vested right when the employment agreement creating the right so provides). Here, claimant's employment contract defines sick leave as a benefit that replaces lost wages when an employee cannot work due to sickness or injury. Short-term disability benefits provided by employer are an income protection plan that is available when an illness prevents an employee from working. However, the analogy stops there. Sick leave can accumulate under the employment agreement. In contrast, the short-term disability benefits at issue here cannot, and do not, accumulate. If available, those benefits last for a discrete period of time and are supplemented by sick leave. Moreover, the short-term disability plan distinguishes between the sick leave benefits and the short-term disability benefits. The plan states, "[employer] will not subtract from your gross disability payment income you receive from, but not limited to, the following: * * * sick pay." Employer also distinguished between short-term disability benefits and sick leave payments that it paid. Accordingly, we conclude that the short-term disability benefits at issue here are not the same as sick leave.

Nonetheless, employer argues that the rule encompasses more than ordinary sick leave, because post-injury wages include "any" sick leave payments received and short-term disability benefits are analogous to sick leave. That is, employer argues that the term "any" preceding "sick leave" expands **1208 the definition of "sick leave" to include short -term disability benefits. "Any" is commonly "used as a function word esp. in interrogative and conditional expressions to indicate *one that is not a particular or definite individual of the given category* but whichever one chance may select." *Webster's Third New Int'l Dictionary* 97 (unabridged ed. 2002) (emphasis added). Thus, in the context of this case, "any" is open-ended with respect to quantity but it is closed with respect to category; the use of the term "any" does not represent an intent to make the category *nonexclusive* as to the category of benefits. By contrast, for the reasons explained above, the use of the term "includes" makes a category *non*exclusive, and the Department of Consumer and Business Services (DCBS) used that nonexclusive term in the same rule, OAR 436–060–0030(8) ("[t]his includes but is not limited to"), demonstrating that it knew how to make a list nonexclusive. Thus, we conclude that DCBS intended to make the list exclusive as to sick leave.

Returning to our interpretation of "post-injury wages," we focus on the term "any." That term functions to extend the definition of "post-injury wage earnings" to all sick leave payments received without limit as to how many sick leave payments were made. "Sick leave" is limited to that particularly described term. It does not extend to terms that are analogous to but are not "sick leave." And, as we discussed before, "sick leave" may be comparable to short-term disability benefits, but short-term disability benefits are not a type of sick leave. We conclude that short-term disability benefits are not sick leave as used in the definition of "post-injury wages" in the administrative rule; and, therefore, short-term disability benefits are not "post-injury wages."

In short, the board did not err in ordering employer to pay claimant temporary partial disability without a deduction for the short-term disability benefits claimant received.

Affirmed.

INTRODUCTION TO THE EXERCISE

Note to students: You have all the tools required to deconstruct this opinion.

Knowing what you already know about reading cases, use the notions of CREAC or IRAC, PASS, and The Three C's as a guide through the court's opinion in *Safeway Stores, Inc. v. Martinez*. Pay particular attention here to the court's application of statutes, administrative regulations, and common law precedent. The court applied Oregon state statutes—a code—to define "wages." It applied Oregon administrative regulations—from that state's Worker's Compensation Division, which is an agency of the executive branch of the state government—to determine whether the employer-sponsored short-term disability payments were "wages" that would reduce the state-mandated short-term disability payments the employer was required to pay the plaintiff.[16] The amount of money in dispute here is probably not particularly

---

[16] Not every employer offers its employees short-term (or long term) disability benefits for off-the-job injuries, but every employer of a certain size is required to pay short-term disability for on-the-job injuries. Workers' compensation laws and regulations provide a steady stream of income for lawyers who specialize in those cases because there is a never-ending conflict between the amount of money employers think they should pay and the amount of money their employees think should be paid. In Workers' Compensation cases, the employees' lawyers' fees are usually paid by

large, but it would be important to an injured, unemployable worker. At its core, civil litigation in the United States tends to be ultimately about money, and the quantity of money does not necessarily determine the rigor of the fight. In some legal systems there might be a different motivation for bringing a civil action, but in the United States money is usually the ultimate issue.[17]

Oregon's code (the legislatively enacted statute) defines "wages" as "the money rate at which . . . service is rendered . . . including reasonable value of board, rent, housing or similar advantages received from the employer [including] tips. . . ." Here, the employer argued that the short-term disability payments provided through its own program were the same thing as wages.

Note the court's explanation of the manner in which it would interpret the state statute: "[w]e examine the text of that statute in context and any helpful legislative history. . . ." This is one of many methods of "statutory construction," the catch-all term that describes courts' methods of interpreting and applying laws created by a different branch of government. There are many "canons" of construction, and courts are generally free to apply whichever one seems most appropriate in the circumstances of a given case. Here, the court specifically wrote that its "paramount concern" was to interpret the statute according to the intent of the enacting body, the legislature of the state of Oregon. Legislative intent is frequently referred to but not always easy to discern. Our books and files are filled with appellate court opinions derived from cases in which a party argued that a lower court misinterpreted or misconstrued a statute or administrative regulation. This requires more of the appellate court that is assigned to review the appealed decision. When a case is appealed, another layer of analysis is required to determine the standard of review; standard of review is the notion that applies only in appellate cases to describe the degree of deference an appellate court gives to a lower court's decision. Standard of review should never be confused with canons of statutory construction.

In addition to applying the statutory definition of "wages" to the plaintiff's employer-sponsored short-term disability benefits, the court was also asked (by the employer) to find, in the alternative, that the benefits were a type of "post-injury wage" as defined in the workers' compensation regulations. Arguing in the alternative is common practice in the U.S. It is considered good lawyering because an advocate never knows whether a court will be persuaded by any given argument. Smart advocates will come prepared with an alternative argument just to be safe. In this case, Safeway's lawyers hedged their bets[18] by giving the court a credible legal reason to find that Ms. Martinez received "wages" when she received the short-term disability benefits provided by

---

the unsuccessful employer, making this a relatively steady stream of income for many lawyers across the country.

[17] This is not an unnecessarily harsh depiction of the U.S. legal system. The reality of civil litigation is that an award of money is presumed to be the desired outcome unless the pleadings say otherwise. Injunctive relief and specific performance are two exceptions to this general rule.

[18] This is another idiom, and one that might make sense to any reader who is familiar with gambling. It is used to mean, quite simply, to play it safe.

Safeway's program. Unfortunately for Safeway, neither argument was persuasive to the court. But nobody could credibly say Safeway's lawyers had not done their jobs.

The court eventually agreed with the plaintiff, and with both the Worker's Compensation Board and the ALJ, that short-term disability payments are neither wages nor "post-injury wages" like sick leave.[19] Students should notice the court's use of case law to support its application of both the statute and the administrative regulation in the Safeway case: the court cited two cases just for the principles of statutory construction, and another one to support its interpretation of the statute's use of the word "including" in its definition of "wages." Law students are frequently tempted to either overlook the need to define a term like "including" or to turn to a secondary source, such as a legal dictionary, if a definition is even recognized as necessary. Students can learn a valuable lesson by observing the Oregon court's use of primary binding authority, in the form of case law, as it logically and methodically worked through the statutory interpretation process. Good legal writers leave no terms undefined; just as importantly, good legal writers never cite a secondary source unless there is no primary source on-point.

The court also cited three cases in support of its interpretation of the administrative regulation that defines "post-injury wages." The regulation lists things that would be post-injury wages, and employer-provided short-term disability benefits are not on that list. Sick leave is not defined in the regulation, but the employer's alternative argument was that the disability payments were a form of paid sick leave. The court turned to precedent cases when it said "sick leave" should be given its "common meaning" as a contracted-for benefit that was defined in the employee's contract as a replacement for wages that are lost when the employee is too sick to work. The employer's disability program, on the other hand, was described in the contract as an "income protection plan" that lasts for a defined period of time, cannot be accumulated in the same manner as sick leave, and is distinguished from sick leave in the very terms of the employee's contract. These characteristics of the short-term disability benefits thus distinguished them from sick leave, a separately defined benefit that was also included in the employment contract.

Without understanding the court's references to precedent cases, a reader could not fully understand the court's reasoning. When reading case law, the court's reasoning is always more important than how the court ultimately disposed of the case. In the Safeway case, the court affirmed both lower tribunals. But that holding, "affirmed," needs the context provided in the court's reasoning to have any meaning for a reader. When reading case law, remember that the court's analysis (including its citations to authority) are

---

[19] "Sick leave" is almost always an optional benefit paid by some employers to some full-time employees. Some benefits are required of every U.S. employer who employs a certain number of workers, such as family leave, following the birth or adoption of an infant, but most benefits are entirely optional. Many workers in the United States lack health care benefits, vacation leave, sick leave, and disability benefits because employers limit employees to part-time work; an employee who works less than forty hours per week is a part-time employee and almost never receives the benefits associated with good full-time employment.

always more important than its holding. The court's reasoning becomes part of the common law; its holding does not.

Court opinions are written primarily for the benefit of the losing party, in an effort to explain to that party precisely why and how it lost. (This is the courts' way of demonstrating that the justice system works, and it helps forestall further appeals.) In the Safeway case, the court's explanations and analyses are designed to tell Safeway why it was losing its appeal. This is true of trial court opinions as well as appellate court opinions. The prevailing party (the "winner") does not generally need an explanation for its victory, but the losing party does. The citations to authority are a substantive part of every judicial opinion's purpose, so the reader needs to pay attention to, and understand the significance of, every citation.

YOUR ASSIGNMENT: SOME EXERCISES IN CAUTION

1.　Look carefully at the citations to authority in the Safeway case.

　　A.　List, in proper format, the two cases cited for the rules of statutory construction:

　　　　_____

　　　　_____

　　　　_____

　　B.　Do the same for the three cases in support of its interpretation of the administrative regulation that defines "post-injury wages."

　　　　_____

　　　　_____

　　　　_____

　　C.　Using your citation manual, identify the components of each citation. Are there any non-binding sources cited? To answer that question, you may need to look up the Oregon court system; every jurisdiction in the United States is different, and each has its own official web site to explain the structure of its court system. If you are using the ALWD Citation Manual, Appendix One lists every U.S. jurisdiction alphabetically and tells writers how to cite the sources that are binding in that jurisdiction. Every legal writer should get in the habit of checking the sources of primary binding authority and how to correctly cite those sources. Answer the following for any of the cases listed above:

　　　　1.　Parties' names in correct citation form:

_____

2. Reporter volume, Reporter abbreviation, and initial page number:

_____

3. Parenthetical with court abbreviation (if needed) and year of decision):

_____

D. The first case cited by the court is *Stone Forest Industries, Inc. v. Bowler*, 934 P. 2d 1138 (Or. App. 1997). The citation alone tells a trained reader that the cited case (*Stone Forest*) was decided in 1997 by the Oregon intermediate court of appeals, the same court that was citing it. Note the distinction between the cited case (*Stone Forest*) and the citing case (*Safeway*). Using the resources available to you, determine whether Oregon has more than one intermediate court of appeals.

Yes _____ No _____

Correctly answering this will tell you, as the reader, whether the cited case is binding authority in the citing case. Some states, like Florida, have multiple intermediate courts of appeal, not all of which will bind the others. How many intermediate appellate courts does Oregon have, and is the cited case primary binding authority for the citing case?

E. Finding statutes and administrative regulations is not difficult, thanks to the Internet. A jurisdiction's official web site will almost always provide (free and reliably) the full text of all statutes and regulations. But if, as a writer, you want to find more sources that address the same legal issues that prompted you to look for the statute or regulation in the first place, an *annotated* code or regulation is an essential tool to use. This probably requires using a commercial legal database, which will more than likely not be free. One efficient method of conducting statutory or regulatory research is to use the jurisdiction's official web site to locate the citation and text of the statute or regulation (for free) and then go to the commercial database, such as Westlaw, to find the *citing references*. Citing references will lead you to every published source, in any jurisdiction, that has cited the statute, regulation, case, constitutional provision, or whatever else you may be researching. Looking at the citing references is the one sure way to determine, if nothing else, that any authority you intend to cite has not been reversed or overruled or superseded—and your responsibility as a writer includes verifying that every single source you cite is current and correct. Failure to do this is generally considered malpractice. Computerized legal research makes this process quick and easy, and there is no excuse for failure to do so.[20]

Using the citing references for *Stone Forrest*, find at least one other primary binding source that cites the Oregon statute (Or. Rev. Stat. § 656.005 (2015)) and the administrative regulation (Or. Admin. R. 436–060–0030 (2015)). Look carefully for citing references that would be binding on an Oregon appellate court. Write the full citation for at least one such citing reference. If you find no citing references, explain why that might so (other than a misstep in your own research process).

_____

_____

_____

_____

_____

* * *

Citations to authorities are more than mere technicalities in legal writing. Citations tell a reader where to locate the cited authority. Citations tell the reader how current the cited authority is, as well whether it is primary or secondary, binding or persuasive. In other words, citations convey substantive information about a writer's assertions. Without citations, those assertions look like the writer's personal opinion. In legal writing, the writer's personal opinion is of absolutely no value. Citations must be clear, correct, and concise (as you will see when you work with the short form citations). Sloppy, incorrect, or missing citations say as much about a writer as do the written words, and what those sloppy citations say is not favorable. Every legal writer is responsible for including clear, correct, and concise citations because they are as much a part of the work product as anything else. Lawyers and law students pay the price for sloppy writing and careless citations. Do not let that happen to you; you have been warned.[21]

---

[20] Google Scholar is making progress in reproducing the text of legal authorities from across the United States. But like the jurisdictions' own web sites, Google Scholar does not yet include the annotations or citing references. Google Scholar is working on this, and students looking for free electronic legal research data bases should bear in mind that Google Scholar may soon be a reliable free option.

[21] To see just one example of what happens when a lawyer's written documents are incomprehensible, including deficient or missing citations, *see In re Shepperson*, 674 A.2d 1273 (Vt. 1996) (noting that the lawyer could represent himself incompetently but could not be allowed to represent members of the public incompetently).

RECOMMENDED READING

When it comes to legal citations, most writers need all the help they can get. In addition to a reliable citation manual, students may benefit from perusing some or all of the following articles:

Darby Dickerson, *Citation Frustrations—And Solutions*, 30 Stet. L. Rev. 477 (Fall 2000).

Timothy D. Blevins, *A Hallmark of Professional Writing Citation Form*, 29 T. Marshall L. Rev. 89 (Fall 2003).

Scott A. Moss, *Bad Briefs, Bad Law, Bad Markets: Documenting the Poor Quality of Plaintiffs' Briefs, Its Impact on the Law, And the Market Failure it Reflects*, 63 Emory L.J. 59 (2013).

CHAPTER 3

COMMUNICATING WITH COURTS AND OPPOSING COUNSEL

■ ■ ■

A. COMMUNICATING WITH COURTS

Every case or controversy that arises in the United States stems from its own unique set of facts. Like snowflakes, no two legal actions are ever exactly alike. On a more practical level, and snowflakes aside, if a legal question arises between two parties and that issue has already been very clearly answered by existing primary, binding authority, no lawyer will file another lawsuit. Most states require new lawyers to take an Oath of Admission before being admitted to the Bar and allowed to practice law within that state. Lawyers are generally prohibited, either by this oath or by the Rules of Professional Responsibility, from pursuing frivolous cases. If the answer to any legal issue can be definitively ascertained from diligent legal research, it would be frivolous to pursue a new legal action. Of course the facts will always look at least slightly different from previously decided cases, because every person, like every snowflake, is unique—and so are their problems.

It is not uncommon for new legal writers to make the mistake of paying too much attention to the facts of a case and too little attention to the legal question(s). Thorough legal research will show that Carl Miles is the only person to have filed a lawsuit objecting to an ordinance that required a business license for a talking cat. Other lawsuits may have been filed that involved talking cats but different legal issues—say, for example, copyright infringement. If the legal issue of the case is different, the fact that it involves a talking cat is not at all important, and the talking cat makes no difference whatsoever. As a general rule of thumb,[1] the law of any case is more important than its facts. When researching, try to focus on the legal issue(s) rather than the facts. Focusing on the facts is almost always a frustrating and inefficient use of time, and it frequently ends badly for the law student or lawyer who has diligently researched and then analyzed the wrong issue.

---

[1] This is another expression used regularly in the United States: a "rule of thumb" is a generally followed practice or principle that is not guaranteed to work every time. Its origin is uncertain, according to Wikipedia, but it probably stems from the notion of a builder who will guess, or measure by "rule of thumb," rather than taking the time to actually measure before cutting or building.

Carl Miles may have been the one and only person to sue a city over the business license required for his talking cat, but remember that there was a First Amendment Freedom of Speech argument Mr. Miles tried, without success, to raise in the Eleventh Circuit Court of Appeals. The legal issue there was whether the cat was a "person" who would be protected by the U.S. Constitution's Bill of Rights. That is not a unique issue; the rights of animals (if there are any) are, as we shall see, the subject of litigation more often than one might imagine.

1. THE COMPLAINT

Every court case in the United States begins with the filing of some written document with some court. Remember that there are courts at every level, from small claims courts all the way up to the U.S. Supreme Court, at the local, state and federal levels, and there are both civil and cases decided at every level. In a criminal case, charges are filed by a prosecuting attorney alleging that a named defendant (or multiple defendants) committed some crime—a crime might be anything from insider trading by a wealthy Wall Street mogul to a simple assault (with or without any physical injury) by one citizen against another, to the first-degree murder that might carry the possibility of a sentence of execution. No matter how serious or how trivial the alleged crime may have been (and until there is a conviction, the crime is, indeed, only "alleged") the legal action begins with the filing of a written document, usually an Indictment or an Information, by a prosecuting official who represents the government (state or federal) in a court that has jurisdiction to decide the guilt or innocence of the accused.

> As of 2015, thirty-one of the fifty United States allow the death penalty to be imposed, as does the federal government and the courts of the U.S. military. Nineteen states, and the District of Columbia, have outlawed the death penalty. The death penalty is a very controversial issue in the United States, and it is generally wise to avoid engaging in conversations about it unless you are curious about an individual's views. Never get into an argument with an American about the death penalty; nobody will walk away happy from that argument.

Similarly, every civil suit (which, you should recall, means any legal case that is not criminal in nature) begins with the filing of a document of some sort in a court that has jurisdiction. Unlike criminal cases, not every civil suit involves a governmental entity, although many do.[2] Any

---

[2]   U.S. citizens have the right to sue their governments, whether local, state, or federal, with some caveats. The concept of "sovereign immunity" protects many public agencies and officials from liability, and special rules require giving any government agency or official advance notice of an intent to sue. Despite these limitations, however, it is a fundamental rule in the United States that the government is not above the law and may be held accountable by the court that has

individual or legally recognized entity may file a civil lawsuit against any other individual or entity—the entity might be a for-profit or non-profit corporation, a public official, a government agency, or a unit of government itself, such as the state of Florida or the U.S. government. The document that initiates the lawsuit must be filed in a court that has jurisdiction to decide the case.

> Jurisdiction is a tough concept for every law student in the United States. There are state and federal Rules of Civil Procedure and of Criminal Procedure, and even of Appellate Procedure, that specify which courts may decide which cases. If you have the opportunity to take a course in Civil Procedure, you should do so; every U.S. law student is currently required to take at least one course dedicated entirely to Civil Procedure. Most of it has to do with jurisdiction. It is a fundamentally important principle of how lawyers work in the United States.

Most civil suits begin with the filing of an initial Complaint or Petition, written by the lawyer(s) who represent the plaintiff or petitioner—the person initiating the case. These documents can take many forms depending on the nature of the case and the rules of the court. But here is one example of a document that initiated a civil lawsuit in a case that is, on one level, related to Carl Miles and Blackie, his talking cat: *Tilikum ex rel. People for the Ethical Treatment of Animals v. Sea World Parks & Entertainment, Inc.,* 842 F. Supp. 2d 1259 (S.D. Calif. 2012).

YOUR ASSIGNMENT: REVIEW CASE CITATION BASICS

Before proceeding, use the list below to identify all of the pieces of the citation above. Who filed the lawsuit against whom, in which court, and when? Name the Reporter in which the court's opinion was published. Which courts' decisions are published in that Reporter? Remember that citations convey substantive information.

a. Plaintiff

b. Defendant

c. Court

d. Year

e. Reporter

f. Type of cases published in that Reporter

---

jurisdiction to hear the claim. In some parts of the world, citizens may sue each other but never their government; the U.S. Constitution was written to ensure that the government, like any citizen, may be held accountable for misdeeds.

Jeffrey S. Kerr (to be admitted *pro hac vice*)
Martina Bernstein (State Bar No. 230505)
PETA Foundation
1536 16th Street NW
Washington, DC 20036
Tel: 202-483-2190
Fax: 202-540-2207
JeffK@petaf.org
MartinaB@petaf.org

Matthew Strugar (State Bar No. 232951)
PETA Foundation
2898 Rowena Avenue
Los Angeles, CA 90039
Tel: 323-739-2701
Fax: 202-540-2207
Matthew-s@petaf.org

UNITED STATES DISTRICT COURT FOR THE

SOUTHERN DISTRICT OF CALIFORNIA

Tilikum, Katina, Corky, Kasatka, and Ulises, five orcas,	Case No.: 11-cv-
Plaintiffs,	**Complaint for Declaratory and Injunctive Relief**
by their Next Friends, People for the Ethical Treatment of Animals, Inc., Richard "Ric" O'Barry, Ingrid N. Visser, Ph.D., Howard Garrett, Samantha Berg, and Carol Ray,	**'11CV2476 JM WMC**
v.	
SeaWorld Parks & Entertainment, Inc. and SeaWorld, LLC,	
Defendants.	

NATURE OF THE CASE

1.   In this case of first impression, five wild-captured orcas named Tilikum, Katina, Corky, Kasatka, and Ulises (collectively, the "Plaintiffs"), seek a declaration that they are held by the Defendants in violation of Section One of the Thirteenth Amendment to the Constitution of the United States, which prohibits slavery and involuntary servitude. Plaintiffs were forcibly taken from their families and natural habitats, are held captive at SeaWorld San Diego and SeaWorld Orlando, denied everything that is natural to them, subjected to artificial insemination or sperm

This is the first page of the initial Complaint filed on behalf of a group of orcas (sometimes called Killer Whales but actually members of the dolphin family). The orcas, obviously, did not file the lawsuit on their own behalf. Instead, an animal-rights organization called People for the Ethical

Treatment of Animals (PETA) filed the lawsuit as the "next of friends" of the Orcas. In the U.S. legal system, a party who is not legally competent to file a lawsuit, a child, for example, may participate in a lawsuit as a party who is represented by a guardian or "next of friend." This is how PETA framed its Complaint, the opening document in its lawsuit opposing the manner in which the Sea World parks in Florida and California capture and then treat wild orcas.

Look at the information contained on the first page of this Complaint. Note not just the information that is provided, but the order in which it was provided, the font in which it was prepared, and the numbered lines. None of these things was decided randomly by the lawyers for the plaintiffs; the content and format of all documents filed with courts are dictated by rules of civil procedure—here, the applicable rules would be both the Federal Rules of Civil Procedure and the "local rules," if any, for the U.S. District Court for the Southern District of California (a federal trial court).

This document is titled a "Complaint for Declaratory and Injunctive Relief." Without attempting to teach the rules of Civil Procedure here, suffice it to say that the people who filed this lawsuit (PETA) did so in an effort to have the federal court "declare" that Sea World was violating the law, and in doing so PETA sought "injunctive relief" in the form of an order from the court that Sea World needed to stop what it was doing because the harm being caused by its conduct could not be compensated by money. When money is an adequate remedy (when a person's car is damaged, for example), injunctive relief is not appropriate. It is only when the alleged wrongdoing could never be compensated by money (if, for example, a corporation's regular business practices involved exposing employees to poisonous gas) that injunctive relief may be granted. PETA sought declaratory and injunctive relief on the grounds that Sea World kept the orcas in slavery and forced them into indentured servitude. Even if a court agreed with PETA and awarded monetary damages to the orcas, as opposed to declaratory and injunctive relief, that would not help the orcas: what would a group of orcas do with money? They don't even have pockets, much less bank accounts, in which to keep it—and they lack the opposable thumbs that are required for every financial transaction. The point is that PETA sought a particular type of relief based on the nature of its case, and that relief is clearly identified on the first page of the Complaint filed in the federal trial court.

The Complaint's first page also identifies the parties, and includes the names and contact information for the plaintiffs' lawyers; this is standard information, but many courts have rules that would place it somewhere other than at the top of the first page. The court itself is clearly identified, as is the case number that was assigned to the case when it was filed with the clerk of the court; the clerk's office receives all documents that become part of the court file, and most jurisdictions now provide for electronic filing. However, none of this should be taken for granted. A proper approach is to find the applicable rules of civil procedure—local, state, and/or federal—and make sure that any document submitted to any court is in compliance with those rules. The U.S. Supreme Court, for example, does not (as of this writing) have rules providing for the electronic filing of briefs; the Court specifies the size and type of paper on which all documents must be presented, as well as the font style and size and the word limit. It even has rules about the color for the cover page of any brief filed with the court: an appellant (the party that lost in the lower court and thus is initiating the appeal) must use a red cover page for its initial brief, while an appellee (the party that won in the lower court and is therefore responding to the appeal) must use a blue cover for its reply brief. It is always the lawyers' responsibility to know and to follow the rules of any court; failure to do so is malpractice.

> PETA sued Sea World parks in both California and Florida. The decision to file the lawsuit in California was probably a tactical one made by PETA's lawyers in one of the few situations in which lawyers have some choice about jurisdiction. When a corporation conducts business in more than one state, the Federal Rules of Civil Procedure provide for "diversity jurisdiction," giving plaintiffs some leeway in deciding where to file the lawsuit. This is a complicated question of jurisdiction that can be studied in a Civil Procedure course.

The first substantive part of this Complaint begins at the bottom of the first page, with a summary of the Nature of the Case. This is presented in two numbered paragraphs, and summarizes the plaintiffs' arguments. Not every court will require or even accept a summary like this; many trial courts at the state level want all written documents to be as concise and efficient as possible. This is where it is the lawyer's job to know what his or her audience (reader) wants and needs to see. The lawyer's personal preference is completely insignificant; the rules of procedure must be followed to the letter, or the court may simply decline to consider the lawyer's document at all.

YOUR ASSIGNMENT: RULES OF PROCEDURE

Using the identifying information on the first page of the *Tilikum* Complaint, prepare a first page that would comply with the rules applicable if you were one of the lawyer's filing this case in federal court in **your** jurisdiction.

This exercise requires that you identify the federal trial court that would have jurisdiction to decide this case if you were to file it where you are currently a student. If you happen to be within the jurisdiction of the court that actually decided this case, the U.S. District Court for the Southern District of California, use a different jurisdiction; you might use the Middle District of Florida. All of these skills are transferrable from one jurisdiction to another within the United States.

The next part of this exercise requires you to determine which rule(s) of civil procedure are applicable in your jurisdiction. We accept that this is a federal case, so the Federal Rules of Civil Procedure apply, but which ones, and what do they require? Also, be sure to look for local rules that may have been enacted by your local federal trial court.

When you have determined the jurisdiction and have located all of the applicable rules of civil procedure, prepare and print (or submit electronically) a first page that would be acceptable for filing in your jurisdiction. Maybe it will look very similar to the one PETA's lawyers prepared for the U.S. District Court for the Southern District of California; maybe it will have some significant differences. You might find sample filings if you are looking up cases on Westlaw or Lexis. Remember that not everything filed and available is accurate or correct. Yours, however, must be.

The lesson to take from this exercise: know your reader, and give your reader what he or she wants, needs, and expects to see. Nothing more and nothing less.

Now, locate and read the Complaint filed in this case so you are prepared to follow along as we deconstruct its parts and their purposes.

The *Tilikum* Complaint next contains specific statements and citations regarding jurisdiction and venue. This is a standard requirement for federal courts and most state courts, because if the court lacks jurisdiction, it lacks any authority to hear or decide a case. This, if nothing else, is reason enough for every advocate to research and verify jurisdiction before filing any legal action of any kind. The venue question is a nuanced version of the jurisdiction question: as noted previously, Sea World operates parks in both California and Florida; a federal lawsuit could therefore be filed against Sea World in either state. The venue statement written by PETA's lawyers is designed to persuade the California federal court that it should hear the case because a "substantial part" of the defendants' actions took place within the geographic boundaries over which that court has jurisdiction. The lawyers may have chosen to file suit in California rather than Florida because California courts are generally thought (rightly or wrongly) to be more liberal or permissive than the courts in many other states, while Florida courts, in general, are thought to be more conservative. And on a very practical level, having chosen to sue in California, PETA's lawyers would not have wanted to be rejected and forced to start all over again in a court on the other side of the continent. From a writer's perspective, you should note that everything the lawyers have written thus far is designed to persuade the court to agree with PETA's position—and that position has not yet even been argued.

The next requirement for the Complaint is to identify the parties—the plaintiffs and the defendants in a civil suit, or the prosecution and the defendant in a criminal case. Identifying the parties does not, in most cases, require much persuasion on the part of the lawyers who write the pleadings. In this case, however, identifying the parties is a primary legal issue because, as noted, orcas do not really have any track record of successfully filing lawsuits in the United States. The PETA lawyers therefore had to expend considerable effort in this section of the Complaint where very little would normally be required. As writers, you should note that this section strives to persuade the court that there are federal laws that allow a non-profit organization, PETA, and several named individuals who have "a genuine concern for Plaintiffs' well-being," to file a lawsuit on behalf of the orcas. If you have already looked at the court's opinion in this case, you know that the lawyers were unsuccessful in this (and every other) endeavor. But they tried, and that is the advocate's job: not to judge or decide a case, but to give his or her client the best possible representation. Obviously, no lawyer wins every case. Good lawyers, however, having committed to represent a party, always provide the best possible representation for that client.

The next section of the Complaint describes the facts of this case, from this party's perspective. Good legal writers use the Facts section of any document to tell the client's story accurately and honestly, yet persuasively. Being persuasive does not mean omitting facts that make your client look bad, or attributing actions to any party when those actions simply did not take place. Persuasive legal writing is an art, and it takes practice. At its core, however, it must be accurate. A lawyer's credibility and professional responsibility are on the line with every written document that lawyer prepares. Any deviation from the truth in a Statement of Facts, or elsewhere, can cause irreparable damage to the lawyer who wrote it. Even if it takes years of practice to become a skilled persuasive writer, every writer, no matter how new or inexperienced, can abide by this universal requirement of truthfulness. If, in your legal writing, there is any uncertainty about the truth of a statement, it must not be treated as a truth. In any Facts section, there is room only for fact. Nothing else is permissible.

In the Facts section of PETA's Complaint, you may be able to discern the attorneys' efforts to tell the plaintiffs' story truthfully but certainly from the perspective most likely to persuade the court to hear the case and decide in the plaintiffs' favor. The Facts are organized topically, and describe at great length the sophisticated cognitive, social, and familial qualities of wild orcas. The Facts section then proceeds to tell the story of each individual orca, again in a manner that is both truthful and designed to give the court good reason to agree with the PETA petition on behalf of these orcas. Note that in paragraph 44, the PETA lawyers truthfully disclose that Tilikum, the first named plaintiff, killed a Sea World trainer in 2010, and in paragraph 60 the Complaint refers to another orca, Corky, having been involved in an altercation with another captive orca that resulted in the other orca's "fatal hemorrhaging," which is a nicer way of saying the other orca died. To have ignored or omitted these facts would have brought the lawyers' credibility into question. Instead, the lawyers used a common method of persuasive legal writing by placing these unfortunate facts deep within the Facts section. Research shows that readers tend to remember best what they read first and last, and that the material they read in the middle of a document tends to get "lost" in the readers' mind. It was probably no accident, then, that the facts about Tilikum having killed a human and Corky having killed another orca were included but were certainly not placed in prominent positions. If it was an accident rather than an intentional use of persuasive writing techniques, the PETA lawyers were lucky. It would not be hard to read this entire Complaint and miss the two facts that cast the orcas in the worst light.

The Facts section in *Tilikum* is definitely not typical for any trial court pleading in any court in the United States. You may have noted that the Facts section begins on page 3 of the Complaint and ends on page 17, thus clearly comprising the vast majority of the plaintiffs' Complaint. Such a detailed Facts section may have been necessary because this was an unusual case, and one of first impression, and the PETA lawyers knew they had an uphill battle[3] if they were to have any chance of persuading the court to accept these orcas as plaintiffs. The details about wild orcas' lives, and about the lives in captivity of the plaintiff orcas, as well as the details about PETA and the individual humans who filed the lawsuit, could not have appropriately been included in any other section of the Complaint. It is true, as seen in the court's opinion, that this attempt at persuasion was unsuccessful, but the PETA lawyers did their jobs.

YOUR ASSIGNMENT: EFFICIENTLY STATING FACTS

Re-write the Statement of Facts using no more than half the words the PETA lawyers used. Be persuasive; do not omit any relevant or necessary facts; instead, reduce the clutter and get to the point. Imagine that there is an eleven-page limit for the entire Complaint, so the Facts should not exceed five pages.

---

[3] An "uphill battle" is another commonly used idiom. It probably dates back to the ancient Greek myth of Sisyphus, who was doomed for eternity to push a boulder up a steep hill, only to have it roll back to the bottom each time it reached the top. Fighting an uphill battle, or waging an uphill war, may also have been in use in a military context for hundreds of years. It may mean a task is impossible, or simply very difficult. Learning to write like a U.S. lawyer might be an uphill battle for many international students, just as it is for most U.S. students, but that does not mean it is impossible—it's difficult and time-consuming, but not impossible.

There is an actual legal argument beginning on page seventeen of the Complaint. As stated in the "Nature of the Case" section on the very first page, the legal argument is based on alleged violations of the Thirteenth Amendment to the U.S. Constitution, which prohibits both slavery and involuntary servitude. In more detail, the plaintiffs argued that the Thirteenth Amendment never mentions "persons"; it simply declares that "neither slavery nor involuntary servitude . . . shall exist within the United States." This is a legitimate framework for what was, by the plaintiffs' own admission, a "case of first impression," meaning that the plaintiffs acknowledged they were asking the court to do something that has never been done in the U.S. legal system. The U.S. Constitution, in particular, is designed to be adaptable to new circumstances, as is the entire common law system under the concept of "*stare decisis*": case law becomes precedent, perhaps binding precedent, every time any court in the nation issues an opinion on any legal issue. Americans are very proud of our Constitution and its ability to remain relevant after 250 years. If courts were unable to accept previously unacceptable legal arguments, as the court was asked to do in *Tilikum*, our hybrid of constitutional, statutory, administrative, and common law could not survive. This explains why a case of first impression is an acceptable legal action (so long as it is not brought in bad faith and is not frivolous).

> Other issues could foreseeably arise, of course, such as how a "person" is defined. This legal issue is at the heart of every abortion-rights case filed in the United States. This is an entirely different issue than the one decided in *Tilikum*. Remember, precedent applies to future cases that revolve around the same legal issue. It takes practice to consistently identify the actual legal question(s) in a case; three years of law school is a good start, but many more years of practice may also be needed.

Obviously, however, the PETA lawyers' argument asked too much of this court. The Thirteenth Amendment might not specifically prohibit the enslavement or involuntary servitude of humans, but the court declined to apply that prohibition to orcas. The court established precedent when it decided that only "human beings or persons" are protected by the Thirteenth Amendment. This means that, at least within the jurisdiction of the U.S. District Court for the Southern District of California, it would be frivolous (and therefore prohibited) for any lawsuit to be filed claiming that any non-person—animal, vegetable, or mineral—has "standing" to sue for violation of its constitutional rights, whether through a "Next Friend" or any other legal representative. That question has been asked and answered within this court's jurisdiction; thus, unless the PETA lawyers had filed an appeal, which they did not, there is no longer any credible legal argument to be made that the Thirteenth Amendment's protections should be applied to anything other than a person.

2. THE DEFENDANTS' RESPONSE TO THE COMPLAINT

Having dissected the Complaint that began this lawsuit, turn now to the Defendants' response. Here is what the first page of the Defendants' first document looked like:

KELLEY DRYE & WARREN LLP
  Michael J. O'Connor (STATE BAR NO. 90017)
  Edward E. Weiman (STATE BAR NO. 193290)
10100 Santa Monica Boulevard, Twenty-Third Floor
Los Angeles, California 90067-4008
Telephone: (310) 712-6100
Facsimile: (310) 712-6199
moconnor@kelleydrye.com
eweiman@kelleydrye.com

Attorneys for SeaWorld Parks & Entertainment, Inc.
and Sea World LLC

FULBRIGHT & JAWORSKI L.L.P.
  Richard R. Mainland (STATE BAR NO. 36055)
555 S. Flower Street, Forty-First Floor
Los Angeles, California 90071
Telephone: (213) 892-9200
Facsimile: (310) 892-9494
rmainland@fulbright.com

Attorneys for SeaWorld Parks & Entertainment, Inc.
and Sea World LLC

UNITED STATES DISTRICT COURT

FOR THE SOUTHERN DISTRICT OF CALIFORNIA

TILIKUM, KATINA, CORKY, KASATKA, AND ULISES, five orcas, Plaintiffs, by their Next Friends, People for the Ethical Treatment of Animals, Inc., Richard "Ric" O'Barry, Ingrid N. Visser, Ph.D., Howard Garrett, Samantha Berg, and Carol Ray, v. SEAWORLD PARKS & ENTERTAINMENT, INC. AND SEAWORLD, LLC, Defendants.	CASE NO. 11-CV-2476 JM WMC (The Honorable Jeffrey T. Miller) **DEFENDANTS SEAWORLD PARKS & ENTERTAINMENT, INC. AND SEA WORLD LLC'S MEMORANDUM OF POINTS AND AUTHORITIES IN SUPPORT OF DEFENDANTS' MOTION TO DISMISS THE COMPLAINT** *[Notice of Motion; and [Proposed] Order filed concurrently herewith]* Date: February 6, 2012 Time: 10:30 a.m. Courtroom: 5190 Action Filed: October 25, 2011 Trial Date: None Set

DEFENDANTS' MEMORANDUM OF POINTS AND AUTHORITIES IN SUPPORT OF DEFENDANTS' MOTION
TO DISMISS THE COMPLAINT

A defendant's first pleading is usually styled as an "Answer" to the plaintiff's Complaint. Here, however, Sea World's lawyers filed a twenty-five page Motion to Dismiss the Complaint on the grounds that the lawsuit had no possible merit and therefore violated two of the Federal Rules of Civil Procedure. First, Sea World argued that the plaintiffs, as orcas, lacked the standing required for any court to have jurisdiction to hear any case. Second, Sea World argued that even if the plaintiffs had standing (which Sea World argued they did not), the Complaint should be dismissed because of the plaintiffs' "failure to state a cause of action upon which relief can be granted."[4]

It's important to pay attention to the cover page of the Motion to Dismiss, as well as the Table of Contents and the Table of Authorities that follow the cover page. These are among the most formal of all legal documents in the United States. Federal court judges and state appellate court judges will expect to see all of this information presented in compliance with the rules of procedure (civil, criminal, or appellate). The tables can be frustrating and tedious, but if they are not prepared properly the document looks careless from its very beginning. That is never the impression an advocate wants to give a court. Every detail of citation and organization really does make a difference in legal writing.

Turning to the substance of the Motion to Dismiss in *Tilikum*, the unusually strong language Sea World's lawyers used is noteworthy. Strong language that criticizes an opponent and/or the opponent's argument is generally frowned upon by courts. Most legal writers in the United States would avoid references to the Complaint's "utter lack of merit," as well as characterizing the Complaint as "offensive." It is risky to take a tone this strident in any legal document. Compare the tone of the Motion to Dismiss to that of the Complaint. You should be able to see that the Complaint maintains a formal yet persuasive tone, while the Motion to Dismiss is more argumentative. In this case, Sea World's lawyers were successful: the court agreed that the Complaint lacked merit because the Thirteenth Amendment only protects humans from slavery or involuntary servitude. It seems reasonable to assume that Sea World would have prevailed on the merits of its motion without adopting an aggressive tone.

---

[4] Such motions are commonly referred to as "12(b)(6) Motions;" they are frequently the first documents filed by a defendant in a civil suit in federal court. The essence of a 12(b)(6) Motion is that the plaintiff has not written anything in the complaint that might give the court grounds to agree with the plaintiff or to grant any form of relief—it is a request for the court to dismiss the complaint, and the lawsuit, because whatever the plaintiff claims happened was not, in fact, illegal.

Courts do not respond well to aggressive tactics from lawyers. Over-zealous advocacy can work against the lawyer's client if it crosses the line between persuasion and derision. One often-quoted opinion from the federal Sixth Circuit appellate court put it this way:

> "There are good reasons not to call an opponent's argument 'ridiculous' . . . [T]he better practice is to lay out the facts and let the court reach its own conclusion' " [presumably by applying cited law to those facts]. *Bennett v. State Farm Mut. Auto, Ins. Co.*, 731 F. 3d 584, 584 (6th Cir. 2013) *quoting Big Dipper Entertainment, L.L.C. v. City of Warren*, 641 F, 3d 715, 719 (6th Cir. 2011).

The Sixth Circuit judges may have been reacting to "cognitive dissonance": "Once a message recipient's cognitive dissonance leads her to believe that the message is flawed (by bias or coercive tactics), the message recipient is likely to reject the message." Kathryn Stanchi, *What Cognitive Dissonance Tells Us About Tone In Persuasion*, 22 J.L. & Pol'y. 93, 102 (2013). An argument that is rejected, for whatever reason, by its intended audience, is an argument that need not have been written in the first place. Professor Stanchi's article warns lawyers against "cross[ing] from zealous advocacy into obnoxiousness." *Id.* at 93. International students must remember that what might have been zealous advocacy at home could be considered obnoxious in the United States, and nobody likes an obnoxious advocate.

YOUR ASSIGNMENT: REVISING AND POLISHING

Rewrite the "Introduction" to the Motion to Dismiss using fewer and less argumentative words. The original Introduction is reproduced here for your reference. It is about one and one-half pages long. Rewrite it so the tone is professional and the necessary information is made clear, but use no more than one page, preferably less than one page. The purpose of this exercise is to emphasize the importance of clear, concise, and correct legal writing. More words are not always better than fewer words. The legal writer's job is to make the necessary point(s) as efficiently and effectively as possible, and that does not normally involve using strong language toward any other party, no matter how frustrated or outraged the writer (and/or the client) may feel.

INTRODUCTION

Defendants SeaWorld Parks & Entertainment, Inc. and SeaWorld, LLC (collectively "SeaWorld") hereby move to dismiss the Complaint brought against them by People for the Ethical Treatment of Animals, Inc., Richard "Ric" O'Barry, Ingrid N. Visser, Ph.D., Howard Garrett, Samantha Berg, and Carol Ray (collectively, "PETA"), as "Next Friends" of the killer whales, *i.e.,* the orcas, known as Tilikum, Katina, Corky, Kasatka, and Ulises ("Orcas") (collectively "Plaintiffs") pursuant to Federal Rules of Procedure 12(b)(1) and 12(b)(6).

PETA readily admits that this is a "case of first impression." *See* Compl. ¶ 1. But it is not a case of first impression because the law is unsettled, but only because PETA's claims that the Orcas have rights under the Thirteenth Amendment are so baseless that no party has ever wasted the time, energy and expense of any court in making such claims in a lawsuit. Thus, SeaWorld finds itself obligated to address the Complaint, notwithstanding its utter lack of merit.

The Thirteenth Amendment only protects people, not animals, from slavery and involuntary servitude. PETA's argument to the contrary is offensive. As a matter of law, the Orcas have no rights under the Thirteenth Amendment, and the Complaint should be dismissed on that ground alone. Moreover, there is no authority for the Court to read or expand the protections of the Thirteenth Amendment to apply to animals, as PETA advocates. Taking that unprecedented step will certainly open a veritable "Pandora's Box" of inescapable–problems and absurd consequences. Further, in the unlikely case that the Court were to illogically construe the Thirteenth Amendment to apply to animals (which it does not), that Amendment still does not provide for a direct cause of action and, therefore, the lawsuit must be dismissed.

Lastly, PETA's Complaint does not meet the threshold requirements of standing, or the prerequisites of the Federal Rules of Civil Procedure, for invoking this Court's jurisdiction. The Orca "plaintiffs" do not qualify as *bona fide* plaintiffs that may seek redress within our judicial system – nor may PETA bring this suit on behalf of the Orcas. The Court, therefore, may also dispose of the case for lack of both:

1

- **Article III constitutional standing.** There is no such standing because the Orcas have no "legally protected interest" at stake, and thus there is no "injury;" and,

- **Prudential standing.** Such standing is wanting because:

  (i) PETA cannot bring this suit as a "next friend' under Federal Rule of Civil Procedure 17 which applies only to representatives of a "real party in interest" – a "person," not an animal; and,

  (ii) the Complaint's allegations do not fall within the zone of interests of the Thirteenth Amendment.

In the end, any one of the above flaws in the Complaint is a sufficient basis for the Court to dismiss the case. Taken together they are so insurmountable as to expose the case for what it apparently is: a transparent attempt to garner press coverage.[1] For all the foregoing reasons, and for those set forth in greater detail below, SeaWorld's motion to dismiss the Complaint should be granted, with prejudice.

3. PETA'S RESPONSE TO SEA WORLD'S MOTION TO DISMISS

After Sea World's Motion to Dismiss was filed, but before the court decided the case, PETA's lawyers had another opportunity to try to convince the court that the Complaint should not be dismissed. This is the usual practice in the United States: an opposing party is given the opportunity to respond to a Motion to Dismiss, especially in federal courts where the judges are more likely to have full-time law clerks, and thus the time to review and research each side's arguments. In a state trial court, there might simply be a Motion to Dismiss followed by a "hearing," at which the trial court judge (only one, rather than a panel, and usually one without a full-time law clerk) would hear the arguments for and against the motion. Some state court judges will issue verbal decisions immediately after the hearing, asking the prevailing party to draft an Order reflecting that decision. Other judges will "take the matter under advisement," meaning the judge will review, research, and examine the validity of each party's arguments at some future point in time, and will then deliver his or her written Order to the parties. But in some state courts, as well as in federal courts and in any appellate court, these arguments may be decided based solely upon the parties' written documents, or upon a combination of the written documents and oral arguments.

In *Tilikum,* the plaintiffs' lawyers wrote and filed a formal argument in support of their opposition to the motion to dismiss their Complaint. The response is thirty pages long, which would probably exceed the allowable length for most courts, and it includes the Tables of Contents and Authorities in the same formats the Defendants used in their Motion to

Dismiss. The Table of Contents provides an outline of the plaintiffs' arguments, and the Introduction provides a Summary of the Argument. So the plaintiffs' actual response to defendants' motion does not begin until page 7 of the Response.

Look at the tone of the plaintiffs' Introduction, and compare it to the tone of the defendants' Motion. The tone of the plaintiffs' Response is in striking contrast to the defendants' tone of outrage at the "offensive" nature of the Complaint's "utter lack of merit." The plaintiffs' lawyers carefully and logically constructed an argument that, if the court had been persuaded, would have made it possible to interpret the Thirteenth Amendment as applicable to orcas as well as humans. If you notice nothing else about the differences in these Introductions, note the number of legal sources cited by the plaintiffs: there are citations to the U.S. Constitution and to two landmark decisions from the U.S. Supreme Court. The defendants' Motion cites no law.

> A "landmark" decision is sometimes referred to as a "seminal" case, or a "leading" case. It means the case has a significant history in U.S. jurisprudence. In plaintiffs' response, Marbury v. Madison, one of the earliest decisions of the U.S. Supreme Court, and a case that is as important today as it was hundreds of years ago, is cited in support of the argument that courts are supposed to interpret the Constitution in ways that are relevant at the time of the decision. This concept relates to the separation of powers in the U.S. legal system, and the cited law of *Marbury v. Madison* is beyond any reasonable disagreement. It is definitely a "landmark" case. The other case cited in the plaintiffs' response, the *Dred Scott* case, is also a "landmark" case, but for a different reason: It is one of a very small number of U.S. Supreme Court cases that has been specifically overruled by that Court itself as a reflection of an evolving society. *Dred Scott* is no longer "good law," but its name would be recognized by lawyers and law students across the U.S. as an example of the flexibility courts should employ to keep our Constitution a "living" thing: courts are supposed to make sure the Constitution's application reflects current, not outdated, social and legal values in the U.S.

Normally, valid legal arguments must be supported by citations to primary, binding authority. In *Tilikum*, the plaintiffs' Introduction did so, while the Defendants' Motion did not. But the Motion was granted, which means the defendants "won" and the plaintiffs "lost." The court's opinion tells the reader why: the court was not willing to take the leap in logic that would be required to read the Thirteenth Amendment as applicable to non-persons, and without a human being who was a "real party in interest," the court decided that it lacked jurisdiction to decide the case. But let's look at how that happened.

Both the Motion and the Response consist of around thirty pages of material, so it should be clear that using more words is not the answer to winning an argument. Both parties presented detailed, organized arguments, so it is not as if there were some obvious defect in the plaintiffs' Response. Plaintiffs did cite more binding case law than Defendants, but apparently that was not a ticket to success. Of the 80 cases cited by the plaintiffs, only nine were non-binding precedent for the U.S. District Court for the Southern District of California, meaning 71 of the plaintiffs' cited cases were decided by the district court itself, the Ninth Circuit Court of Appeals, or the U.S. Supreme Court. This is impressive, and it looks like a well-researched and well-supported legal argument (however, if you look carefully at the citations within the Table of Cited Authorities you will find several that are not in their correct forms according to any legal citation manual). Defendants' Motion cites only 53 cases, 15 of which are non-binding (and again, many of the case citations listed in the Table are just wrong). Yet, the defendants won. A winning argument cannot be identified by simply calculating the quantity or the quality of cases cited, or the number of words used, or even the organization of the argument itself. Here, the defendants were ultimately more persuasive than the plaintiffs even if they cited fewer binding authorities. How does this happen? Read on for the final pleading in this case.

4. SEA WORLD'S REPLY TO PETA'S OPPOSITION TO SEA WORLD'S MOTION TO DISMISS THE COMPLAINT

There is one more legal document in this lawsuit that might explain why the court ruled in favor of the defendants. It is the final pleading the court permitted, and it is the defendants' Reply to PETA's Response to Defendants' Motion to Dismiss. Yes, legal pleadings are a constant back-and-forth process until a court says "Enough!" and renders its decision in a case. Reviewing the pleadings filed in this case, remember that PETA started the action with its Complaint. Sea World then filed its Motion to Dismiss that Complaint, including its memorandum in support of the Motion. Then it was PETA's turn again, and it filed its Response to Defendants' Motion to Dismiss. And finally, Sea World got the last word when it filed its Reply to PETA's Response. Each party had, by that point, filed two substantive pleadings, and the party that did not initiate the action was allowed to have the final word before the court decided the case. Here is what Sea World's Reply looked like (after the customary cover page and tables):

INTRODUCTION

PETA's Opposition ("Opp.") sets forth a variety of irrelevant arguments that attempt to obscure the central issues before this Court, namely: (i) whether the Thirteenth Amendment applies to animals and (ii) whether animals are legal persons for purposes of standing. Notwithstanding the Opposition, the answers remain "no." As SeaWorld demonstrated in its Memorandum of Points and Authorities in Support of Defendants' Motion to Dismiss The Complaint ("SW Mem.") and as it further establishes below, this Court must conclude that the Constitution does not grant rights to animals such as the Orcas, and further that there are no rules or statutes that treat animals as legal persons for purposes of standing here.

PETA contends that the Thirteenth Amendment should be judicially "expanded" to encompass the captivity of animals. To support this proposition, PETA submits a litany of broad brush arguments based on sweeping principles of constitutional construction found in inapposite cases. In short, PETA apparently argues that if *any* court has interpreted the Constitution at *any* time in *any* way that expands the reach or nature of its protections, it necessarily follows that the prohibitions on slavery and involuntary servitude found in the Thirteenth Amendment are properly construed to extend to animals. The absurdity of this conclusion is apparent on its face, but it is even further belied by the very authority PETA relies upon in support of its argument.

SeaWorld does not question the judiciary's centuries-old power to "interpret and expound" constitutional rights. Nor does SeaWorld challenge the notion that certain constitutional rights have been, and may be, construed in a way that extends their application to reach new circumstances unforeseen by the Framers. The issue before this Court is not, as PETA suggests in its Opposition, whether courts must adhere to the original intent of the Framers, or alternatively, whether courts can construe the Constitution to reach new circumstances beyond those foreseen by the Framers. Either way, the Constitution has boundaries, and courts simply are not empowered to rewrite or amend the Constitution to apply the Thirteenth Amendment to animals.

The reason why the Court cannot accept PETA's interpretation of the Thirteenth Amendment is because the rights and protections under the Constitution generally, and the Thirteenth

Amendment specifically, apply only to *people*, and (absent a constitutional amendment) cannot be held to extend to animals. That much is evident from every case PETA cites in support of its arguments. In all of those cases – whether dealing with the important issues of privacy, equal protection, cruel and unusual punishment, discrimination or slavery – courts only extended constitutional rights and freedoms to *people*. This is necessarily so. The Constitution is a document written to provide a government of the people, by the people, and for the people, to protect the rights of *the people*.[1] Although non-human entities, such as corporations and partnerships, have been defined as legal "persons" and have been granted some constitutional rights, these entities were created by *people* and are ultimately associations of *people*.[2]

PETA does not, and cannot, cite to a single case where Congress or any court has recognized animals as "persons" for purposes of the Constitution or standing; indeed, PETA does not even argue that the Orcas are (or should be) "persons." Instead, PETA asks this Court to effectively amend the Constitution by holding that it applies both to legal "persons" *and* animals – a holding that would greatly exceed the Court's power to "interpret and expound" the Constitution and would encroach on the power reserved by Article V to the people of the United States, through their duly elected representatives, to amend the Constitution. This the Court may not do. PETA's case must, therefore, be dismissed with prejudice.

Look carefully at the tone of this Introduction, and compare it to the tone of the Introduction to Sea World's Motion to Dismiss the Complaint. Yes, there is still some strong language: it is unpleasant to read a lawyer's criticism of an opponent's argument, even when that criticism is ultimately deemed correct. Sea World's lawyers wrote that PETA's response consisted of "a litany of broad brush arguments based on sweeping principles of constitutional construction found in inapposite cases," and referred to the "absurdity" of PETA's conclusion that the Thirteenth Amendment could apply to people. This is, in itself, a "broad brush" criticism of PETA's Response, and it's important to know that using negative adjectives is generally not an effective tool of persuasive writing (and neither is the use of italics for emphasis: sentence structure is more persuasive than italics).

And then Sea World's lawyers appear to settle down, adopting a more reasonable tone of argument. Point by legal point, Sea World substantively deconstructs PETA's arguments, citing primary binding authority and employing recognizable forms of logic. This is what wins cases, as indeed it did in *Tilikum*. U.S. legal writers use factual analogies and distinctions, as well as syllogistic reasoning, to construct arguments that cannot be chipped away by an opponent. Here, Sea World had the last word in its Reply, and it gave the court every reason to agree with its conclusion that the Thirteenth amendment simply cannot be construed as applicable to anything but humans.

YOUR ASSIGNMENT: TYPES OF REASONING

Familiarize yourself with the concepts of both factual analogies and distinctions, as well as syllogistic reasoning. Then identify one example of each in Sea World's Reply (its final pleading). Factual similarities and differences are usually easier to spot than syllogisms, and they are also easier to write. Sea World used many distinctions to demonstrate that the Thirteenth Amendment cannot be applicable to non-humans. But good legal arguments focus more on the law than on the facts of any case. Sea World used syllogistic reasoning (major premise, minor premise, conclusion) to demonstrate what the law says (major premise), how that law should be applied to this case (minor premise), and the only logical conclusion that could flow from this reasoning. In syllogistic reasoning, there must be a major premise, a minor premise, and a conclusion, every time. Without those three logically related pieces, there is no logical argument. The purpose of this assignment is to train your eyes to recognize a good argument when you see one, so that you will be better able to write such arguments.

Remember, as well, that a solid legal argument anticipates and refutes an opponent's arguments. Note the shift from affirmative arguments in the initial Complaint to responsive arguments by the time Sea World filed its final document. Train yourself to identify analogies, syllogisms, affirmative and responsive arguments, and you will become a stronger legal writer.

B. COMMUNICATING WITH OPPOSING COUNSEL BEYOND COURT DOCUMENTS

Because opposing lawyers have to communicate with each other long before a case goes to trial (if it ever does), there are both formal and informal rules about how to do so. Many times, the first step is simply to make sure there is an opposing counsel. Many litigants represent themselves, whether by choice or from necessity (lawyers are expensive). The rules of professional responsibility prohibit lawyers from communicating directly with a party whom that lawyer knows is represented by counsel: the interests of fairness and justice mandate that lawyers communicate with other, similarly trained lawyers, rather than with non-lawyers (no matter how sophisticated or experienced those non-lawyers may be). The ultimate outcome of any case may depend on how opposing lawyers communicate with each other from the very beginning of any legal dispute, civil or criminal, state or federal.

In many cases, a few telephone calls can set a case on the road to an amicable resolution. More experienced lawyers who know many of their counterparts in the community are frequently able to engage in polite, even friendly, conversations that lead to a resolution of the case with which all parties can live. This is a wonderful skill to develop, especially as the courts become more crowded and actual trials become more rare. A quick, informal resolution saves everyone time and stress, and it is always the lawyers' duty to do what is in their clients' best interests. Sometimes that means explaining the unpleasant realities to a client so that he or she can understand and accept resolving a dispute without taking chances on a decision imposed by a judge or jury. Seasoned lawyers agree that even a "bad" settlement is better than a "good" trial, although the rules of professional responsibility require clients' consent before accepting or rejecting any settlement offer.

When informal conversations do not accomplish amicable resolutions, most civil litigators will proceed with a formal letter to opposing counsel (or to the opposing party if that person does not yet have counsel). In a criminal case, a conversation or letter is less likely to resolve the case because busy prosecuting attorneys rarely have the time or the authority to engage in out-of-court communications, much less settlements. Furthermore, criminal defendants are guaranteed certain "speedy trial" rights, so the lawyers and their clients[5] may be less motivated to settle than in a civil case, where getting to court may take years. Criminal prosecutors also consult with the victim before engaging in any plea bargaining with the defendant. In civil cases, a written statement of the client's position or demands is a good starting point. Again, U.S. lawyers who find themselves on opposite sides of a dispute are expected or required to communicate in polite, professional terms, even when making a demand; the rules of professional responsibility require civility.

Formal letters are an integral part of resolving legal disputes in the United States. Many young lawyers and law students come to law school with no experience in writing formal letters or even email correspondence. This is an era of text messages and social media, such as Facebook, Twitter, Tumblr, and Pinterest. Proper punctuation and grammatical precision are irrelevant in most social media, but in legal correspondence precision is every bit as important as it is in documents filed with a court. Carelessness in any written form, from one lawyer to another, may have serious substantive consequences. A misplaced comma can change the meaning of an offer or demand. Much has been written about the million-dollar comma that was misplaced in a contract written by one lawyer, and was the subject of litigation by other lawyers. One misplaced comma did, in fact, cost the U.S. Treasury over one million dollars in revenue when the Tariff Act was intended to exempt from taxes certain "fruit plants," but instead exempted "fruit, plants," and certain other plants.[6] That misplaced comma broadened the category of exempt imports, thus costing the Government over one

---

[5]   In a criminal case, the prosecutor's client is "the people": The citizens of the jurisdiction in which the prosecution is taking place, local, state, or federal.

[6]   *Pineapple Growers Co-Op Ass'n. of Puerto Rico v. U.S.*, 24 Cust. Ct. 133 (1950).

million dollars in lost tariffs before the errant comma could be put back in its intended place. In at least one other case, a fourteen-page contract contained one misplaced comma that changed the terms of the contract to the tune of over one million dollars (Canadian), much to the dismay of one party to the contract.[7]

When it comes to proper grammar and punctuation, the current generation of U.S. J.D. students may be at a disadvantage to international students who have more recently studied English as a second, third, fourth, or even fifth language. International students should feel confident that their awareness of the importance of clear, correct, and concise language surpasses that of their U.S. born classmates. The experience and education that come with any international lawyer or exchange student who has recently studied English will probably be superior to that of the U.S. students because most secondary and post-secondary schools in the U.S. today do not emphasize writing, grammar, punctuation, or technical accuracy beyond the grammar school classes.

Remember that it is not necessary to memorize the rules of grammar and punctuation; the important thing is to remember that there are, in fact, rules that dictate how to communicate clearly and correctly, and any law student or advocate in the United States needs to look up the rules. This applies to the rules of English language usage and of legal citations. A good writing style manual, written specifically for lawyers or law students, will contain every rule that any lawyer or law student needs in order to communicate effectively. Citation manuals, particularly The Bluebook and the ALWD Citation Manual, are required, not optional, and must be consulted: they do not help if they are sitting unopened on the desk. Students who are enrolled in a legal writing class are undoubtedly already in possession of a style manual and/or a citation manual, and those books must be consulted. No written communication can afford to be written casually, and writers must assume that everything put in writing, whether in a text message, an email, or a printed letter, can and will be viewed as a reflection on the writer's professional competence. Be correct, and be accurate, or do not put it in writing. The best thing one might hope for from inaccurate writing is that the writer looks ignorant, careless, and/or under-educated. The worst thing that can happen is that the writer finds him or herself facing a legal malpractice suit and professional ethics complaints filed with the appropriate bar association(s). Lawyers lose their licenses, and their livelihoods, when their written communications do not reflect the highest standards of care and attention to detail. This is a very high price to pay for making the choice to ignore style and citation manuals.

---

[7] The decision was rendered by the Canadian Radio-television and Telecommunications Commission in 2007, in a 2007 case involving a petition filed by Rogers Communications, Inc., Telecom Decision CRTC 2007-75. The opposing party was Aliant Telecom, Inc.

Of course, grammar, spelling, and punctuation are only the beginning tools of effective writing. More advanced tools for effective writing should become standard equipment in every legal writer's repertoire. The conventions of effective writing can be mastered with practice, and most can be identified through careful reading of others' good legal writing.

Writing Rules of Thumb

Being good readers makes us all better writers. Think about the differences between the tone of the Complaint in *Tilikum* and the tone of the defendants' Motion to Dismiss. If you were on the receiving end of a written communication from another lawyer (or anyone, for that matter) that was written in the tone of the Motion, it seems unlikely that you would be open to engaging in any sort of meaningful conversation with that writer. Nobody appreciates being insulted, and the offense is even great when the insult is part of a legal document. Bear in mind that in the United States good legal writing relies on logic rather than strong emotions or adjectives, and consider the following writing tips:

1. Write sentences with **parallel structure:**

    Do This: The defendants moved to dismiss the complaint based on its lack of merit and the plaintiffs' lack of standing.

    Not This: The defendants moved to dismiss the complaint based on its lack of merit and because the plaintiffs did not have standing.

2. Use **direct quotes** with care, and use only those parts of any quote that are truly important:

    Do This: Any party sued in a civil action may move for dismissal if the plaintiff has "failed to state a claim upon which relief can be granted."

    Not This: Defendants may file a Motion to Dismiss because "[e]very defense to a claim for relief in any pleading must be asserted in the responsive pleading if one is required. But a party may assert the following defenses by motion: . . . failure to state a claim upon which relief can be granted."

3. Write **efficiently:**

    Do This: New law students may believe that using many words is a sign of intelligence, but experienced writers will use fewer words rather than more.

    Not This: It may be the firm belief of many new law students that their use of many words is a clear sign of superior intelligence, but at this particular point in time writers ought to use as few words as possible in an effort to make any and every particular point.

a. American English allows using the **possessive apostrophe** with inanimate objects:

Do This: The Complaint's allegations lack merit.

Not This: The allegations of the Complaint lack merit.

b. Avoid using the **passive voice** unless it is a tool of persuasion:

Do This: Sea World treated the orcas with care and respect.

Not This: The orcas were treated with care and respect by Sea World (unless the emphasis is supposed to be on the orcas' treatment rather than on Sea World).

c. Be aware of **absolute adjectives:**

Do This: The complaint is without merit.

Not This: The complaint is utterly without merit.

4. Do not confuse **punctuation** marks:

Do This: The complaint should be dismissed because it lacks merit—utterly—and the plaintiffs, as non-humans, lack standing.

Not This: The complaint should be dismissed; because it lacks merit–utterly–and, the plaintiffs, as orcas lack standing. [Note the differences between an em dash and an en dash, as well as between commas, colons, and semi-colons. When in doubt, keep it simple, and refer to a legal writing style manual for help.]

5. Do not mangle, misplace, or leave dangling any **modifiers:**

Do This: Sea World finds itself compelled to respond to the complaint, despite the utter lack of merit in the claim.

Not This: Sea World finds itself compelled to respond to the complaint despite its utter lack of merit. [What lacks merit? The complaint or Sea World? Any sentence that raises more questions than it answers needs to be repaired.]

6. Be **specific;** refer to people, places, or things (but not, in most legal documents, to yourself):

Do This: Sea World respectfully requests that this Court dismiss PETA's Complaint because the plaintiffs lack standing.

Not This: I (or we) respectfully request that the Complaint be dismissed because there is no standing. [Anything that makes the reader's job harder rather than easier should be removed.]

7. Avoid vacuous words or sentences of **introduction or transition;** make every word pull its weight:

Do This: PETA argued, as "next friend," that the Thirteenth Amendment applied to the orcas, and that Sea World violated the orcas' rights to be free from slavery or involuntary servitude.

Not This: Peta made several arguments. First, PETA argued that it had standing as the orcas' "next friend." PETA then argued that the Thirteenth Amendment applied to the orcas. Third and finally, PETA argued that Sea World violated the orcas' rights. In summary, PETA argued that Sea World's treatment of the orcas violated those orcas' Thirteenth Amendment rights to be free from slavery or involuntary servitude. [This is consistent with the notion of writing efficiently; use fewer words, not more, to say the same thing.]

8.   **Demonstrate,** don't describe:

Do This: Specific acts of domination, exploitation, and coercion violate the Thirteenth Amendment; Sea world dominates, exploits, and coerces the orcas by separating them from their families and holding them with no means of escape, forcing the orcas to perform tricks in front of audiences who have paid almost $100.00 per person to visit Sea World, and subjecting the orcas to forced artificial insemination; therefore, Sea World has violated the orcas' Thirteenth Amendment rights. [This "demonstration" is also a good example of syllogistic reasoning, one very useful form of logical analysis. It contains a major premise, a minor premise, and a conclusion, and this will never leave a writer stranded.]

Not This: Specific acts of domination, exploitation, and coercion violate the Thirteenth Amendment; Sea World holds the orcas captive, makes the orcas perform tricks, and subjects the orcas to artificial insemination; therefore Sea World violates the orcas' Thirteenth Amendment rights. [Here there is a major premise, followed by some facts, and ultimately a conclusion. The missing link is the minor premise that demonstrates application of the major premise to the facts. There is no logic here.]

9.   Make sure **pronouns and nouns are in agreement, as are verbs and subjects:**

Do This: The corporation's lawsuit was dismissed because it failed to state a cause of action.

Not This: The corporation's lawsuit was dismissed because they failed state a cause of action. [In American English, collective nouns, such as "court," use singular, not plural, pronouns. No word processing system will catch these mistakes, but they ruin any sentence in which they appear; ruined sentences ruin their writers' credibility.]

a. **Collective nouns** use singular, not plural, pronouns:

Do This: The members of the jury said they were in agreement, and the appellate court agreed in its opinion.

Not This: The jury said they were in agreement, and the appellate court agreed in their opinion. [International students who learned British English will have to adjust their writing for U.S. readers.]

b. Be aware of **gendered pronouns:**

Do This: Only a human being may be held involuntarily because the word "involuntary" can only refer to a person, and that person's ability to make decisions based on free will.

Not This: Only a human being may be held involuntarily because the word "involuntary" can only refer to a person, and his ability to make decisions based on free will. [Older legal writing may use only the masculine pronoun, but in current writing it is a mistake to do so. Astute writers have a variety of options: make the noun plural and use the plural pronoun; alternate between using the masculine and feminine pronouns; write about specific actors whose gender can be identified; or, as a last resort, use "he or she" in place of either a masculine or a feminine pronoun—but do not resort to the use of "s/he," as many first-year law students do in frantic, last-minute efforts to comply with an assignment's word-count requirement.]

10. If nothing else, **be internally consistent:** This final tip does not lend itself to good and bad examples because this is an all-encompassing tip. In any piece of writing, the writer's credibility may hinge on internal consistency. If you use the Oxford comma one time, use it throughout the document, letter, or email. If your document begins in Times New Roman font, use that same font all the way through; nothing looks worse to a critical reader than a sudden and unexplained change of font style or size. If numbers are spelled out from one through ninety-nine, do not throw in the occasional 30 or 75 (this does not apply to citations). If you learned British English and are either unable or unwilling to adapt to American English, at least be consistent: spelling and punctuation cannot alternate, within the confines of any one piece of writing, between British and American English. Internal consistency assures the reader that you wrote with care. Without that assurance, the reader will have no choice but to assume that the writer was simply careless. And if the writer doesn't care, why should the reader? Write correctly, or do not write at all.

YOUR ASSIGNMENT: DEMAND LETTERS

Based on what you now know from the pleadings in *Tilikum*, put yourself in the place of Sea World's lawyers, who must respond to the letter below from PETA's lawyer. PETA's letter would have been written and delivered months, if not years, before any lawsuit was filed; once a suit has been filed, any settlement the parties might reach must be approved by the court, but prior to litigation lawyers can, and do, negotiate settlements every day in this country. Write a response to PETA's letter, making clear your client's position (which is easily discerned from the pleadings you have already read). Note that a demand letter or a letter of intent to sue is not always required. In some cases, however, such as when a party intends to sue a governmental entity, such a letter must be sent at least thirty days before any lawsuit is filed. Most civil litigation lawyers will send a demand letter as an invitation to opposing counsel to begin negotiations before initiating litigation. Litigation is expensive, stressful, and time-consuming for the parties involved (and for the lawyers, even though this is traditionally how lawyers make their money). If a clear, specific, reasonable demand letter might prompt an amicable settlement, it is well worth investing the time and thought to craft it carefully, correctly, and concisely. When writing to opposing counsel, some citations to authority might be appropriate, but they should be used sparingly: remember the intended audience (opposing counsel, not a court) and include just enough citations to demonstrate to opposing counsel and his or her client that you may indeed have a winning argument, and that everyone will be better off if the dispute is resolved without litigation. Here is a fictitious sample demand letter from PETA's lawyer to Sea World's lawyer in *Tilikum* to provide one example of the proper format, structure, and tone for a demand letter. Note the confident but not necessarily argumentative tone and the specific relief sought by a specific date. An empty demand letter will accomplish nothing. When you write your response on behalf of Sea World, you should try to match the tone and confidence of PETA's lawyer, and you should counter with a clear indication of your client's intention to dispute this demand; that intention, again, is discernable from the pleadings filed by Sea World, which you have already studied. Your letter should not exceed one page. Letters are typically single-spaced, with two spaces after each paragraph, using eleven or twelve point font. The address information for the Los Angeles PETA attorney from whom the letter below was sent is: Mr. Matthew Strugar, PETA Foundation, 2154 W. Sunset Blvd., Los Angeles, CA 90026.

Remember, your assignment is to respond to the following letter:

Richard R. Mainland
PETA Foundation
555 S. Flower Street, Forty-First Floor
Los Angeles, CA 90171

Dear Mr. Mainland,   June 26, 2015

Please be advised that our firm has been retained by the Los Angeles office of People for the Ethical Treatment of Animals to pursue legal action against your client, Sea World, LLC, on behalf of seven orcas currently held in captivity by Sea World. PETA has retained this law firm because Sea World's capture and subsequent treatment of the orcas is in direct violation of the Thirteenth Amendment to the United States Constitution, which explicitly prohibits both slavery and involuntary servitude in any form.

PETA is fully aware that its claim will be one of first impression, but as you know this is the nature of every Constitutional issue: Courts are allowed, and even required, to interpret the United States Constitution in ways that are reflective of current social values, morals, and laws. As the Supreme Court observed over one hundred years ago, a constitutional protection, "to be vital, must be capable of wider application than the mischief which gave it birth." *Weems v. U.S.*, 217 U.S. 349, 373 (1910). The current culture in the United States makes it probable that a court can and will interpret the Thirteenth Amendment's prohibitions of slavery and involuntary servitude as applicable to the wild orcas captured and detained by Sea World, forcibly separated from their families, and made to perform mindless tricks in order to line the pockets of Sea World's officers and employees. There can be no doubt that such treatment of a human would be prohibited, and there is no reason such prohibitions should not extend to these noble wild animals.

PETA is prepared to file suit in the appropriate Federal District Court as the legal representative of the orcas whose lives are at the heart of this horrific case. If your client is prepared to discuss measures that must be taken to protect the orcas, PETA is willing to offer specific requirements that must be met. The orcas must be evaluated by an independent expert who can determine whether the animals are suited to be returned to their homes in the wild. Those who are fit must be released. Those who are not capable of surviving in the wild after so many years of maltreatment at the hands of Sea World must be transferred to suitable facilities immediately, where they might have some hope of living out their lives in conditions that more closely resemble their natural habitats. Sea World has made untold millions from the enslavement and servitude of these orcas, and now Sea World must prepare itself to make amends.

Our firm stands ready to meet with you or your representatives immediately to begin negotiations that will lead to justice for the orcas. However, if Sea World declines to enter into discussions, we are similarly prepared to proceed with appropriate, and merited, litigation. The current situation is completely unacceptable and must be corrected immediately. We look forward to receiving your response no later than July 15, 2015 and trust that your client is ready and willing to do the right thing.

Sincerely yours,

____/s/_____

Matthew Strugar

CHAPTER 4

DRAFTING SPECIFIC DOCUMENTS (CLIENT LETTERS AND MEMORANDA TO THE FILE)

. . .

A. PROFESSIONAL RESPONSIBILITIES

Practicing law in the United States is a hard-earned privilege that must be exercised with great care. Just as there is no one body of "U.S. Law," there is no one set of "U.S. Rules of Professional Conduct." Every one of the fifty United States, every federal court, has its own rules of law, rules of court, and rules of professionalism. Even smaller geographic units, such as counties and cities, may have local bar associations and local rules. In order to practice law in any jurisdiction, the advocate must be admitted to the bar.[1] Bar admission generally requires three years of successful post-university full-time study at a law school and, in almost every jurisdiction, that law school must be accredited by the American Bar Association.

> A very small number of states, including California, New York, and Tennessee (as of this writing) do not require graduation from an ABA accredited law school. However, international LL.M. students, in particular, must pay strict attention to the requirements of any jurisdiction in which they aspire to practice law.

After graduation from law school, in every jurisdiction in the United States, the would-be lawyer must sit for, and pass, the State Bar Exam, which usually consists of at least two days of essay and multiple-choice questions. (Some states that are geographically close to each other allow admission through "reciprocity" to lawyers who have successfully passed the state bar exam in a reciprocating state.) Every state requires bar applicants to pass a "character and fitness" check, but the rigor of those

---

[1] And no, when lawyers refer to the "Bar," we are not (usually) referring to an establishment in which alcoholic beverages are purchased and consumed. The term "Bar," or admission to the Bar, originated in the physical set-up of courtrooms in England and the United States. There is a wooden railing in every courtroom that separates the participants (judges, lawyers, parties, juries) from spectators. In order to be on the same side of that "bar" as the judge, an advocate must be a member in good standing of the Bar for that jurisdiction, so being a member of the Bar gains one entrance to the area that separates the players from the observers in any courtroom. There is a literal bar, the railing, and a virtual bar, the association that qualifies people to practice law in the jurisdiction.

checks varies widely. For example, Florida, the Sunshine State, is a very attractive relocation spot for lawyers from across the United States. With eleven law schools of its own, Florida is already turning out more lawyers than it needs every year. Therefore, Florida's character and fitness, or background, check is quite thorough, and the scores required to pass the Florida Bar Exam continue to be raised. Florida does not have reciprocity with any other jurisdiction; Florida has more than enough lawyers already licensed to practice law, and it does not want or need any more, so it makes the process as difficult as possible for even the most eminently qualified applicants. Other states, with smaller general populations and fewer practicing attorneys, are less rigid: Minnesota and Wisconsin, for example, have mutual reciprocity, meaning a lawyer admitted to the Bar of Minnesota may also appear before the courts in Wisconsin, and vice versa. International lawyers and law students who wish to sit for any state Bar Exam need to research the regulations that govern the practice of law in any given state because they vary widely and change frequently.

Most law schools' international LLM programs are not designed to prepare anyone to sit for a Bar exam, because it generally does take three years of full-time study to understand the law well enough to pass such an exam. But international lawyers who are interested in sitting for a Bar Exam may sometimes tailor their LLM course selections to better prepare them if they are determined to take a state Bar Exam. More and more law schools also have "accelerated" J.D. programs for international lawyers who wish to become licensed attorneys in the United States. Again, international students should do their research thoroughly before undertaking their studies, regardless of their goals but especially if they hope to become eligible to sit for any state's Bar Exam.

> There is a popular myth that the U.S. has more than enough lawyers to go around, and that there are more than enough qualified applicants for every job available on the legal market. This may be true in some areas of practicing law, such as corporate law or mergers and acquisitions law. It is not true, however, when it comes to what we call "public service" jobs. Working for a governmental entity or a legal aid program does not appeal to everyone, and it almost always pays less than working in the private sector. There may be too many lawyers in private practice in the United States, but public sector legal positions are generally understaffed (in addition to being underpaid).

Just as only members of the Bar are allowed to cross the physical bar that separates the courtroom into two distinct sections, only a person who is a licensed attorney may purport to represent a client at any level of any legal dispute. Documents might be researched and written by non-lawyers (clerks or paralegals), but only a licensed attorney is allowed to give legal advice, verbally or in writing. The unlicensed practice of law is a crime in many states. If you are asked to provide legal advice in the United States but are not yet licensed to do so, just say no.[2]

Licensed attorneys who interact with clients or potential clients have professional responsibilities that begin with their very first contact with any actual or potential client. Each state's rules of professional responsibility vary slightly but it is safe to assume that a privileged attorney-client relationship is established as soon as a potential client makes an appointment with a lawyer. Wise lawyers treat even the briefest contact with a potential client as the beginning of a formal relationship, and assume that the "client" will rely on any and every thing the lawyer might say. Even the most experienced lawyers take notes during every client meeting, and follow-up with a written letter confirming the course of that conversation. Whether the client's file is electronic or paper, every contact with the client is recorded and then confirmed in writing with the client.

B. CLIENT LETTERS

Documenting advice given to clients is important for at least two reasons. First, non-lawyers need written confirmation because they cannot be expected to remember or absorb and retain information or advice given during a conversation with a lawyer. Second, written confirmation protects a lawyer whose client acts on ignored, misunderstood, or misinterpreted advice and then blames the lawyer for any negative consequences. A lawyer who has not followed up with a written **confirmation or advice** letter may be personally and professionally liable for the client's loss. Writing advice and/or confirming letters is a good investment of any lawyer's time.

The components of a good advice letter are generally the same regardless of the context. If the letter is confirming a conversation that has already taken place, that should be the first sentence of the letter: "This letter will confirm our conversation of June 23, 2016, during which we discussed. . . ." This should be followed by a short summary of the key facts as told to the lawyer by the client. This ensures that any mistakes or misstatements of fact by the client are duly recorded and attributed to the client rather than to the lawyer. After summarizing the facts of the client's situation, the lawyer will then demonstrate, in writing, the basis for his or her advice to the client. For example: "Based on the information you provided, and on the language of the city's ordinance, there appears to be no merit to a claim that the city may have somehow exceeded its authority

---

[2] "Just say no" was a popular slogan in the late Twentieth Century, as part of Former First Lady Nancy Reagan's nationwide campaign to stop the use of "recreational drugs." The phrase has worked its way into the lexicon of American English, although it is not entirely clear that the anti-drug slogan had any effect on the use of illicit drugs in the United States, particularly among younger people.

in requiring that you obtain a business license." Citations to authority are not generally appropriate or necessary in a letter to a client, who will not understand or recognize the importance of the citations.

When writing to a non-lawyer, the tone must be formal but appropriate for the reader. A client letter is neither persuasive nor objective; it is informative, and it must be logical and understandable in order to meet its goals. Lawyers who write to clients with needless jargon and "legalese" often find themselves on the receiving end of Bar complaints or malpractice suits because the client could not, or did not, understand what the lawyer wrote. Constant attention to the purpose, audience, scope, and stance are the keys to all successful legal writing, and never more so than in a letter to a client. Sensitivity to clients' problems and mindfulness of their sophistication, and writing to clients with accuracy and empathy, will make every lawyer-client relationship more productive and less stressful for everyone involved.

YOUR ASSIGNMENT: ADVICE LETTERS

Return now to Carl Miles, with his talking cat. Assume you are a sole practitioner in Augusta, Georgia in 1981, and Mr. Miles comes into your office for advice. He asks whether the city has the right to force him to pay for a business license before he can resume collecting money on the streets from people willing to pay to hear Blackie speak. Assume that you research the city ordinances for Augusta and find the same ordinance that was cited by the federal trial court in Mr. Miles' case. It seems clear to you that the city ordinance authorizes imposing a business license requirement on anyone who is engaged in any activity for profit within the city limits. During your conversation with Mr. Miles you showed him the ordinance and told him that you did not think he would have a valid legal argument in opposition to the city's ordinance. Mr. Miles did not like your advice, and he left your office without signing a retainer agreement or entering into a formal attorney-client relationship; you did not charge him for the initial consultation, and you never expect to see him again. You know, however, that you need to confirm your advice to him in writing.

YOUR ASSIGNMENT: CONFIRMING LETTERS

Write a letter to Carl Miles at 123 Main Street, Augusta, Georgia 30901, dated June 23, 1981. Keep the tone, sentence structure, and wording appropriate for a client with Mr. Miles' apparent levels of sophistication and education. The letter should be typed in twelve-point Times New Roman font, single-spaced, with a double space between paragraphs. The entire letter should not exceed a page and a half. Think about sentence and paragraph structure as well as word choice, and remember the purpose, audience, scope, and stance. Write clearly, correctly, and concisely. Use logic to explain your conclusion, knowing that Mr. Miles will not readily accept your advice.

For additional practice, put yourself in the position of an assistant city attorney for the City of Augusta, Georgia. Assume the City Council has asked for advice in responding to a complaint from Mr. Miles about the business license requirement. (With or without legal representation, Mr. Miles would be allowed to pursue his complaint against the business license ordinance.) For this part of the exercise, write a letter advising the City Council how to appropriately respond to Mr. Miles' argument that he should be exempt from the license requirement. The city attorney's job here would be to advice the City Council of the city's potential liability, or lack thereof, in language that is appropriate for sophisticated members of the community with no legal training.

By completing both of these assignments, students will write two different advice letters to the clients on opposite sides of the same dispute. This will demonstrate a key point about legal analysis in the U.S.: The opposing parties use the same law, because they must address the same issues, but they demonstrate logical reasons why that law, when applied to the same facts, might lead to opposite conclusions. In other words, this exercise demonstrates that the advocates' job is to find and apply the relevant law, and the applicable law is the same regardless of who the advocate represents. Effective legal writers formulate reasonable arguments on their clients' behalf by using the tools of logical analysis. The legal writer who tries to manipulate the law, or who searches high and low for some law that might be favorable to his or her client, is not an effective writer. True advocates are good writers who find the applicable law and demonstrate the application of that law in support of their clients' cases. Novice writers who confuse logical analysis with emotional or fact-driven arguments leave themselves open to charges of incompetence.

C. MEMORANDA TO FILES

At almost every law school in the United States, first-year students are required to successfully complete a full year of some form of legal research and writing instruction. Some schools require more, and some less, but almost every first-year law student experiences this "rite of passage."[3] Those of us who teach such classes are highly cognizant of the fact that the Legal Writing class is frequently the most painful and difficult class in any law school's required curriculum. Students are shocked and appalled by the quantity and quality of the work that is expected of them in this class. Almost all of them, however, work very diligently, learn more than they realize they are learning, and eventually come to see the value of the skills they acquire in this class (but it may take several years and a few jobs in the legal field, before this realization occurs). Different schools

---

[3]   This is another idiom; writing assignments are not, of course, rites of passage in the literal sense of that phrase. The memorandum is not a cultural or religious ritual that denotes the passage of a child into adulthood, although it may feel that way to some law students. For most first-year law students it is generally a stressful, difficult, and disappointing challenge, a rude awakening to the shortcomings of their secondary and post-secondary educations in the context of law school.

use different names for these classes. They might be called any of the following, or some combination of these, or even something else entirely: Legal Research & Writing; Legal Reasoning; Lawyering Skills & Values; Legal Writing & Reasoning, etc. The names may differ, but the purpose is essentially the same: to teach law students how to approach legal problems in the same way U.S. lawyers and judges do, which requires significantly changing the way students think and write.

During the first semester of law school, most legal writing classes include an exercise in writing an objective memorandum. Successfully doing so requires some understanding of all of the writing and analysis principles covered thus far in this book. For this assignment, students are usually assigned a fictional client, and are instructed to research that client's legal question(s)—the issue(s)—and then write a formal memorandum for the "client's file" that evaluates the merits of the client's case. This type of predictive legal writing is quite different from persuasive writing, and there is some question every year about whether this is a skill that law students actually need to acquire. Whether lawyers and law firms today still use this type of predictive memo is a good question. However, there is no question whatsoever that students acquire valuable, and transferrable, skills by engaging in this legal writing exercise.

Purpose, audience, scope, and stance are, of course, determined by the nature of any document. When assigned an internal memorandum to a client's file, students' focus must identify the purpose (evaluating the merits), audience (the client and the writer's colleagues), the scope (defined by the issue(s)), and the stance (objective. This is necessarily a different approach than would be the focus when writing a persuasive memorandum or brief to a court. The file memorandum must honestly and objectively weigh the strengths and weaknesses of the client's position, regardless of the nature of the case. Completing such an exercise should familiarize students with some of the more common areas of legal practice. For example, it is not uncommon for faculty to assign analysis of the criminal issues that comprise the bulk of many lawyers' daily practice. Driving Under the Influence of alcohol or drugs, trespassing, and burglary cases all offer a manageable context for first-year students' analysis.[4]

---

[4]   Criminal cases in the U.S. are handled differently than in much of the world. Keeping accused criminals in jail is expensive, so not every person who is arrested and charged with a crime is kept in jail until his or her trial date. Our criminal justice system operates with a concept called "bail." Every person arrested is brought before a judge within 24 hours of arrest; judges have the authority to release non-violent, or first-time, criminal defendants if they or their friends or family are able to deposit the amount of money—the bail—set by the judge during the first-appearance hearing. If the accused is considered a "flight risk," bail is usually withheld. Many accused criminals are released either on bail or on their own recognizance. If they are eventually convicted, or if they agree to plead guilty to some or all of the charges against them, these accused defendants may be ordered to voluntarily surrender themselves to serve any jail time to which they might be sentenced. This system can minimize the trauma and disruption that usually follow an arrest. It also provides a flourishing trade of business for "bail bondsmen": companies that will post a person's bail if that person (or the family and friends) is able to pay a percentage of the bail set by

Whatever the nature of the assigned case, students will be given access to information obtained during an "initial meeting" between a lawyer and a hypothetical (potential or current) client. Entire law school courses are devoted to the skill of interviewing and counseling clients. The initial client interview should ideally leave the lawyer (or law student) with a complete and accurate description of the legal problem(s) raised by the client's circumstances. Sometimes there really is no legal problem, just an upset person who wants the legal system to offer a solution. Sometimes there are multiple legal problems implicated by one set of facts. Not all clients are sophisticated, highly educated, or trained as lawyers. It is a mistake to assume that all clients will know a legal problem from a non-legal problem, and it is the advocate's job to make that determination.

In traditional U.S. law firms, the initial client interview was handled by a senior lawyer, who might then hand the file over to a newer lawyer for follow-up. Most U.S. lawyers are extremely cautious about offering any client legal advice during the initial interview: there are too many unknowns, in both the law and the facts. It is a very rare client who will offer an honest, unbiased version of events to his or her new lawyer. The law is a complex creature, and most lawyers are wise enough to not trust their memories or experience by offering off-the-cuff advice without engaging first in research and investigation.[5] Therefore, the senior attorney might interview the client, but the junior attorney would be the one to formulate answers to the client's questions. This involves legal research and, in the traditional model, writing the memorandum to be placed in the client's file that summarizes the facts as the client related them, the legal issues raised by those facts, the primary binding authorities that could be applied to those facts, and the demonstration of how the court with jurisdiction would most likely construe and apply the law to the facts of the client's case, concluding with a prediction (which is why this is called "predictive" writing) about how this client's case is most likely to be resolved.

There are at least two reasons to write a memorandum to a file: first, the memo demonstrates to a senior attorney what to advise the client; and second, the document memorializes the facts as related by the client, the research conducted on the client's behalf, and the careful, logical analysis of the client's case in light of its facts and the applicable law. The memorandum has at least two audiences, just as it has two purposes. It

---

the judge. The bail money is returned to the bail bondsmen when the bailee appears for subsequent court proceedings.

    5   "Off-the-cuff" means without preparation. The origin of this idiom seems to be traceable to a long-gone practice of men using the starched, or even disposable, cuffs of their white shirts for jotting notes. Never in my relatively long life have I ever seen anyone write anything on the cuff of a shirt; I've seen many people write a note on either the palm or the back of a hand, but never on a shirt. Perhaps a better expression of this notion of speaking or acting extemporaneously, with no advance preparation, would be "off the hand." However, while "off-hand" is an easily understood and often-used phrase, "off the hand" makes no sense to any English speaker. Thus, off-the-cuff it is.

will be read by other lawyers in the firm, probably both the lawyer who conducted the initial client interview and other lawyers in the firm who need to understand the nature of the case and its predicted outcome. The memorandum will be read by still more people if, for any reason, the client complains in the future about not understanding the outcome of the case, or why he or she must pay the lawyers' fees, or if the client complains about any of the myriad other things about which clients eventually do complain. The memo is the tangible work product for which the lawyer is entitled to be paid. Beyond the firm, the client, and possibly a professional grievance committee, there should be no other audience.

The scope of the memo is determined by the legal issues presented in the client's case. The stance of the memo is objective and predictive: the internal office memo should not argue on the client's behalf, but should instead be an honest evaluation of the merits (if any) of the client's position in the legal dispute. This stance may not make the client happy because most people who find themselves embroiled in the U.S. legal system do not want to be told that there is no merit to their position. But at this early stage of the attorney-client relationship the lawyer's job is not to make the client happy; the lawyer's job is to give the client realistic expectations in the form of advice based on competent research and application of primary binding authorities to the client's facts.

Again, it is certainly possible that the formal office memo is not as common in today's fast-paced legal world as it may have been just a few years ago. But the research, analysis, and writing skills that first year law students develop when they engage in this assignment will never go out of fashion. Furthermore, most law students are, also at some point in the first year, required to write an appellate brief, regardless of whether they will ever, as lawyers, write such a brief. Again, the skills thus acquired are necessary and transferrable to other contexts. Lawyers and law students cannot function without these skills.

Therefore, the occasional debate amongst professors in this field about the practicalities of writing office memos and appellate briefs is irrelevant. Every student enrolled in a U.S. law school has to somehow learn to conduct legal research, how to reason, and how to write like a lawyer. These skills are gained through some instruction and guidance from the professor (or other mentor or supervisor) but ultimately they can only be acquired through extensive practice. This is the reason we teach this way; legal writing classes are not designed for the sole purpose of tormenting students (despite students' beliefs to the contrary). The only way for students to adapt their existing writing skills to meet the needs of U.S. legal writing is for them to practice. That practice has to begin somewhere, and in most legal writing classes the internal office memorandum is where it begins.

D. PARTS OF THE OFFICE MEMORANDUM

Every document prepared on behalf of a client, whether in anticipation of litigation or before or after litigation, must be clearly identified as a confidential piece of attorney-client privileged work product. Failure to so identify a document means that the opposing party is entitled to see that document when and if pre-trial discovery takes place. This means, essentially, that the opposing party receives, for free, the work product paid for by your client. Clients will not pay their lawyers to do the other side's work, so lawyers and their employees cannot forget to label all written communication "Confidential." That is a universal fact of practicing law in the United States. After that, with some variations, these are the parts and purposes of the internal, objective, predictive memorandum to a client's file:

1. HEADING

The heading identifies the document's recipient, author, subject, and date. The goal of the heading is to identify the specific purpose of the document, partly for the client's benefit and partly so the research and analysis contained in the memo may be used for future reference when other clients' cases raise the same, or similar, issues.

Perhaps the most important part of the heading is the "Re:" line, sometimes referred to as the subject line, which must provide enough information to identify the parties (all of them, not just the client, in order to avoid possible conflicts of interest) and the nature of the dispute, but which cannot possibly summarize all aspects of the client's legal problem. Crafting a good "Re:" line takes thought, time, and practice. Many times that line will change once the entire memorandum has been written, because the writer's focus is sharpened as he or she goes through the process of identifying the issue, conducting the research, and then drafting the analysis. Again, re-writing is not just normal, it is indispensable. It is always easier to re-write the subject line than to re-write the entire memorandum.

This is what a typical memorandum heading might look like:

CONFIDENTIAL: Attorney/Client Work Product

To: Supervising Attorney

From: Associate Attorney

Re: Bobby Browning v. Christina Andrews, Client File No. 15123. Dissolution of Marriage, Equitable Distribution of Jointly Owned Hobby Farm Purchased With Funds In Wife's Possession Prior To Marriage

Date: July 12, 2016

Note that the heading is single spaced, even though the remainder of the document will be double-spaced. Not also that the "Re:" line comprises three lines, rather than one, and identifies the parties, the cause of action, and the element(s) in dispute; this is appropriate format because it suits the purpose of identifying with particularity the contents of the document.

2.   ISSUE(S)

If the subject line is the most important part of the heading, the Issue statement is the most important part of the memorandum. Some memoranda have a single issue; others may have two or more. An issue is a distinct legal question, so not every element of a cause of action will amount to a separate legal issue. Based on the memo's purpose, audience, scope, and stance, the Issue statements define the parameters of the entire document. Issues should be written specifically for the case being analyzed, should not exceed one sentence, should be answerable with a "yes" or "no" but never a "maybe," and should end with a question mark because, by definition, the issue is a question.

The most straightforward way to ensure an effective issue statement is to frame each issue as some variation of an "under-does-when" question. This format provides the structure required to clearly, correctly, and concisely identify the jurisdiction and subject matter ("under"), the precise legal question ("does"), and the outcome-determinative facts of this client's situation ("when"). All of this information must be conveyed in one question, preferably one that makes it easy for a reader (client, colleague, or supervisor) to understand why the memorandum was written. Below are three sample Issue statements from objective office memos. Note that each one identifies the jurisdiction, the relevant area of the law, the precise legal question (or element in dispute) and the few outcome-determinative facts; each issue can be answered with a simple "yes" or "no."

Under South Carolina burglary law, did Carl Smith "break" and enter the home of another when he reached one arm through an open, unscreened window of Katherine Clark's house and removed her jewelry box from a table inside the house just under the window?

Under California divorce law, is Bobby Browning entitled to one-half of the fifty-acre hobby farm purchased by his wife during their marriage, paid for with funds she inherited from her father during the marriage, and titled in both spouses' names?

Under the Fourteenth Amendment to the Constitution, does PETA have standing to file suit on behalf of seven captive orcas when the Constitution grants equal protection under the law to "all men"?

3.   FACTS

The Facts section of any document, whatever its purpose, audience, scope, or stance, is the only place in U.S. legal writing that allows the writer to tell a story. Students who have experience with Creative Writing will enjoy this opportunity for storytelling. The rest of us can simply start at the beginning and work our way through the client's situation until we reach the final event in any sequence of events. The biggest challenge in writing a Facts section comes with knowing what to include and what to omit. Not everything a client tells his or her lawyer can or should be included in a Facts section: some things are unimportant on any level, some things are opinion rather than facts, and some things are, unfortunately, simply not true. Good writers make the tough decisions about what to include, and they indicate the source of their facts even when the source is simply a conversation with a client. In court documents, there will be a transcript or other record of a legal proceeding to cite as the source of any facts, but in a memo written for internal purposes, before any transcripts have had occasion to be created, the writer should indicate by text, rather than citation, the source of the information. There is no set rule for the length of a Facts statement because the complexity of each issue will dictate the required depth of the Facts section, but more than two pages is probably too long.

In general, a Facts section begins with an introduction of the parties and the nature of their dispute. It is a good rule of thumb that the first sentence of the Facts section should provide this information, identifying which party the lawyer or law firm represents, who the opposing party is, and what the cause of action is likely to be, if any. The legal context may be stated broadly, keeping in mind that the primary audience consists of the writer's colleague(s) and client. This information must be written clearly, correctly, and concisely, and it should be the first sentence because the intended audience includes the typical busy lawyer who needs to know, up front, what the case is about. Identifying the writer's own client as well as the opposing party is essential because law firms encounter serious professional responsibility problems, and possible civil liability, if they are engaged to represent a client who has previously been an opposing party, or if they take action against an opposing party who has previously been a client. Naming names will help prevent future problems for everyone involved.

After the parties have been introduced and the general subject of their dispute has been explained, it is easiest for most writers to present the facts in chronological order, beginning with the incident or exchange that started the dispute. This starting point will vary tremendously depending on the nature of the dispute that necessitates writing the memo. If, for example, the issue is whether the accused committed burglary by "breaking and entering," the facts section should focus specifically on the acts that may, or may not, have amounted to "breaking." On the other hand, the same set of facts may give rise to an entirely different legal issue, such as whether the alleged burglary happened "at night," as some jurisdictions require. If the issue is the time of the incident, the facts describing the precise hour and/or the amount of daylight at that precise hour will be the outcome-determinative facts and should be the focus of the Facts section. This Facts section would necessarily look different from the Facts section of a memo focused on the issue of "breaking and entering." Both involve the crime of burglary, and both may even be analyzed in the same memorandum, but the writer must strategically address the outcome-determinative facts for the element(s) in dispute.

The outcome-determinative facts—those that would change the outcome of a case if they were changed—obviously need the most attention in a Facts section, which usually means prominent placement at the beginning of sentences and paragraphs. But in order to tell a complete story and give the outcome-determinative facts appropriate context, other facts are also needed: there are background facts that provide the necessary history, and there are emotionally relevant facts that might not change the outcome of a case but might change the way the case is perceived. The writer's job includes knowing what to include and what to omit, and this requires writing, re-writing, and re-writing again. Often the writer does not fully appreciate the significance of a particular fact until after the analysis has been written. Any fact that finds its way into the analysis must be included in the Facts section or its introduction will just confuse the reader. (Why bother to tell the story and then spring new facts on the reader when it's time for the analysis?) But not every fact that makes its way into the Facts section must also have a place in the analysis. Thinking about the purpose of each section will help the writer decide what to include and where to include it.

There is no such thing as a representative Facts section because of the individualized nature of every memorandum. It may thus be helpful for students to engage in preliminary legal research before you attempt the following drafting exercise.

YOUR ASSIGNMENT: HEADING, ISSUE, AND FACTS

For this exercise, students will act as new attorneys who work as law clerks for a firm in Miami, Florida. A new client has hired firm to represent her in appealing the final order entered recently in the dissolution of her marriage (divorce). The supervising attorney has handed you, the student, this client's file, asking you to review it and then prepare a memorandum for the file that may be referred to when the client returns in two days for her follow-up appointment. Students have one day to complete this assignment, and the entire memorandum may not exceed seven pages. Based on the information in the client's "file," reproduced below, each student should first draft the

heading, the **issue,** and the **Facts Statement** for an internal office memorandum that analyzes the potential merits of the client's case. Do not exceed 1000 words.

CLIENT FILE

Client: Martha Edward Chapman

Interview Date: July 8, 2016

Interviewer: Matthew Richards, Senior Partner

Interviewer's Notes: *Martha Chapman, referred by mutual acquaintance Barry Black (I play tennis with Barry, and Martha went to school with him). Client wants to sue for modification of recently entered court order dissolving her marriage to Christopher Bailey. Marriage duration: 12 years; no children; marital home currently under contract for sale per order of trial court w/in part 30 days. Property in dispute now is 2000 acre "hobby farm" located near Ocala, Florida, purchased by client three years ago with money client inherited from deceased father. Client paid cash for farm, no mortgage, and title is held in her name only. Sole source of funds for purchase was client's inheritance. Husband claimed farm was marital asset, trial court agreed, ordered farm sold and proceeds divided on grounds that farm was a "marital asset" purchased during the couple's marriage. Trial court heard wife's testimony that farm was purchased outright by her from proceeds of inheritance, and titled in her name only, but trial court made specific finding that farm was marital property, thus ordered its sale and division of proceeds, 50% to wife, 50% to ex. Trial court specifically found that purchase of farm during course of marriage made it a marital asset. Client has fired her divorce lawyer, seeks representation in appeal of order only insofar as regards farm. Client is outraged at notion her ex might be entitled to money her father's will left specifically to her alone, not to her and her then-husband. This is a very quick turn-around, as deadline for filing appeal is approaching. Final order of divorce attached.*

IN THE CIRCUIT COURT OF THE ELEVENTH JUDICIAL CIRCUIT,
IN AND FOR DADE COUNTY, FLORIDA

Case No.: 16-123
Division: Fam.J

In re the Marriage of:

Martha Edward Chapman,

>   Wife

vs.

Christopher Bailey,

>   Husband

FINAL JUDGMENT OF DISSOLUTION OF MARRIAGE
WITHOUT DEPENDENT OR MINOR CHILD(REN)

This cause came before this Court for a trial on a Petition for Dissolution of Marriage. The Court, having reviewed the file and heard the testimony, makes these findings of fact and reaches these conclusions of law:

1.   The Court has jurisdiction over the subject matter and the parties.

2.   At least one party has been a resident of the State of Florida for more than 6 months immediately before filing the Petition for Dissolution of Marriage.

3.   The marriage between the parties is irretrievably broken. Therefore, the marriage between the parties is dissolved, and the parties are restored to the status of being single.

SECTION I. MARITAL ASSETS AND LIABILITIES
A.   Date of Valuation of Property. The assets and liabilities listed below are divided as indicated. The date of valuation of these assets and liabilities is, unless otherwise indicated:
a. _____ date of filing petition for dissolution of marriage.
b. _____ date of separation .
c. _____ date of final hearing .
d. __X__ other: {specify date} **Date of Entry of Final Order**

B.   Division of Assets.
1.   The assets listed below are marital assets, and will be divided as follows:
50% to Husband and **50% to Wife:**
a.   Marital home
b.   One 2000 acre section of horse farm land located in Marion County, Florida, purchased in 2013 and currently titled in the wife's name only.

SECTION II. EXCLUSIVE USE AND POSSESSION OF HOME
[Indicate all that apply]

1.   The   **X**   Husband _____ Wife, as a condition of support, shall have exclusive use and possession of the dwelling located at the following address: **123 Biscayne Blvd.,**

until: {date or event} **Entry of Final Order**

2.   The _____ Husband   **X**   Wife may make visits to the premises described in the paragraph above for the purpose of obtaining any items awarded in this Final Judgment. These visits shall occur after notice to the person granted exclusive use and possession of the dwelling and at the earliest convenience of both parties or as ordered in paragraph 4 below.

3.   Upon the termination of the right of exclusive use and possession, the dwelling shall be sold and the net proceeds divided **50% to Husband** and **50% to Wife**, with the following credits and/or setoffs being allowed:

N/A _____

_____

_____

_____

4. _____ Other:

_____

_____

SECTION III. THERE ARE NO MINOR CHILDREN OF THE MARRIAGE, AND THUS NO CUSTODY, VISITATION, OR CHILD SUPPORT IS AT ISSUE.

SECTION IV. NO ALIMONY WAS SOUGHT AND NONE IS ORDERED.

SECTION V. THE PARTIES HAVE AGREED TO EACH PAY HIS AND HER OWN ATTORNEYS' FEES, COSTS, AND SUIT MONEY.

DONE AND ORDERED at Dade County, Florida, on June 30, 2016.

_____ /S/_____

CIRCUIT JUDGE

A copy of this Final Order was {Choose one only} (X) mailed ( ) faxed and mailed ( ) hand delivered to the parties listed below on {date} June 30, 2016 by {clerk of court or designee}

4. DISCUSSION

Having laid the groundwork by presenting the Heading, the Issues, and the Facts, the writer of an internal office memorandum must then engage in the research required to demonstrate the predicted outcome of the issues. The Issues are determined by reviewing all available facts presented by the client's situation. It is not yet even a "case," because that term implies a pending court action, and the office memo would normally be written prior to the filing of any legal action. The Discussion section is the heart of any memo, and it will determine whether the memo as a whole succeeds or fails in accomplishing its purpose. The writer will spend more time researching and writing a Discussion section than writing the rest of the memo as a whole.

The first step in writing a Discussion section is conducting the legal research required to understand the issues that have been identified, at least preliminarily, as the focus of the memorandum. Identifying issues includes identifying the jurisdiction, and the jurisdiction determines which sources will be primary binding authority. Remember that the researcher's goal is always to find on-point primary binding authority.

Here are some of the **common pitfalls for legal researchers,** and how to avoid them:

- Be certain to answer the question you were actually asked to answer. Do not get sidetracked; repeatedly refer back to the assigning materials.

- Look for statutes first and then cases. Applicable statutes that are annotated can then be used to locate every other source that has ever cited that statute, including cases, administrative regulations, and secondary sources.

- Focus on the legal issue(s) rather than the facts of your client's case. The law is always more important than the facts.

- Update all research results by looking at citing references, or KeyCite, to verify that any source on which you might rely is still good law.

- Research is most effective when it begins with the broader issues. Effective researchers then work down to the exact, specific issue that needs to be answered in any memo. Effective research requires understanding the big picture before attempting to engage in any legal analysis.

- Headnotes or KeyCites are excellent finding tools, but they are nothing more than that. Quoting or citing headnotes is malpractice. Only the opinion written by a judge or judges is actual law, and it is the writer's responsibility to locate and cite only primary binding authority.

- Occasionally, but infrequently, the best research will turn up no binding authority. Then (and only then) it may be appropriate and necessary to look at the law in other jurisdictions. The ideal goal is to find jurisdictions that are geographically close and have laws that are similar to the writer's own. Non-binding authority may be persuasive, but never the other way around, and the closer the non-binding authority is in terms of both law and geography the more persuasive it will be.

- Secondary sources enable a researcher to become educated about an unfamiliar area of the law. Secondary sources are also excellent finding tools. Most, such as Law Review articles, legal encyclopedias, and treatises, cite some primary authority, enabling efficient researchers to use them accordingly.

- Effective researchers keep a research log, or trail, avoiding the need for unnecessarily repetitive steps in the process. This does not mean copying every source that is found; it simply means keeping track of every source consulted. Research notes should include the reason the source might be helpful and its citation, so it can be found again.

- Research results must, eventually, be copied and compiled. They should be organized by topic so the writing process will be more efficient. There is wisdom in the notion that no piece of paper should be handled more than once in order to deal with it. Many researchers use a binder or computerized folders; any organizational method is acceptable so long as the resources are easily accessible.

- At some point, the research must end and the writing must begin. It does not take long for the research process to become a place of comfort, one that is much less risky than the writing process, and lawyers as well as law students frequently postpone writing in favor of research. Effective advocates establish internal deadlines, and force themselves to stop researching and start writing with enough time to write, re-write, polish, self-edit, and re-write again. Do not procrastinate; it does not work, ever.[6]

---

[6] The first time I taught a university-level course, a student assured me his paper would be finished in plenty of time but that he had not actually started writing until shortly before the paper was due because, according to him, "I work best under pressure." He learned with that assignment that he did not, in fact, work best under pressure; none of us do. Time pressure just adds

When the research process is well underway, the writer must start organizing thoughts into some form of a written outline. It is almost impossible to wrestle large quantities of complex ideas into any organized form without using an outline. With just a little extra effort, that outline can become a first draft before the writer knows it. Students are well-advised to keep the outline in front of them as they progress with the writing, but should give themselves permission to revise it as they write. In legal writing, it is impossible to know exactly what will ultimately need to be written. At the same time, it is a serious mistake to wait to start writing until the writer believes he or she thoroughly understand the issues. No one will ever know everything, but at some point, everyone has to write something. Again, it is always easier to re-write than it is to write, so just start somewhere. Some people find it easier to start with the Discussion, and to write the Issues and Facts sections later; others prefer to frame the issues before embarking on the Discussion. That is the writer's choice to make, as long as he or she does, in fact, begin somewhere.

Begin the Discussion with a broad statement of the applicable law that will then be broken into smaller statements, each of which will be analyzed separately. This is where CREAC comes into the equation: a memorandum's Discussion section is one large CREAC filled with smaller forms of CREAC that define and analyze the key terms of the larger CREAC. The depth of the analysis is dictated by the complexity of the issue(s), and will vary widely from one memo to the next. The important thing to remember is that the Discussion's purpose is to explain the law, demonstrate the application of that law to the client's situation, and then reach some logical conclusion. Because the stance is predictive rather than persuasive, there is never a wrong conclusion unless it is illogical. Any conclusion that stems necessarily from the application of law to new facts is a logical conclusion. Worry less about where the analysis takes you than how you get there.

When writing predictive analysis, use **CREAC**:

C: In writing a predictive memorandum based on the preceding drafting exercise, the logical starting point of a Discussion, using CREAC, would be to predict, or conclude, the answer to the client's question: "Ms. Chapman should have a meritorious appeal of the trial court's decision that the farm in Ocala was marital property." No citation is needed for that sentence, because it is a prediction—there is no crystal ball to cite for a predicted outcome.

R: The rule of law might come from one or several sources, but it makes sense to begin with a statute if one is applicable. Here, Florida has a comprehensive dissolution of marriage statute, Florida Statutes Section

---

unnecessary stress to already stressful situations, and it is so easily avoidable that there really is no reason to subject oneself to that additional stress. Write early and write often.

61.075: it provides the language that a court would apply if an appellate court is asked to decide whether the trial court erred in determining that the farm was marital property. The key language of the statute is that which defines marital as opposed to non-marital property in any Florida divorce case. The statute defines real estate as marital property if it is "held by the parties as tenants by the entireties." Non-marital property, on the other hand, is defined as "assets acquired . . . by either party by . . . bequest, devise, or descent." If the farm is indeed held by Ms. Chapman in her name only, rather than being held by her and her former husband as tenants by the entireties, Ms. Chapman should be advised by her lawyer that she likely prevail if she appeals the final order of divorce that found the farm was marital property. If that is the case, it would be quite straightforward to appeal on the grounds that the trial court's order was clearly erroneous because the statute's definition of marital property was not met. But if the farm was, in fact, held by Ms. Chapman and her former husband together, as tenants by the entireties, there is a reasonable dispute about whether the trial court erred in its determination that the farm was marital property. Knowing the applicable rule of law, then, and citing it, either as a direct partial quote or as a paraphrase, sets the stage for the writer to predict a logical outcome for this case.

> Some readers dislike too many direct quotes, which is something a writer must keep in mind even as he or she decides whether the quote is more effective than a paraphrase. There are times when only a quote will do, and there are times when a paraphrase is more efficient and effective. The decision is the writer's.

Legal research would reveal whether there is binding case law on this legal question. The legal question is not about the divorce itself: it is about marital versus non-marital property and its distribution during a divorce. To look for binding case law, the researcher must know what jurisdiction's decisions are binding in Miami. There are several ways to determine what would be binding precedent. Almost every governmental entity in the United States has a web site that will include the legislatively enacted laws of that jurisdiction. Appendix One of the ALWD Citation Manual lists every jurisdiction alphabetically and its sources of primary law. Having determined the source of binding authority, the researcher can identify the search terms, or key words, in an online database limited to the binding sources of law.

When identifying the "R" in CREAC, there may be several sources, either separately or combined, that make up the applicable rule. A synthesized rule is one that takes pieces from more than one source and combines those pieces into one comprehensive whole. Rule synthesis might happen at the beginning, or it might be a cumulative effect after the separate pieces of a bigger rule have been stated and cited. If a synthesized rule derives from an ordinance plus a precedent case that applied that ordinance, both sources must be cited after the synthesized rule sentence. It may take a short paragraph to articulate a synthesized rule, in which case each sentence requires a citation. However it is presented, the writer must bear in mind the ultimate purpose, audience, scope, and stance: if the intended reader cannot follow the writer's train of thought, it is the writer's problem, not the reader's.

> Computerized legal research using Boolean searches is more efficient than using plain-language searches. Westlaw and Lexis provide the terms and connectors used in Boolean searches if the researcher clicks on either "terms & connectors" or "advanced search terms." If nothing else, the researcher may type the key words or phrase(s) in quotation marks to eliminate all search results that might include one word in the term but not necessarily the terms that are required. The sources can also be restricted by indicating the relevant jurisdiction. The goal in legal research is not to find as many sources as possible but to find only the primary binding sources that actually address the client's legal issue(s). Keep narrowing the search result, or try different search terms, until the results are down to a manageable number, never more than one hundred, because no researcher wants to read or cite more than a few of the most applicable sources.

E: The explanation of the rule provides its context. The depth of explanation required depends on the number of sources cited for the rule and the directness with which the cited sources support the writer's proposed use of the rule. If the rule comes from a statute or ordinance or regulation, its explanation may be limited to legislative history, which is helpful but not necessarily definitive. Legislative history takes many forms, depending on the enacting body. A federal statute, for example, might have legislative history in the form of committee hearings, testimony of expert witnesses, congressional debates, etc. But a local ordinance may not have any available legislative history at all.

The language of legislative or administrative law does not provide context. In a jurisdiction without common law the statutory (or code) language alone defines the law, but in the United States it is only the beginning of defining the law. Cases explain how codes are interpreted and applied. Cases provide context for statutory language. Describing a court's opinion is the best way to explain the law—the E in CREAC.

A writer can easily describe a case by using one formula, no matter how complicated the case itself might be. First, the writer identifies the general legal principle from the precedent case that could or would be applied to a client's new case. That general legal principle is the "rule" for the writer's purposes, and it is the first sentence in a paragraph devoted to describing one case. That rule sentence is always followed by a citation to its source so the reader knows exactly how authoritative the cited rule is, based on the court that decided the precedent case and when it was decided.

After the rule and its citation, the description of a precedent case continues, when doing so is helpful, by summarizing only the most important facts from the precedent case. This might be one sentence, or two, or even three, each of which is followed by a pinpoint citation that tells the reader the location of the cited fact within the precedent case.[7] After the rule and the facts, with their corresponding citations, a case description tells the reader what the court decided in the precedent case (its holding) and why the court decided that way (its reasoning). This case description makes a tidy, well-organized paragraph of anywhere from three to six sentences, plus citations. The most important parts are the first and the last: the rule and the court's reasoning.

The "E" in CREAC might consist of one case description or it might include more, depending on the number of sources that contribute to a synthesized rule. A paragraph might begin with a statutory rule and then explain that rule with a case description, including the case rule, key facts, holding, and reasoning. Every piece of analysis has its own level of detail and depth depending on its complexity. The pitfall to avoid in describing cases is the temptation to focus too much on the facts of a precedent case when the rule and the reasoning—the law of the precedent case—are almost always much more important than the facts. The facts are easier to see, but that does not make them more important.

More sophisticated legal writing may not include any case descriptions at all. Briefs to the U.S. Supreme Court are unlikely to include case descriptions, for example, because at that level the analysis is strictly legal rather than factual. Case descriptions enable the writer to make factual analogies and distinctions, which are appropriate in the early evaluative stages of analysis. But more complex legal issues lend themselves to syllogisms rather than analogies, and syllogisms depend on legal principles rather than facts.

---

[7] Pinpoint cites, remember, are important to a reader who wants to see for herself what the cited authority addressed. Providing a pinpoint cite is part of the writer's job of giving the reader what he needs to see, making the reader's job easier even if it makes the writer's job harder. Pinpoint cites seem picky, but they are among the required tools of a writer who is effectively providing everything the reader needs.

Syllogisms are tools of persuasive writing that are more fully addressed in the chapter covering appellate arguments. In broad terms, a syllogism consists of a major premise (think of this as a rule of law), a minor premise (this can be viewed as application of that rule of law to a new set of facts), followed by the logical conclusion that arises from the major and the minor premise. The classic example is something like this: A = B, and B= C; therefore, A = C. Or, in another form: All men are mortal (major premise/rule); Socrates is a man (minor primes/application); therefore, Socrates is mortal (the only logical conclusion to be drawn from the two premises).

A: The "A" in CREAC refers to the Analysis, which means the Application of the cited law to a new set of facts—a new client's legal problem. U.S. legal education always stresses the importance of analysis. Without analysis, students are left with rules and conclusions, followed by more rules and conclusions, none of which is enough to be effective. Analysis is what separates the successes from the failures in legal practice and in law school, but it is a very difficult concept to master. It requires demonstrating, not just talking about, how the law could or should be applied in a new case. Application of the law provides the support for any conclusion. Without that support, the conclusion has no credibility. There is no reason to engage in the process of legal writing without analysis.

Below is a deconstructed piece of analysis that might find its way into a predictive office memo:

Ms. Chapman would likely succeed in appealing the trial court's decision that her farm was marital property. **[This is the predicted outcome of the client's case, the initial "C" in CREAC, and it requires no citation to authority because there is no authority for a prediction.]** Real estate that is owned by one party to a marriage, rather than owned by both as tenants by the entireties, is specifically identified as non-marital property. Fla. Stat. Ann. §61.057 (West 2016). **[This is the rule from the state statute, the "R" in CREAC.]** Only when both spouses contribute to the enhancement in value of non-marital property may it be transformed from non-marital to marital property. *Barner v. Barner*, 716 So. 2d 795 (Fla. 4th DCA 1998). In *Barner*, the Fourth District Court of Appeal determined that a trial court erred in finding that a wife's income from non-marital property was marital property because the husband had contributed to the financial appreciation of the property throughout the marriage. *Id.* at 798. In reversing the trial court's decision, the District Court of Appeal explained that "only where appreciation occurs as a result of . . . marital effort or funds [may] the enhancement of nonmarital assets . . . be considered a marital asset." *Id.* at 797–98. **[These sentences contain the rule from the case and a description of the case: rule, facts, holding, reasoning—the E in CREAC.]** Unlike the spouses in *Barner*, Ms. Chapman and her former husband did not work together to increase the value of the farm she purchased in her own name only, so there is nothing that might have been transformed from non-marital to marital property. **[This applies the cited law to the facts of the client's case—the "A" in CREAC.]** *Barner*, 716 So. 2d at 798; Fla. Stat. §61.057. **[These are short, rather than full, citations to both authorities incorporated in the Application.]** The facts of our client's case are distinguishable from *Barner* because our client purchased the farm near Ocala with funds that she inherited during the marriage, separate from her husband, and the husband made no contribution to that property that could have converted the farm to a marital asset. **[This is a factual distinction, the opposite of an analogy, that demonstrates how the client's situation is distinguishable from the cited case law.]** *Barner*, 716 So. 2d at 798. **[This is another short cite to the precedent case, required because the case name and its facts are incorporated in the preceding sentence of text.]** Therefore, because there is nothing in our client's case that would have justified the trial court's finding that the farm was marital property, and absent such a fact the farm fits the statute's definition of non-marital property. **[This is the final "C" in CREAC, the conclusion, reiterated for emphasis and to bring the analysis full-circle back to its starting point.]**

You can see that the example above is an abnormally long paragraph, and that the actual analysis is limited to two sentences, one of which applies the cited law and the other of which compares the facts of the current case with those of the precedent case. Law students are frequently nervous about having only one or two sentences of analysis, but the goal is quality, not quantity. The paragraph above could have been broken into smaller pieces, perhaps even one piece per element of CREAC, but a long paragraph that clearly and efficiently accomplishes its purpose is perfectly acceptable in legal writing; there is no magic number of sentences per paragraph so long as the writer is giving the reader everything that reader wants or needs, in a clearly recognizable form that is written with purpose, audience, scope, and stance in mind, and that is clear, concise, and correct. This CREAC structure can be repeated as many times as necessary within a Discussion section in order to address the issues raised by the client's legal problem.

C: The final "C" in CREAC is included to draw the logic to its natural end, which reinforces its beginning. This brings the logic full circle. It is necessary because it signals to the reader that the analysis is finished by reminding the reader of the bottom-line answer to the client's question. It is the final piece in the process of analysis, in which the writer has told the reader the answer to the issue(s), then demonstrating why that is the answer, and finally reminding the reader, again, of that answer. This formula will make it easier for a reader to understand and follow the writer's thought processes, and for that reason it is absolutely necessary. One sentence, usually with no citation, and perhaps beginning with the word "Therefore," will be enough to bring the reader along to the writer's conclusion.

5. CONCLUSION

In an internal office memorandum, the Conclusion should devote one short paragraph to each issue addressed in the Discussion. Each paragraph should be constructed as a crystal-clear syllogism for the major premise of each issue. If you find yourself rehashing every point in the Discussion, rein yourself in. The purpose of the Conclusion is to provide the bottom-line answer to each issue, without citations or unnecessary sidetracking. Below is an example of a Conclusion to an objective memorandum to a client's file.

Real estate that is purchased by and titled in the name of only one spouse during a marriage is non-marital property; even if the other spouse has expended time or money toward its improvement, only the value of any appreciation in the property's value might be transformed into marital property. **[Major premise]** Ms. Chapman's farm was purchased by her with money she inherited three years ago, and is titled in her name only. Her former husband made no contributions that might have increased the value of the property. **[Minor premise]** Therefore, the trial court probably erred when it decided that the farm was marital property, and Ms. Chapman is likely to prevail if she files an appeal of this aspect of the divorce order. **[Conclusion]**

YOUR ASSIGNMENT: RESEARCHING THE LAW AND WRITING THE DISCUSSION

Find the South Carolina (state) statute that defines first-degree burglary (§ 16–11–311). Identify the elements of first-degree burglary in South Carolina, and then read the facts below.

Assume you are enrolled in an internship at a State Public Defender's office in Myrtle Beach, South Carolina. Your supervising attorney just met a new client, a young woman who has been charged with first-degree burglary. You must determine whether the State is likely to obtain a conviction of first-degree burglary based on the following facts:

Client name: Dawn Harrellson

Age: 24

Criminal Record: None

Client Statement: Client seeks representation in criminal case currently pending against her. Arrested July 13, 2016 at 11:48 p.m. by Myrtle Beach Police Officer David Brown. Arrest report says client was in her ex-husband's condo without consent, and was in the process of taking his Rolex wristwatch, valued at over $100,000.00, from his closet when neighbors called police because they could hear someone moving around in what was supposed to be an empty apartment; ex-husband/victim, Phillip Freiman, was travelling on business at time of incident. Client is very recently divorced and is still a recorded owner of the condominium but was arrested for burglary. Client has not lived in the condo since separating from Mr. Freiman three months ago (separated as of April 11, 2016, divorce finalized Sept. 10, 2016).

It should not take you more than ten minutes to locate South Carolina's statute defining first-degree burglary. If you do not locate the statute within ten minutes, use different search terms or change the database being searched. Remember to search the smallest possible data base by limiting the jurisdiction (here, South Carolina) and the type of law (here, state statutes).

The text of the statute is the source of the elements of first-degree burglary: "A person is guilty of burglary in the first degree if the person enters a dwelling without consent and with intent to commit a crime in the dwelling, and . . . the entering or remaining occurs during the nighttime." Complete the following list to organize your thoughts and verify your understanding of the law:

a.   **Elements** of first-degree burglary (enters; dwelling; without consent; with intent to commit crime; in the nighttime)

b.   **Corresponding facts** of Ms. Harrelson's case (entered; condo co-owned by her and ex-husband; while he was out of town; with intent to steal wristwatch; at 11:48 p.m.)

Now use the statute as a finding tool to locate one South Carolina Supreme Court decision that will help you predict whether Ms. Harrelson is likely to be convicted of burglarizing a condo when she and her husband are the joint owners of the condo.

Reading case law defines the elements and reveals that some statutory elements are beyond any reasonable dispute: Yes, Ms. Harrelson "entered" a "dwelling" in the "night-time," and apparently she did so with the "intention" of taking her ex-husband's expensive wrist watch. (These four elements might be referred to as elements that are beyond reasonable dispute, or undisputed elements.) The only element in dispute is whether she had "consent" to enter the dwelling.

Burglary laws are historically designed to give people a sense of security in their own homes, especially at night, so normally a defendant should not be convicted of burglarizing her own home. For example, homeowners or renters do not need their own consent to enter their own homes regardless of the time of day or of any intent they might have in doing so. The element in dispute in this hypothetical case is whether Ms. Harrelson's entry into the condo that she still co-owns with her former husband was "without consent."

If a researcher spends more than ten minutes looking for case law, that researcher should stop. It is far better to ask for help from a reference librarian, a teaching assistant, or a professor than to waste time, because if case law has not been found within the first ten minutes the key words and/or data base should probably be changed. The researcher may have narrowed the field too far and therefore be unable to find an applicable case, or the search terms may need to be changed.

With practice will come greater research efficiency. Remember to try looking at the statute for key words and phrases that will help you through the initial research process. State statutes are available free on the Internet, but finding a case that cites that statute might require using Westlaw or Lexis. Google Scholar is improving its legal research capabilities, and when that system is more fully developed it will be free. But for now, a commercial legal database is probably necessary to find citing cases (and to verify that an applicable statute is still good law).

Return now to the hypothetical client charged with burglary. When you have located a South Carolina Supreme Court case that you think will be helpful (and there are several), begin writing the Discussion section of a predictive memorandum of law. Start with the statute's definition of first-degree burglary. Next, explain which elements are beyond reasonable dispute and why (for example, Ms. Harrelson's attorney could never argue that it was not "nighttime" when she entered the condo because she was arrested just a few minutes before midnight in South Carolina, which is not the land of the midnight sun.)[8] It is never acceptable in the United States to make an argument that clearly has no merit; doing so is unethical. It is wise to address the elements that cannot be disputed first, before getting into the analysis of any elements that might be subject to dispute.

Before anything can be written, the writer must have a sense of what will be written, and in legal writing that means attaining a preliminary understanding of the applicable law. As a law student or lawyer, you should expect to read cases more than once in order to learn the law. This may feel tedious, but it is always a good investment of one's time. If, at this point in your education, you want to write analysis of the hypothetical client's case but do not feel that you understand the issue, stop and talk it through with a teaching assistant or professor. Even if only one case will be cited, the writer will, at least initially, want to read many cases in order to begin writing with some assurance that the predicted application of the law is based on sound analysis.

---

[8] Only those few places located at the Earth's poles are truly lands of the midnight sun, although any northern area with extremely long summer days might be referred to in that way. Finland calls itself the land of the midnight sun, but so do Norway and Alaska.

Do not hesitate to conclude that Ms. Harrelson might be found guilty of burglary even though she is still an owner of the condo (the dwelling) that she entered at night with the intent to take a very valuable wrist watch that did not belong to her. Clients frequently do not like what they hear from their lawyers, but the lawyer's professional responsibility requires that the client be told what the law says and how that law is likely to be applied to the client's legal problem. Ms. Harrelson might think she cannot be convicted of burglarizing a home she co-owns, but she has not been trained to find, read, and analyze the applicable law. It is never easy to give a client bad news, but it is far worse to mislead a client.

Students who are prepared to complete the assignment to write a Discussion for Ms. Harrelson's file must remember the purpose, audience, scope, and stance of the memorandum, and must think about writing clearly, correctly, and concisely. The Discussion section must be organized with CREAC as the framework. Starting with the statute, the Discussion must explain the uncontested elements before moving on to analyze the elements in dispute. Writers must always use a legal citation manual and include proper citations to statutes, cases, or any other source that is referred to or relied on in any way. Syllogistic reasoning will always make it easier for the reader to follow the writer's thought processes: major premise, minor premise, and conclusion. Taking the time to do this assignment well now will ensure that the writer is better equipped to tackle future, more complex assignments.

E. ALTERNATIVE DISPUTE RESOLUTION

There is another arena in which much U.S. legal writing takes place: there are many different types of alternative dispute resolution, and each might involve different kinds of written documents. Most legal disputes in the United States, whether state or federal, civil or criminal, are settled before they go to trial. Many of those cases are settled with the help of a neutral third party, an arbitrator or mediator, or through the parties' attorneys acting as negotiators. Many contracts include a provision for mandatory arbitration of any disputes that might arise under the terms of the contract. But when there is no contract, or no binding arbitration, and the parties or their lawyers have been unsuccessful in negotiating with each other, the parties might turn to a mediator for help settling their dispute. Some courts require mediation before approving any settlement or signing any final order. As the courts' workloads rise, so does the use of alternative dispute resolution. Research shows that people are generally happier with a mediated settlement than with a court-imposed disposition of their cases.

If a mediator will be used to help settle any case, the parties must agree on which mediator to use. Most jurisdictions in the United States require specialized training before a lawyer can be called a "mediator." In

Florida, for example, certified mediator training is forty hours long, with regular refresher courses required. Mediators, like lawyers in other fields, tend to specialize in one area of the law: criminal law, domestic relations (divorce) law, estate planning, tax law, personal injury law, patent law— these are just some of the areas of specialization. A good mediator, with an established practice and a proven track record, can become highly sought-after; many lawyers prefer mediation to litigation because the results come more quickly and tend to be better received by their clients.

When mediation or arbitration is successful, the parties go through a series of negotiations in order to reach an agreement with which they can all live. Sometimes the parties, or their lawyers, sit at a table with each other and the mediator. In more contentious cases, the mediator keeps the parties in separate rooms but moves back and forth between them as the negotiations proceed. Any negotiated settlement must then be put in writing. A settlement agreement that is approved by a court with jurisdiction over the case has the force and effect of any other court order, but it is reached by the parties and their lawyers rather than being imposed on them by a court.

Settlement agreements are as complex as the cases they resolve, and there is no general rules for the length or form of settlement agreements. Without a sample to follow, newer lawyers might be hesitant to memorialize any agreements in writing. But using the same general principles as are used in writing a predictive memorandum to a client's file, readers of this book can now write anything. Remember to write with an eye towards the document's purpose, audience, scope, and stance; write clearly, correctly, and concisely; and use CREAC to keep the document organized.

F. CONTRACT DRAFTING

In the United States, as in most of the world, legally binding contracts generally require a written document that sets forth the parties' agreement. Law students throughout the United States spend at least one semester, and frequently more, studying the law of contracts. And the first-year course is generally just the theory of contract law; upper level classes may focus on Contract Drafting, the process of writing contractual agreements. Law libraries and legal databases contain form books that are helpful for specific types of contracts in specific jurisdictions, but writers must proceed with caution: pitfalls abound when it comes to drafting contracts.

The nuances and requirements of contract drafting are complex and are unique to this area of the law. Contracts that are not well written can costs clients millions of dollars. The requirements of a contract for the sale of goods might be quite different from those of a contract for the sale of real estate or a contract for services. This is not an area of legal work that is forgiving of any mistakes, so only skilled and knowledgeable lawyers should venture into contract drafting. As Contracts professors like to say, "If you write at all, write it all." Unless the writer is licensed to practice law in the jurisdiction, he or she should not attempt to write a contract at all.

CHAPTER 5

AFTER THE COURT DECIDES:
APPELLATE PRACTICE

■ ■ ■

After a trial court makes a final decision in any case in the United States—state or federal, civil, administrative, or criminal—the losing party must decide whether to pursue an appeal.

> Appeals may be filed only from "final orders," but sometimes a "final order" is issued by a trial court before the underlying case has been decided. When this happens, the losing party may file an "interlocutory appeal": an appeal may be filed when a trial court rules on a motion during or before a trial, if that ruling has the effect of a final order. Otherwise, both parties need to wait until the trial court has made a final decision on the case as a whole before filing any appeal. What constitutes a "final order" for purposes of an appeal can be quite controversial, and is part of learning the rules of appellate procedure in any jurisdiction in the United States.

Appeals are only guaranteed in certain criminal cases, where a convicted criminal is said to have an appeal "as of right." In the United States, criminal cases generally implicate more constitutional rights than do civil or administrative cases, because only after conviction of a crime may a losing party be sentenced to serve time in jail or prison. There is no "debtors' prison" in the United States, and civil liability does not come with jail time. There are some exceptions, of course, because there are always exceptions in the U.S. legal system which is why it is almost always correct to answer any legal question by saying, "It depends"). For example, a non-custodial parent who fails to pay child support can be sentenced to stay in jail until he or she has the money to pay past-due child support, either fully or to the extent required by a court order. In some scenarios, willful disobedience of a court order is considered "contempt of court," which is punishable by imprisonment. If, for example, a news reporter is ordered by a judge to reveal the source of published information, and the reporter refuses to do so because she promised that source that the source's identity would not be revealed (think of a low-level drug dealer revealing the name of his supplier, which information is then published in a newspaper as part of the reporter's story about organized crime in a big city), the reporter may be found to be in contempt of court for willfully disobeying the court's order, and the reporter may find herself in jail until either she reveals her source or the court changes its mind. But in general only conviction on criminal charges results in anyone spending time behind bars.[1]

When an individual's right to personal freedom is involved, so is the U.S. Constitution. This is why many criminal convictions come with an automatic right to appeal. When a losing party is ordered to pay money or make other reparations to a prevailing party, fewer constitutional rights are involved, meaning there is not always an automatic right to appeal. In the United States, we are very serious about protecting the right to liberty; personal liberty is considered irreplaceable in a way that money or other property is not. Thus in most courts, and particularly in federal courts, appeals are more likely to stem from criminal convictions than from losing a civil suit.

Appellate practice requires a set of skills that are transferrable from pre-trial or trial practice. In today's legal culture, however, appellate lawyers do not usually litigate in trial courts, and trial lawyers do not usually argue appeals. Practicing law has become quite specialized in the United States, and while there is not always a line that separates appellate lawyers from trial lawyers, there are very few lawyers who try to cross that line. For students' purposes, however, it is helpful to look at the similarities rather than the differences between the realms of pre-trial, trial, and appellate practice.

Every good lawyer in the United States starts from the same point, whatever the context of the particular case might be: The starting point is always jurisdiction.[2] The first question, therefore, is which court has jurisdiction to hear any dispute in which the lawyer has agreed (or might agree) to represent any party? As readers saw in *Tilikum*, if the court decides it lacks jurisdiction the case cannot proceed. A lawyer who files a lawsuit or brings criminal charges in a court that lacks jurisdiction, whether intentionally or inadvertently, is a lawyer who is likely to face disciplinary charges and/or a malpractice suit. Only very experienced lawyers can safely memorize jurisdictional rules. Newer lawyers, and

---

[1]   This is yet another kind of "bar," not to be confused with either the kind of bar where alcoholic beverages are sold or the kind of bar to which lawyers are admitted to practice. "Behind bars" means in jail. "Jail" is a local imprisonment, and in most parts of the United States a convicted criminal can be held in jail for up to one year; if the term of imprisonment will exceed 365 days, the prisoner is usually confined in a "prison." Jail and prison are not synonymous, and should not be used interchangeably.

[2]   Most U.S. law students study jurisdiction as part of a course entitled Civil Procedure. This course is a requirement for first-year J.D. students across the United States, and international students who aspire to take a state bar exam would do well to take at least one course on civil procedure and one on criminal procedure, at a minimum; most law schools also offer higher-level courses on appellate practice and procedure. An international lawyer or law student cannot hope to understand how the U.S. legal systems operate without studying the rules of procedure just like every J.D. student in this country is required to do.

certainly law students, need to conduct legal research just to ensure that any legal action is brought in a court that has the jurisdictional power to decide the case.

Having determined an appropriate appellate court, the lawyer who seeks to appeal any decision rendered by any trial court must begin the arduous process of substantive legal research. Knowing the correct jurisdiction tells the lawyer what authorities will be binding on the appellate court. The lawyer's goal is always to engage in legal research that leads to primary (not secondary), binding (not merely persuasive) authorities to cite to the appellate court (just as it would have been with the trial court). Primary binding authority might come from case law, statutes, administrative regulations, or constitutional law—but without correctly answering the question of jurisdiction, the lawyer cannot determine what authority will be binding.

Assuming the jurisdiction has been correctly identified and the lawyer (or law student) is ready to engage in the process of substantive legal research, the difference between a good advocate and a bad or mediocre one comes down to pinpointing the legal issue(s) and engaging in efficient legal research. Most lawyers in the United States rely on electronic databases to conduct their research, whether commercially or publicly published.

Research, writing, and citations are the three strands of the braid of effective advocacy. No matter how brilliant or engaging a lawyer's arguments might be, those arguments will have no value in a U.S. court unless they are thoroughly researched, persuasively written, and appropriately cited. This is probably as new and unexpected for the international lawyer studying U.S. law as it is for the American J.D. student. No other discipline in the United States approaches its work the way lawyers do, so this is a new skill for everyone. International students might face the language barrier, but every student in every classroom of every law school in the United States faces the same hurdles when it comes to the approach to legal issues.

When the jurisdiction and the issues have been identified correctly, the substantive research revolves around more than just finding authorities that support what the lawyer intends to argue. Good legal research requires finding and evaluating a spectrum of authorities rather than limiting the search to finding sources that support the lawyer's arguments. In most fields, the writer decides what he or she wants to argue and then researches to find sources in support of that position, but in law it should be the other way around: Good legal researchers start with a question, find all possible answers, and then craft arguments based on the results of their research. In other words, the research determines what arguments may be made rather than the arguments determining what research is conducted.

It may be helpful to envision a legal argument as a circle: a completely logical argument incorporates even those authorities that seem to work against your position. Ignoring adverse authorities brings its own set of problems because it leaves the legal writer unprepared to respond to any opponents' arguments. Researching every side of every issue ensures that the writer is prepared to make all valid arguments (but none that rely on anything other than primary, binding authority) and also to rebut any valid arguments that an opponent might raise. A writer who stops researching when he or she finds authorities that agree with a client's position is a writer who has only drawn half the circle. The first half should always be the affirmative arguments that best support the writer's client, but to close the circle it is imperative to anticipate and refute all equally logical opposing arguments. Only a complete circle will leave the arguments unassailable and thus with a better chance of persuading a court that the writer's position is the best approach to whatever issues are before the court.

Not every trial court decision results in a written opinion that might become the subject of an appeal, but without an appealable order from a trial court there can be no appeal. State and local trial courts typically file their decisions in the form of Orders that have been drafted by the lawyer(s) for the prevailing party. For example, when a motion is granted, either before or during a trial, the prevailing party's lawyer is usually asked to write the order granting that motion. Federal trial courts, with more resources and time, are more likely to write their own opinions, usually with the assistance of one or more law clerks, leaving little doubt about the basis for those decisions. Whether there is an order or an opinion or both, only a final order is ripe for appeal by the losing party.

The first step in an appeal is a timely filed Notice of Appeal filed with the appellate court. The time for filing an appeal varies with different jurisdictions. Appeals are limited to the issues preserved for appeal and raised by the appealing party. There is a common misconception that appeals give the losing party a second shot at winning, but in reality every appeal is limited to the issues raised on appeal. An appellate court's function is not to re-try a case, but is instead to review the legality of the lower court's order that forms the basis of the appeal.

The scope—or standard—of review is determined by the nature of the question being appealed. The standard of review describes the window, or lens, through which the appellate court reviews the legality of the lower court's decision. If the appeal is based on a decision of fact (For example: Was the defendant the person who possessed the drugs? How many minutes passed between the time the defendant was stopped and the time the arresting officer found the drugs in the defendant's car?), the appellate court has a very limited window through which to review the decision of the trial court. But if the issue on appeal is a question of law (i.e., does the constitutional prohibition of illegal searches extend to a defendant who is stopped for breaking the traffic laws but then arrested for being in possession of drugs?), the appellate court has more latitude, and a wider window, through which to review the trial court's decision. Most appeals, in reality, involve mixed questions of fact and of law, leaving the appellate court with a standard of review somewhere between that which is used for questions of fact and that which is used for questions of law; mixed questions of law and fact are normal.

It is important to remember that the appeal is not a re-trial. The appeal is confined to a review of the legality of only those parts of the trial court's decision that have been properly **preserved** for appeal. Thus, rather than a re-hearing or re-trial, the appellate case has a limited **scope of review**.[3] And unless the appeal is a matter of right, it will be dismissed if the appellate court determines that it raises no genuine question of law or fact for the appellate court to review. Trial courts see evidence and hear witnesses. Appellate courts only hear the lawyers' arguments, and even those are limited by the court's scope and standard of review.[4] Many U.S. lawyers prefer appellate practice to trial practice for this very reason: only the lawyers and the judges speak during appellate arguments, so the process tends to be smoother and easier to control than a trial. The theatrics that are so prevalent in film and fiction reflect a fictitious version of a trial. Appellate practice is quite sterile by comparison. Trial work can be exciting because of its unpredictability, but appellate work can be challenging on a more cerebral level.

After filing its notice of appeal, the party that lost in trial court gets a new title. Instead of being the plaintiff, prosecutor, petitioner, defendant, or respondent, the losing party that files an appeal becomes the appellant. The party that prevailed at trial becomes the appellee. Any lawyer or judge in the United States will recognize these distinctions, so it is important for the writer to understand their significance. Appellants file appeals; Appellees respond to appeals.

The appellant's Notice of Appeal is followed by the appellant's initial brief. Appeals then proceed in a way that should look familiar from the trial court process: appellant's initial brief is followed by Appellee's Reply brief. There is some advantage to having the first word, and some advantage to

---

[3]   The "scope of review" is limited to the issues preserved at trial and raised on appeal; the "standard of review" refers to the extent an appellate court will defer to the trial court's decisions. Lawyers argue endlessly about the applicable standard of review because it dictates the appellate court's review of the issues on appeal. Standard of review is part of every appellate argument.

[4]   Some people file appeals without lawyers. When this happens, it is called a *pro se* appeal. The same is true at the trial level: a party without a lawyer appears *pro se*. It's a delicate business, and there is a reason for the widely accepted truth that a lawyer who represents himself has a fool for a client. The rules of procedure are difficult enough for lawyers; pro se advocates are rarely successful. However, the U.S. legal system generally allows any party to be self-represented at trial or on appeal.

having the last word. By letting the parties take it in turns, the legal system balances those advantages.

Appellate courts judges are on record as saying that the written arguments, usually referred to as briefs, are more influential than the oral arguments that might follow submission of the written arguments. Oral arguments are not always either allowed or required. Most courts have rules that permit the appellant to request oral arguments, but a request does not always guarantee an oral argument. Lawyers would usually rather have the opportunity for oral arguments in the appellate courts because the oral arguments provide an extra opportunity to persuade the court to see the case from the lawyers' perspective. If the appellate court is not required to hear oral arguments, it might choose to do so because the case raises particularly interesting or novel issues, and the judges of the appellate court want a chance to have a conversation with the advocates.

Appellate oral arguments, when they happen, are conversations, not recitations. Appellate court rules do not allow the type of theatrics that are so prevalent in most fictional depictions of the U.S. courts. In an appellate court, there are between three and nine judges sitting on the bench while the attorneys for both parties are given an equal number of minutes to present their oral arguments. The judges might interrupt the lawyers to ask questions (if there are no questions, there would be no need for oral arguments) but the lawyers are not allowed to interrupt each other for any reason. The party that initiated the appeal argues first, just as it filed its brief first; the party that prevailed at trial argues second, the same order in which its brief was filed. Some courts permit rebuttal and even sur-rebuttal during appellate arguments, but both sides have the same amount of time in total. The system is designed to be fair. It may not be perfect, but it is the best we can do to ensure that every party has the same opportunities to present its arguments.

Appellate oral arguments can be graceful, or they can be disastrous. Not every court allows arguments to be filmed, but the Ninth Circuit (the U.S. Court of Appeals for the Ninth Circuit) has many videos on YouTube for students who want to see what a federal appellate court looks like in action. Most impressive are the arguments that are heard *en banc*, by all of the judges of the Ninth Circuit.[5]

A. APPELLATE BRIEFS

Appellate courts across the United States represent the areas in which lawyers' skills of persuasive writing and speaking are put to their most

---

[5]   An ordinary appellate bench might hold three judges, but when all nine of the judges file in to hear oral arguments it makes quite a formidable sight. Note that trial and appellate court judges are called just that: judges. The jurists on the highest court of any jurisdiction, however, are called "justices." It's an important distinction to make.

challenging tests. Appellate courts are more formal, and formidable, than most trial courts. Rules of procedure must be strictly followed, as must the practices and protocol of each court. While there are always local rules and practices, some general principles apply to appellate writing across the United States.

Appellate writing is the one area of legal writing in which it is most important to keep in mind the importance of the written document's purpose, audience, scope, and stance. The purpose is always to convince the higher court that the lower court's ruling was either in accordance with the binding law or an erroneous application of that binding law, depending on which party the writer represents. The audience includes the panel of judges or justices who will decide the case, as well as any law clerks who conduct the legal research for those judges, but it also includes the opposing counsel and opposing party. A well-written, well-thought-out brief may give opposing counsel reason to reconsider the efficacy of proceeding with any appeal. The scope of an appellate brief is defined by the issues that were properly preserved at trial. The stance is always persuasive. Effective legal writers in the United States never lose track of the fact that appeals are generally won or lost based on the written briefs; rarely, if ever, is an oral argument so persuasive that it might overcome the deficiencies created by a weakly written brief.

Because the right to appeal is only guaranteed in certain criminal cases, it makes sense to use a criminal case as an example. This leads us to *Rodriguez v. United States*—an appeal from a federal trial court, to the federal Eighth Circuit Court of Appeals, to the U.S. Supreme Court. Mr. Rodriguez was driving his car in Nebraska when a local police officer saw him swerve off of, and then back on to, the road. The officer stopped, or "pulled over," Mr. Rodriguez for suspected violation of the driving laws. As is customary with traffic stops, the officer used his patrol car's computer to verify Mr. Rodriguez's driver's license and the insurance and registration for the car; he also checked the identity of the passenger in the car, Mr. Pollman. There were no problems for either of the men or for the car, and the officer issued a written warning (not a ticket) based on his observation of the car swerving. But the officer did not tell the men that they were free to leave. Instead, he asked whether Mr. Rodriguez would give him permission to bring his drug-sniffing dog out of the patrol car to walk around the car. Mr. Rodriguez did not consent, so the officer called for assistance (again, this is standard practice: an officer alone in the dark with two men of whom he was suspicious is expected to call for back-up, for the officer's own safety).

A local sheriff's deputy arrived to assist the initial police officer, and a police dog was brought from the patrol car to walk around Mr. Rodriguez's car. Halfway through the second walk around the car, the dog alerted its handler to the presence of drugs in the car. The officers searched the car, found a "large" bag of methamphetamine, and arrested Mr. Rodriguez, who was ultimately charged with possession with intent to distribute methamphetamine, a felony offense. At his trial, Mr. Rodriguez's lawyer filed a Motion to Suppress the Evidence[6] on the grounds that the search violated Mr. Rodriguez's right to be free from unlawful searches and seizures, as guaranteed by the Fourth Amendment to the U.S. Constitution. The Motion to Suppress was denied, and Mr. Rodriguez was convicted and sentenced to sixty months' imprisonment in a federal prison. He appealed first to the U.S. Court of Appeals for the Eighth Circuit, which affirmed the trial court's denial of the Motion to Suppress, and then to the U.S. Supreme Court, which reversed and remanded the case to the Eighth Circuit.

The format of the appellate briefs in this case should look familiar to you, based on previous dissections of the memoranda filed in support of and in opposition to the Motion to Dismiss in *Tilikum*. There are substantive differences because the appellate briefs in Mr. Rodriguez's case were written with a different purpose, audience, scope, and stance in mind. But all of these documents, from the pre-trial memoranda in *Tilikum* to the appellate briefs in *Rodriguez*, include cover pages, tables of contents and authorities, summaries of the facts of the underlying cases, and logically organized legal arguments that apply primary binding authorities to new facts in an effort to demonstrate to the intended audiences that the writers' conclusions are supported by the application of law to facts. The name of the document changes, but there is nothing new here: the substance of these documents illustrates the core qualities of effective legal writing in the United States, and all of the research and writing skills utilized in a trial court memorandum are transferrable to the appellate brief. With all of this in mind, it is time to deconstruct selected parts of Mr. Rodriguez's initial brief in his appeal to the Eighth Circuit.

---

[6] A "Motion to Suppress" is very common in any criminal trial when a defendant objects to the way evidence was obtained. The root of every Motion to Suppress is in the Fourth Amendment to the U.S. Constitution, which protects citizens from "unreasonable search and seizure." The Fourth Amendment raises many issues in criminal law, and is the subject of much study in law school courses devoted to criminal law, criminal procedure law, and the law of evidence. These constitutional protections might be familiar from American movies or television shows, but keep in mind that they involve complex legal questions that require extensive study.

STATEMENT OF THE FACTS

At approximately 12:06 a.m. on March 27, 2012, Officer Morgan Struble of the Valley Police Department was traveling westbound on Highway 275 near the Meigs Street intersection. (Supp. Tr. 3-4)[1] Struble had been a law enforcement officer for almost two years. (Supp. Tr. 31) Struble had his certified canine with him. Struble initiated a traffic stop of a Mercury Mountaineer after he observed the vehicle's passenger side tires momentarily cross the fog line and then briefly drift off the roadway. (Supp. Tr. 4-5) (Supp. Tr. 5; 28; 30-31) Struble testified that he believed this behavior constituted driving on the shoulder of the road which is a traffic violation[2]. (Supp. Tr. 54 56) Upon stopping the vehicle, Struble contacted the occupants. (Supp. Tr. 6) The Defendant, Dennys Rodriguez, was driving the vehicle, and his passenger was Scott Pollman. (Id.) According to Struble, his first observation was the overwhelming, but pleasant, odor of air freshener coming from

---

[1] "Supp. Tr." refers to the transcript of the July 10, 2012, hearing on Rodriguez's motion to suppress evidence.

[2] The Defendant initially raised the issue that the law enforcement officer did not have probable cause to stop his vehicle because crossing the fog line was not a violation of Nebraska law. After the District Court denied that motion, the Nebraska Supreme Court ruled in State v. Magallanes, 284 Neb. 871, 824 N.W.2d 696 (Neb. 2012) that crossing the fog line constituted driving on the shoulder of the road which is a violation of Nebraska law. The federal courts are bound by the state's interpretation of their statutes. Based on that ruling, Rodriguez is not challenging that issue in this appeal.

the vehicle. (Supp. Tr. 6; 32-31) Struble also testified that Pollman seemed nervous. He wore his cap low over his eyes, was smoking a cigarette and looked straight ahead, making no eye contact with Struble. (Supp. Tr. 7) There is no evidence in the record that Rodriguez showed signs of nervousness. Rodriguez appeared agitated when he was told that crossing the white line was a violation of driving on the shoulder of the road. (Supp. Tr. 31-32)

Struble asked Rodriguez if there was a reason that he drove onto the shoulder, and Rodriguez replied that there was a large pothole in the roadway. (Supp. Tr. 8; 29) Struble obtained Rodriguez's paperwork and then asked him to sit in the cruiser while he conducted a records check. (Supp. Tr. 8-9) Rodriguez exited his vehicle and asked Struble whether he was obligated to sit in the cruiser. (Supp. Tr. 9) When Struble advised him that he was not obligated to sit in the cruiser, Rodriguez indicated that he would rather sit in his own vehicle. (Id.) Struble found this significant because in his law enforcement experience, he has "never had anybody not want to sit in my vehicle with me." (Supp. Tr. 9) Struble then returned to his cruiser to conduct the records check. (Id.)

Upon returning to the vehicle, Struble spoke with the passenger, Mr. Pollman. (Supp. Tr. 9-10). Struble initially asked Pollman for his identification, and then began questioning Pollman about the purpose of their trip. (Supp. Tr. 10). Pollman explained that he and Rodriguez had traveled from Norfolk to Omaha to look at an older model Mustang for sale for $6,500. They did not buy the car because the seller did not have a title. (Id.; Supp. Tr. 40-41) In response to further questioning, Pollman indicated that he had not seen any pictures of the vehicle prior to making the trip to Omaha. (Supp. Tr. 11) Struble testified that he found this to be abnormal; something he would not do. (Id.; Supp. Tr. 41-42)

After obtaining Pollman's driver's license, Struble again returned to his cruiser. (Supp. Tr. 11). At approximately 12:19 a.m., while conducting a records check on Pollman, Struble requested a second officer, admitting that he already had plans to walk his dog around Rodriguez's vehicle but because there were two people involved, he needed backup for officer safety. (Supp. Tr. 12; 47; 50-51) He then began writing a warning ticket for Rodriguez. (Supp. Tr. 12)

After completing the warning ticket, Struble returned to the Mountaineer for a third time, returned all of the documents to Rodriguez and Pollman, and issued the written warning to Rodriguez. (Id.) Struble testified that the warning was completed at 12:25 a.m. and given to Rodriguez approximately a minute or two later. (Supp. Tr. 12-13) Struble spent another two to three minutes explaining the ticket to Rodriguez, until approximately 12:28 a.m. (Supp. Tr. 14) Consistent with his training, Struble returned Rodriguez's documents and then immediately asked Rodriguez whether he had an objection to his drug dog walking around his truck. (Supp. Tr. 14) Rodriguez

told Struble that he did object. (Supp. Tr. 14; 49) Struble admitted that Rodriguez

was not free to leave at that time and would have used his dog no matter what. (Supp.

Tr. 49) Struble then ordered Rodriguez to turn off the ignition and exit his truck and

stand in front of the cruiser until a second officer arrived. (Supp. Tr. 14-15)

Struble then asked Rodriguez if he had an issue with a police service dog

walking around the outside of his vehicle. (Id.) Rodriguez indicated that he did have

an issue with it. (Supp. Tr. 14; 49) At 12:33 a.m., Deputy Decals of the Douglas

County Sheriff's Office arrived at the scene. (Supp. Tr. 16; 48) Approximately one

minute later, Struble walked his dog around the vehicle. (Supp. Tr. 17; 48) The dog

alerted to the front passenger side door. (Id.) Struble estimated that as much as eight

minutes passed from the time he issued the written warning to the time the dog alerted

on the vehicle. (Supp. Tr. 18) A subsequent search of the vehicle revealed a large

bag of methamphetamine. (Id.)

At the conclusion of the hearing on Rodriguez's motion to suppress, the

Magistrate Judge concluded that the officers' actions complied with the Fourth

Amendment. Specifically, the Magistrate found that probable cause for the traffic

stop existed because Struble had an objectively reasonable basis for believing that

Rodriguez had violated Nebraska law. (Supp. Tr. 77-78). The Magistrate made a

7

factual finding that the routine traffic stop concluded at 12:25 a.m. and that the dog indicated on the vehicle seven to eight minutes later. (Supp. Tr. 78). The Magistrate found that Struble did not have reasonable suspicion necessary to detain Rodriguez after the traffic stop concluded. (Supp. Tr. 81-82) Nevertheless, the Magistrate stated that the Eighth Circuit considered a detention of up to ten minutes beyond the conclusion of a traffic stop to be a *de minimis* intrusion on an individual's Fourth Amendment rights. Therefore, Rodriguez's detention of up to eight minutes was *de minimis*. (Supp. Tr. 81-82). The Magistrate voiced his opinion that he did not think ten minutes was *de minimis*, but noted he was required to follow Circuit precedent. Accordingly, the Magistrate recommended that Rodriguez's motion to suppress be denied. (Supp. Tr. 81-82)

The district court further held that the traffic stop was not unreasonably prolonged, and any intrusion on Rodriguez's liberty following the traffic stop was *de minimis*. (Add. at 4) As did the Magistrate, the Court cited <u>United States v. Morgan</u>, 270 F.3d 625 (8th. Cir. 2001) as the source of this ruling. Accordingly, the court denied Rodriguez's motion to suppress. (Add. at 5)

The document above comprised one part of one document in the appeal of Mr. Rodriguez's conviction for possession of narcotics. The question on appeal was the Motion to Suppress the evidence found by the police dog. The trial court denied that Motion, and the evidence was admitted. Mr. Rodriguez was convicted on the basis of that evidence, and he appealed. Now that this much is clear, students should be able to identify the purpose, audience, scope, and stance of the excerpted material. Effective legal writing leaves no doubt in the reader's mind about who wrote the document and for what purpose, its intended audience, its scope, and its stance. Students should note the citations to the trial transcript, which clearly demonstrate that this is a post-trial document. Notice the words and phrases that reveal this document's purpose, even though it is a statement of the facts rather than a legal argument.

In the excerpted document, Mr. Rodriguez is referred to as "the defendant" rather than by his actual name; this choice of word dehumanizes him. The arresting officer, in contrast, is referred to by his name and title, Officer Struble. Officer Struble is described as acting in a manner that was "consistent with his training," while "the defendant" is said to have declined the officer's request to sit with him in the police car while the records check transpired, and is also described as saying that he did, in fact, object to having the police dog circle his car. Mr. Rodriguez is painted as an uncooperative, suspicious criminal, while Officer Struble is portrayed as an officer of the law who did his job according to the manner in which he was trained. The conclusion the writer wants the reader to reach is that Officer Struble was correct in stopping Mr. Rodriguez's car, as demonstrated by the "large bag" of illegal drugs eventually found in that car.

It should be clear by now that this Statement of Facts was written by the State in response to Mr. Rodriguez's appeal of the trial court's decision denying his Motion to Suppress the evidence obtained after the police dog alerted Officer Struble to the presence of illegal methamphetamine in the car. The **purpose** of this description of the facts is, therefore, to persuade the appellate court that the trial court was correct in denying the motion to suppress the evidence. The intended **audience** is two-fold, encompassing both the appellate court and the opposing counsel, both of whom must be persuaded that the trial court's decision was correct. The **scope** of the argument is limited to evaluating the trial court's decision to deny the defendant's Motion to Suppress the evidence—without the evidence, the defendant's conviction could not stand. The **stance**, it should by now be clear, is persuasive rather than objective or predictive.

The issue raised in the appeal excerpted above was limited to whether the trial court was correct in denying the Motion to Suppress the evidence. The rule of law might not be evident from the Facts statement, but the manner in which the facts are presented allows a reader to infer the rule: A police officer may stop a car if there is a reasonable suspicion that traffic laws have been violated, and until that lawful stop's purpose has been completed the officer may also search the car for contraband; any evidence thus obtained is admissible against the defendant.[7]

The Statement of Facts excerpted above uses sentence structure to emphasize those facts that will meet the requirements of the inferred rule. Any fact the writer uses in demonstrating application of the law to these facts must be included in the Facts section. That is the **purpose** of the Facts section. Its **audience** includes both the appellant (the losing party, here the defendant) and the judges on the court of appeal. The **scope** is defined by the issue, and the **stance** must be persuasive. Furthermore, the

---

[7] For the Eighth Circuit's opinion, see *United States v. Rodriguez*, 741 F. 3d 905 (8th Cir. 2014).

Statement of Facts in this document is clear, concise, and correct: nothing is omitted if it is legally relevant, and nothing is included that does not play a role in the analysis that will necessarily follow. This Statement of Facts seems to meet all of its goals for effective legal writing. Note the differences in emphasis between the excerpt analyzed above and this small part of Mr. Rodriguez's failed appeal from the Eighth Circuit Court of Appeals to the United States Supreme Court:

> By the time Officer Struble had returned Mr. Rodriguez's documents and issued the warning, Officer Struble had "[taken] care of all the business" of the traffic stop. J.A. 70. In his words, he had "got[ten] all the reason for the stop out of the way." *Id.* Nevertheless, because of his plan to conduct the sniff regardless of what else happened, Officer Struble did not allow Mr. Rodriguez to leave. Instead, Officer Struble asked Mr. Rodriguez if "he had an issue with [Officer Struble] walking [his] police service dog around the outside of [the] vehicle." J.A. 29, 72–73. When Mr. Rodriguez replied that he did, in fact, have an issue with that, Officer Struble directed Mr. Rodriguez to turn off the ignition, get out of his vehicle, and stand in front of the cruiser until the second officer arrived. J.A. 29–30. Officer Struble acknowledged that at this point Mr. Rodriguez "was not free to leave." J.A. 69–70.[8]

Notice that Mr. Rodriguez's brief emphasizes the notion that the traffic stop's purpose had been accomplished before the officer asked Mr. Rodriguez to consent to the dog's sniff test, as well as emphasizing the amount of time that passed between completion of the traffic stop and the dog's search. These are the same facts as in the government's brief, and both briefs are accurate. The purpose and audience of each document dictates the facts that its author selected to emphasize: the purpose, audience, scope, and stance all dictate how the facts are portrayed.

The difference between the emphasized facts, as seen above, stems from the basic notions of CREAC and PASS. Every case is necessarily different from any case that has come before it: If the cases were identical, the second one would never be brought to court, so students should use these samples as information rather than as templates.

After the Statement of Facts most appellate briefs include a Summary of the Argument, depending on the jurisdiction's rules of appellate procedure. If a Summary is required by the rules, it usually does not involve citing authorities: it is a Summary, and its purpose is to inform a "busy reader" of the lawyer's theory of the case and the applicable legal

---

[8]   The citations to "J.A." are to the transcript of the appellate court's decision. It might be an appropriate reference in an appellate brief, but in general, citations should be to published judicial opinions when possible.

principles. This is one of the very rare occasions when citations are omitted, and most law students (and probably lawyers) enjoy writing the Summary for this reason.

Ultimately, the success or failure of any appellate brief depends on the quality of the arguments section. This is where the lawyer demonstrates for the court and for opposing counsel how the law should be applied in the case on appeal. There are two sides to every story, and if not, there should be no appeal. But if the lawyers do their jobs well, each party in any appeal will have a thoroughly researched, logically organized, and well-written set of arguments.

Logical organization of the arguments requires starting with the broader statements of the applicable law and systematically narrowing the focus of the argument as it is written, point by point, step by step. Effective arguments utilize **point headings** to guide the reader through the argument's logical progression. In Mr. Rodriguez's appeal, his attorney began her written arguments with this point heading:

I.   MORGAN STRUBLE VIOLATED RODRIGUEZ'S FOURTH AMENDMENT RIGHTS WHEN, AFTER THE CONCLUSION OF A TRAFFIC STOP AND WITHOUT REASONABLE SUSPICION OF CRIMINAL ACTIVITY, HE DETAINED RODRIGUEZ FOR EIGHT MINUTES TO WAIT FOR A BACK-UP OFFICER AND DEPLOY A DRUG DOG TO SNIFF RODRIGUEZ'S VEHICLE.

Point headings are the road signs for the reader. They are complete sentences that constitute the first "C" in CREAC. They should be written persuasively in order to make it easier for a reader to agree with the writer. Many arguments proceed directly from a point heading to a legal principle, with citation of course; the legal principle is the rule, the "R" in CREAC. Mr. Rodriguez's lawyer moved from the point heading above to disposing of the undisputed elements of the appeal:

It is undisputed that Officer Struble detained Rodriguez for eight minutes following the termination of the traffic stop. Under this Court's case law, such a detention is justified only if the officer develops reasonable suspicion of criminal activity during the course of the stop or if the driver consents. *United States v. Flores*, 464 F.3d 1100, 1103 (8th Cir. 2007). Nothing occurred during the stop to provide reasonable suspicion of criminal activity, and Rodriguez did not consent to further detention. Nonetheless, the court declined to suppress the evidence, erroneously concluding that the extension was only a permissible "de minimis" intrusion on Rodriguez's Fourth Amendment rights.

First, students should identify in the above paragraph the elements of CREAC" conclusion, rule, explanation, application, and conclusion. Then, students should evaluate the effectiveness of this paragraph's effectiveness in terms of its purpose, audience, scope, and stance. Is the tone persuasive or has it crossed the line into being argumentative?

Compare it to the beginning of the State's initial Reply Brief:

I. THE DURATION OF THE DETENTION FOLLOWING THE TRAFFIC STOP WAS *DE MINIMIS* AND DID NOT VIOLATE THE FOURTH AMENDMENT.

A. STANDARD OF REVIEW.

> A district court's denial of a motion to suppress is reviewed under a two-pronged framework: factual findings are reviewed for clear error, and legal conclusions are reviewed *de novo*. *United States v. Farnell*, 701 F.3d 256, 260 (8th Cir. 2012).

The government's lawyer began by framing the standard of review for the court, which is at the core of every appellate decision. If the government had persuaded the court to apply the standards of review it cited, half the battle would have been won.

Other than their opening shots, the two briefs seem to be on the same track: the issue is whether the duration of the stop was *de minimis*. But look carefully at the two briefs: they are organized differently. The attorney for the petitioner, Mr. Rodriguez, proceeded from the Jurisdictional Statement (required in this and some other jurisdictions) to the Statement of the Issues, to the Statement of the Case (procedural history: how a case came to be on appeal), to the Statement of Facts and the Summary of the Arguments, then to a separate section to address the appropriate Standard of Review followed, finally, by the Arguments. The Government's lawyer arranged things differently: there is no separate section for the Standard of Review; that question is addressed within the Arguments section.

YOUR ASSIGNMENT: PERSUASIVE WRITING

Look up the Rules of Appellate Procedure utilized in the Eighth Circuit. Is there a rule that specifies the required sections of a brief, and if so, which party did it correctly in this case?[9]

Now look at the way each party addressed the precedent cases, particularly *Morgan*.

---

[9] Rule 28 of the Federal Rules of Appellate Procedure lists the requirements for an appellant's and an appellee's brief. After reading the rules, a thorough legal researcher would look for local rules of appellate procedure for the Eighth Circuit, if any. If the writer is using the ALWD Citation Manual, each court's local rules are included in Appendix Two. This is very helpful to newer writers who are unfamiliar with the jurisdictions and courts of the United States.

"When a police officer makes a traffic stop and has at his immediate disposal the canine resources to employ this uniquely limited investigation procedure, it does not violate the Fourth Amendment to require that the offending motorist's detention be momentarily extended for a canine sniff of the vehicle's exterior." *United States v. $404,905 in U.S. Currency*, 182 F.3d 643, 649 (8th Cir. 1999). "Dog sniffs that occur within a short time following the completion of a traffic stop are not constitutionally prohibited if they constitute only de minimis intrusions." *United States v. Alexander*, 448 F.3d 1014, 1016 (8th Cir. 2006). The dividing line separating a constitutionally prohibited detention and a de minimis detention is artificial, and the "constitutional standard is reasonableness measured by the totality of the circumstances." *$404,905 in U.S. Currency*, 182 F.3d at 649. This Court has found that in cases where the K-9 is already present and the time of the search lasted mere minutes, the seizure was de minimis. See *$404,905 in U.S. Currency*, 182 F.3d at 649 (two minute delay to conduct canine sniff was de minimis); *Alexander,* 448 F.3d at 1016 (four minute delay to conduct canine sniff was de minimis); *United States v. Mohamed*, 600 F.3d 1000, 1005 (8th Cir. 2010) (five minute delay to conduct canine sniff was de minimis). *Id.* at 648. Cir. 2010) (five minute delay to conduct canine sniff was de minimis).

In *United States v. Morgan,* 270 F.3d 625 (8th Cir. 2001), a traffic stop was conducted on a van in which Morgan was a passenger. *Id.* at 627–628. The officer conducting the traffic stop was accompanied by his drug detection K-9. *Id.* at 628. Following the completion of the traffic stop, the officer ran his K-9 around the exterior of the van, which alerted to the presence of narcotics. *Id.* The total time between the completion of the traffic stop and the K-9's alert to the narcotics was unclear, but it was "something less than 10 minutes." *Id.* The Court in Morgan addressed whether the length of the time it took to conduct the K-9 search following the traffic stop violated the Fourth Amendment. In doing so, this Court considered two possible exceptions. "The first question is whether [the officer] had a reasonable, articulable suspicion of criminal activity beyond the reason for which he stopped the van." *Id.* at 631. It was determined that reasonable suspicion did exist. *Id.* However, the analysis did not end there. Despite finding that reasonable suspicion existed, the Court continued its analysis by next examining whether the delay was de minimis: Even if the facts had not been sufficient for reasonable suspicion, however, a short detention for a dog sniff would not violate the Fourth Amendment. See *$404,905 in U.S. Currency*, 182 F.3d at 647–49.

Compare the above passage to the following analysis of the same case, but written from the opposing viewpoint:

This Court gave three reasons for its decision. First, while the length of detention is an important factor in the analysis of Terry investigative stops, where officers must "diligently pursue" a given means of investigation, that limitation does not similarly apply to traffic stops. *Id.* at 648. "Given the myriad situations in which traffic stops occur," the Court explained, "it is not reasonable to subject them to the length-of-detention analysis we use in evaluating investigatory stops." *Id.* Second, the decision asserted, "the line [making completion of a traffic stop] is quite artificial." *Id.* "When the constitutional standard is reasonableness measured by the totality of the circumstances, we should not be governed by artificial distinctions." *Id.* Finally, "[the officer's] conduct on the whole was not constitutionally unreasonable." The Court held that a two minute extension of a traffic stop is a "de minimis" intrusion on a person's liberty. *Id.* Since this decision, this Court has been careful to confine its "de minimis" exception to cases where the length of post-stop delay was nearly the same as that approved in *$404,905*. As the chart below [omitted] demonstrates, the Court's definition of "de minimis" extension typically means a 2 to 3 minute delay when a drug dog is immediately available or the officer can easily obtain consent.

It is very important to notice that both parties cite the same law, but that they argue differently because they have opposing purposes and audiences. The briefs accomplish their goals without requiring the lawyers to argue different law. This is the way case law is decided in the United States: the applicable law is not usually debatable, but its application is. The defendant's lawyer, the Federal Public Defender, could have chosen to look for precedent cases with outcomes that supported her argument that her client's constitutional rights had been violated, but that would have been a mistake. In U.S. legal writing, the lawyers do not decide their position and then go look for cases that support that position. Instead, the lawyers engage in the research process and let the results dictate how their arguments are framed. **The research drives the writing rather than the writing driving the research.** The result is that all the lawyers refer to the same legal authorities and the court is then in a position to decide which argument is the most in keeping with the law.

Look at the extent to which each of the lawyers described the facts of *Morgan*. This is from the initial appellate brief filed on behalf of Mr. Rodriguez:

> *Morgan* involved a traffic stop in Nebraska for speeding. Nebraska State Patrol Trooper Goltz stopped a van for speeding and improper registration of the vehicle. There were three occupants. Goltz smelled cigar smoke as well as some kind of deodorizer or perfume as he approached the vehicle. He noticed one of the occupants to be very nervous and made no eye contact with him. He spoke with another passenger who was also nervous and explained a very suspicious story about a visit to Arizona but was not able to provide a name of any other city other than Phoenix. Goltz concluded

the traffic stop by returning documents he had taken from the three passengers. Before they could leave, he approached Morgan and talked to her about law enforcement's role in the war on drugs. She denied that any drugs were in their vehicle but was very nervous as she did so. Goltz asked for permission to search and Morgan responded what would happen if she refused. He answered that he would use the dog anyway. Morgan relented and the dog was walked around the vehicle. It alerted on the vehicle revealing a large quantity of marijuana.

And this is the same case addressed in the Government's brief on the same issue:

In *United States v. Morgan*, 270 F.3d 625 (8th Cir. 2001), a traffic stop was conducted on a van in which Morgan was a passenger. *Id.* at 627–628. The officer conducting the traffic stop was accompanied by his drug detection K-9. *Id.* at 628. Following the completion of the traffic stop, the officer ran his K-9 around the exterior of the van, which alerted to the presence of narcotics. *Id.* The total time between the completion of the traffic stop and the K-9's alert to the narcotics was unclear, but it was "something less than 10 minutes". *Id.*

The Court in *Morgan* addressed whether the length of the time it took to conduct the K-9 search following the traffic stop violated the Fourth Amendment. In doing so, this Court considered two possible exceptions. "The first question is whether [the officer] had a reasonable, articulable suspicion of criminal activity beyond the reason for which he stopped the van." *Id.* at 631. It was determined that reasonable suspicion did exist. *Id.* However, the analysis did not end there. Despite finding that reasonable suspicion existed, the Court continued its analysis by next examining whether the delay was *de minimis*:

Even if the facts had not been sufficient for reasonable suspicion, however, a short detention for a dog sniff would not violate the Fourth Amendment. *See $404,905 in U.S. Currency*, 182 F.3d at 647–49 (two minute delay for a dog sniff a de minimis intrusion). Here, the dog was at the scene from the beginning, and it only took a short time to walk the dog over to the van where it alerted to the presence of drugs. The exact number of minutes is uncertain, but [the officer] testified that 'well under ten minutes' passed between the end of his conversation with Morgan and the dog alerting to the marijuana. We do not believe that the few minutes difference between the time in this case and *$404,905* has constitutional significance. The delay caused by conducting the dog sniff did not violate the Fourth Amendment.

Id. at 631–632.

The facts are less important than the law of any precedent case because it is the law, not the facts, that binds future court decisions. In the passages above, the lawyers are appropriately correct in their descriptions of the precedent case; to mischaracterize the law would be unethical and unwise. Here, both lawyers wrote accurately about the same case, but obviously from different positions. These briefs demonstrate that the lawyers have done their research and are able to craft clear, logical arguments based on that research. The context will change with every case, but the process is the same. This is quite different from most nations' legal systems because U.S. lawyers are not reaching or stretching to find "favorable" precedent cases. The law is the law, and it is up to each advocate to persuade a court that application of that law requires a favorable outcome for his or her client.

YOUR ASSIGNMENT: THE APPELLATE BRIEF

The capstone of almost every legal writing class in a U.S. law school is writing an entire appellate brief, from the cover page through the final conclusion. Legal writing professors generally assign a hypothetical client with a hypothetical appeal for this assignment. Writing an appellate brief provides students the opportunity to demonstrate their acquisition of all of the legal research, writing, and analysis skills needed to function in the U.S. legal system. Even students who may never have an occasion to write a real appellate brief must remember that the skills required in doing so are transferrable to any legal writing context in the United States.

Rather than working on a hypothetical case, students might benefit from researching and writing about a real case. Doing so requires a bit of suspension of disbelief.[10] In the case that follows, the U.S. Supreme Court denied the appellant's Petition for a Writ of Certiorari (the appeal). For the purposes of this assignment, however, students might "suspend their disbelief" and assume the Supreme Court granted, rather than denied, the request to hear the appeal.

The case is a tragic one, as are so many in the United States. This one is particularly distressing because the defendant is a young, single Native American mother of three daughters who was arrested and charged with the murder of her newborn son. Because the infant's body was found on an Indian Reservation, the murder was a federal offense. The United States' legal treatment of Native Americans is not always stellar and is the subject of litigation dating back to the earliest days of this nation.[11] For a variety of

---

[10] "Suspension of disbelief" is a literary term that refers to an audience's willingness to accept a fictional premise or scenario. Film and fiction would not be entertaining if the audience was unwilling to suspend disbelief. For an in-depth analysis of "willing suspension of disbelief," see this essay by The New York Times' language specialist, William Safire: http://www.nytimes.com/2007/10/07/magazine/07wwln-safire-t.html?_r=0.

[11] Some of the most illogical writing to come from the U.S. Supreme Court can be found in *Johnson v. M'Intosh*, 21 U.S. 543, 569 (1823). There, the Court contorted itself to justify its finding that Native Americans were "perpetual inhabitants with diminutive rights" to the land on which they lived; this line of reasoning bolstered the idea that white Europeans had a moral obligation to take this continent out of the hands of the "savages" whose presence predated the first

reasons, some of which make more sense than others,, serious crimes that happen on Indian Reservations are still treated as federal crimes. In the case below the defendant was charged initially with first-degree murder, which she then "plea bargained" down to second-degree murder. (Plea bargains are the criminal equivalent of the settlement agreements that are so common in civil cases.)

To proceed with this assignment, students should first read the Eighth Circuit's opinion in *United States v. Deegan*, 605 F. 3d 625 (8th Cir. 2010). Once they are familiar with the facts and the issues, students should proceed to locate and read the Government's initial brief to the Eighth Circuit, and should then draft at least the Arguments section of a reply brief for the appellant, who was the defendant at trial. The appellate brief must address the issues on appeal, the standard of review, and the scope of the appeal. The appellant, Dana Deegan, never argued that she was not responsible for the death of her newborn son; she argued, among other things, that her sentence of 121 months was unconstitutionally excessive (even though it was the result of her plea bargain). When drafting a reply brief on her behalf, it would be a mistake to argue that Dana Deegan did not cause the death of her newborn son. Instead, the arguments should focus on the issue on appeal, which was the length of her sentence.

This assignment may take several weeks to complete. Ideally, some students would write an initial brief in support of Dana Deegan's Petition for a Writ of Certiorari, and some would write the Government's reply brief in opposition to that Petition. Following completion of the briefs, students would then exchange their written briefs with an assigned opponent, and oral arguments would follow. However, even if a class or group of students is not engaged in an appellate brief assignment, students can practice their research and writing skills with this assignment.

Below is a selection of other cases that might be used as the basis for an appellate brief assignment, along with very short summaries of their substantive issues; these are offered so that professors and their students might choose topics of interest. The issues cover a broad range of topics, from civil rights to employment law, and include criminal as well as civil questions. Most of these cases involve multiple issues. Students and their professors may choose to address some or all of those issues, but at least two issues are identified for each of the listed cases. Students are reminded that using real cases requires a certain amount of suspension of disbelief; for the purposes of these exercises, students should focus on demonstrating their ability to write clear, logical legal analysis, accepting that some suspension of disbelief is necessary. Practicing the skills of persuasive writing and following the rules of appellate procedure will serve all students well, regardless of their future career paths. Some of the cases listed below may require more willing

---

Europeans' arrival. Things have not changed much since 1823. Indian Reservations were established in the Nineteenth Century on some of the least-desirable land in the United States. Today, the reservations are home to the worst poverty in the Country, with some of the nation's highest rates of infant mortality, domestic violence, substance abuse, teen suicide, and depression.

suspension of disbelief than others, but all should provide every learning opportunity any student could hope to find.

1.   *United States v. Washington*, 520 F.2d 676 (9th Cir. 1975). Issue(s) on appeal, hypothetically, to the U.S. Supreme Court: Whether a state may regulate the fishing rights of Indians when those rights are covered by long-standing treaties, and whether the trial court in this case abused its discretion by allocating fishing rights between whites and Indians 50/50.

2.   *Native American Council of Tribes v. Weber,* 750 F. 3d 742 (8th Cir. 2014). Issue(s) on appeal, hypothetically, to the U.S. Supreme Court: Whether a prison policy amounts to genocide, under international law, when it deprives Native American inmates of their ability to engage in the free exercise of their religion, and whether such a policy violates the federal Religious Freedom and Institutionalized Persons Act.

3.   *Bubbenmoyer v. Boca Bargoons of Melbourne, Inc.,* 2013 WL 593814 (M.D. Fla. 2013). Issue(s) on appeal, hypothetically, to the Eleventh Circuit Court of Appeals: Whether an employer violates the federal Fair Labor Standards Act by designating an employee as a "manager" who is not entitled to overtime pay when that employee's primary job responsibilities do not require supervising other employees or exercising independent judgment, but do require day-to-day maintenance activities as well as retail sales, and if such an employer has violated the FLSA whether that employer may offset, against any unpaid overtime it is ordered to pay, the amount of a personal loan made to the employee by the employer.

4.   *Apple v. Jewish Hosp. and Medical Center,* 829 F. 2d 326 (2d Cir. 1987). Issue(s) on appeal, hypothetically, to the U.S. Supreme Court: Whether a party's Motion to Recuse a trial judge must be granted when that judge enters an order requiring the party's attorneys to remain in the courtroom, under threat of arrest, until the case is settled, and whether a trial court has jurisdiction to find that an insurance company acted in bad faith when that company was not a party to the lawsuit before it intervened.

5.   *Thomas v. Mendez,* 2009 WL 89116 (C.D. Cal. 2009). Issue(s) on appeal, hypothetically, to the Ninth Circuit Court of Appeals: Whether a prisoner's Eighth Amendment right to be free from the use of excessive force is violated when prison guards use rubber bullets and a smoke bomb to remove the inmate's cellmate from their cell, and whether those guards showed deliberate indifference to the prisoner by requiring him to remain in the cell during the altercation with his cellmate.

6.   *State v. Elliott,* 2014 WL 2013334 (Minn. Ct. App. 2014). Issue(s) on appeal, hypothetically, to the Minnesota Supreme Court: Whether a state may criminalize drunk driving suspects' refusal to submit to field sobriety, breathalyzer, or blood alcohol content testing when a suspected drunk driver's refusal is granted and no sobriety or other tests are conducted, and whether driving a car is considered a privilege or a right.

B. ORAL ARGUMENTS

If a lawyer has a long and distinguished career, he or she might have an opportunity to participate in a handful of appellate court oral arguments. Even when the lawyers request oral arguments, appellate courts are not generally required to grant such requests. When allowed, an oral argument provides a singularly challenging and rewarding opportunity for any lawyer to have a conversation with the appellate court judges who will decide the lawyer's case. The formality of the proceedings might be intimidating but every lawyer should welcome the opportunity to present oral arguments.

Oral arguments, if they are scheduled, take place after the parties have filed their appellate briefs but before the court has decided which party will prevail. The purpose of the oral argument is not to simply repeat what was written in the briefs; the judges (or their clerks) will have done that before hearing the arguments. The arguments let the judges ask questions that may not have been addressed in the brief. The judges want a conversation with the lawyers, albeit a very formal conversation.

Rules of appellate procedure provide that the time allowed for oral arguments is strictly limited. Even if the appellate court judges ask the lawyer to answer questions and discuss points the lawyer did not intend to discuss, the clock begins running when the lawyer begins to talk, and can only be extended upon a request made and granted by the court. Appellate courts might limit each lawyer's argument to no more than ten minutes total, including any rebuttal or sur-rebuttal allowed. Because the rules may vary from one jurisdiction to another, any lawyer who anticipates having an opportunity for an oral argument must be completely familiar with that jurisdiction's rules of appellate procedure. Students should know that every law school in the United States offers some sort of class in appellate practice, and any student who wants to pursue the intricacies of this topic should enroll in one of those courses. The legal writing course might introduce students to the skills involved in appellate practice, but for a more in-depth experience students are encouraged to enroll in an appellate advocacy class.

YOUR ASSIGNMENT: REQUEST FOR ORAL ARGUMENT

Research the rules of the U.S. Supreme Court for requesting an oral argument. Then draft a written request for oral argument to the Court as if you represented Dana Deegan in her efforts to have the Court reverse the lower courts' decisions about the length of her sentence. By willingly suspending disbelief, complete this assignment as if her Petition for a Writ of Certiorari had been granted, and follow the Court's rules when drafting a request that the Court hear oral arguments in the case.

CHAPTER 6

PROFESSIONAL RESPONSIBILITY IN LEGAL RESEARCH AND WRITING

■ ■ ■

A. OBLIGATIONS TO CLIENTS AND COURTS

Every jurisdiction in the United States requires lawyers to abide by specific rules of professional responsibility. Many jurisdictions' rules are based on the Model Rules of Professional Responsibility. The Model Rules are the subject of an exam that most law school graduates and Bar applicants must pass. Underlying all of these rules is the notion that being a lawyer is a privilege, not a right, and only those who practice law responsibly will be allowed to exercise that privilege.

Lawyers who do not abide by applicable rules of professional conduct are subject to disciplinary actions that are pursued by the relevant bar association. The consequences of violating the professional responsibility rules are determined based on the nature of the rule violation. More serious offenses, like stealing from a client or being charged with a felony crime, may result in disbarment, or loss of the lawyer's license to practice law. A disbarred lawyer is not only forbidden to practice law in one jurisdiction: disbarred lawyers will most likely not be allowed to practice law in any jurisdiction in the United States.

U.S. law students are uniformly required to pass at least one Professional Responsibility course to be eligible for graduation. International students with no plans to practice law in the United States may not be required to take Professional Responsibility, but it might be advisable to do so: ethics, or professional responsibility, is a substantive part of everything U.S. lawyers do. It may be taught as a separate course, but professional responsibility is integral to everything lawyers do.

What does this mean for legal writers? It means knowing and following the rules whenever anything is written to, or for, a client. It means identifying every internal document as privileged, confidential attorney-client work product. It means understanding every facet of every legal issue before undertaking any work on behalf of any client. It means not giving any legal advice unless and until the writer is licensed to practice law in the jurisdiction. It means writing with absolute precision and accuracy. There is no room for any inaccuracy in legal writing.

B. CONSEQUENCES FOR BREACHES OF PROFESSIONAL RESPONSIBILITIES

Lawyers in the United States are generally quite well-paid because they "hold the keys to the court house." It takes years of rigorous study and testing to gain the requisite level of expertise. Non-lawyers lack the background, the skill, and the privileges to access the legal system in this country. Lawyers are responsible for their own conduct and for the conduct of their employees. Any lawyer who responds to a disciplinary action by claiming that the problem is the result of an employee's actions rather than the lawyer's is bound to face difficulties.

A lawyer's words are his or her career: reputation is everything in the U.S. legal system, and disciplinary proceedings will ruin a lawyer's reputation faster than anything else. A good reputation takes years to build but can be dragged down irreparably in one instance of misbehavior. Intention is not generally required for a lawyer to face disciplinary action, so it is not a defense to say the lawyer did not know he or she was violating the rules of professional responsibility. One inadvertent book-keeping or accounting misstep can ruin a lawyer's reputation. Inadvertently sending electronic communications that violate the attorney-client confidentiality is an overwhelmingly damaging mistake. Writing a contract incorrectly, or drafting an invalid will, sending a client written advice that is substantively wrong, not performing adequate conflict of interest checks— all of these things and more might signal the end of a lawyer's career.

Any student, international or domestic, needs to proceed with caution with regard to professional responsibility. The consequences of disregarding lawyers' ethical obligations are not worth any perceived benefit. Disciplinary proceedings are completely avoidable with enough attention to the rules and basic principles of honesty, accuracy, and clear communication with clients, colleagues, and courts.

Writing well is one of every lawyer's professional responsibilities. Clients, courts, and the public must be able to trust lawyers' abilities both substantively and technically. The type of disciplinary measures taken may vary from state to state, but case law confirms that lawyers whose writing is substandard will be, and should be, subjected to discipline. The following are some examples that demonstrate the seriousness with which state authorities have addressed lawyers' incompetency in the area of legal writing.

The Minnesota Supreme Court explained why a lawyer's poor writing warranted disciplinary measures including a public reprimand, if not suspension of the lawyer's license to practice law.[1] The lawyer, Patrick Hawkins, specialized in the area of bankruptcy law, and the Court

---

[1]　*In re Hawkins*, 502 N.W. 2d 770 (Minn. 1993).

acknowledged that Mr. Hawkins' expertise and knowledge of bankruptcy law was adequate to serve his clients' needs, and that no clients were harmed by Mr. Hawkins' representation. However, Mr. Hawkins' inability or unwillingness to follow the bankruptcy court's rules, and to communicate correctly in writing, harmed the courts and the public, and therefore were appropriately the source of the public reprimand.[2] The excerpts below illustrate the seriousness with which courts discipline lawyers whose writing is deficient and who fail to follow the rules.

A public reprimand may be more damaging than one might think. There are very practical reasons to maintain one's reputation, even if the lawyer does not possess the expected sense of professional responsibility. Professional reputations are particularly important because lawyers' advertising is restricted due to the professional obligations that accompany a license to practice law. With only the limited advertising allowed by the Rules of Professional Responsibility, a lawyer's business growth is dependent on his or her reputation. Therefore, a public reprimand is the equivalent of money being taken out of the lawyer's pocket. Unfortunately, if they graduate with nothing else, many U.S. lawyers enter the profession bearing the weight of staggering amounts of student-loan debt, and a damaged reputation means a damaged income. A public reprimand, combined with restricted advertising and damage to his or her professional reputation, can cripple a lawyer's ability to warn enough money to repay student loan debt. Courts do not look kindly on such transgressions:

> [R]espondent's failure to comply with the Local Bankruptcy Rules of the United States Bankruptcy Court, District of Minnesota, and his repeated filing of documents rendered unintelligible by numerous spelling, grammatical, and typographical errors were sufficiently serious that they amounted to incompetent representation.

> On five occasions between January 13 and June 15, 1992 respondent failed to file amended lists of creditors as required by Rule 304(c), Local Bankruptcy Rules. On four occasions respondent failed to include the proof of service required by Rule 304(b), Local Bankruptcy Rules, when filing amended lists of creditors, and at least twice respondent filed amended schedules of exempt property that did not comply with Rule 304(c).

> Respondent also failed to comply with Rule 103, Local Bankruptcy Rules, in attempting to withdraw from representation. Although respondent filed a motion asking for permission to withdraw from a chapter 13 bankruptcy, it was untimely; and the bankruptcy trustee obtained a dismissal for

---

[2] *Id.* at 771.

failure of the debtor and respondent to appear at the creditors' meeting.

In short, the referee found that by regularly filing substandard bankruptcy documents containing numerous errors of various kinds, the respondent failed to represent his bankruptcy clients competently. The referee concluded, however, that respondent was well-versed in bankruptcy law and that his incompetence with respect to documentation had not harmed his clients. Nevertheless, the seriousness of respondent's noncompliance with the Local Bankruptcy Rules and respondent's attitude toward his shortcomings prompted the referee to recommend a three-month suspension followed by two years' supervised probation and completion of educational requirements.

It is apparent to us that Hawkins' repeated disregard of the Local Bankruptcy Rules, coupled with the incomprehensibility of his correspondence and documentation, constitutes a violation of Rule 1.1, Minnesota Rules of Professional Conduct. Although it is quite true that the deficiencies in the documents submitted to the bankruptcy court did not, as the referee concluded, cause harm to Hawkins' clients, the lack of harm is fortuitous. Compliance with the rules of the bankruptcy court ensures discharge of dischargeable debt. Even though Hawkins might be able to prove that a creditor who claims he did not receive notice of the bankruptcy proceedings was in fact notified, in the absence of appropriate documentation of service of proper notification, he might not. Therefore, Hawkins' contention that because there has been "no harm," there is "no foul" is unacceptable.

Moreover, harm has occurred: even though Hawkins' clients have not been harmed, administration of the law and the legal profession have been negatively affected by his conduct. **Public confidence in the legal system is shaken when lawyers disregard the rules of court and when a lawyer's correspondence and legal documents are so filled with spelling, grammatical, and typographical errors that they are virtually incomprehensible.**

We are of the opinion, however, that respondent's misconduct does not warrant suspension at this time. That is not to discount the seriousness of Hawkins' misconduct but only to recognize that suspension does not appear to be required for the protection of the public because, despite Hawkins' disregard of rules of court and lack of writing skill, he does-as the referee concluded-appear knowledgeable of the substantive law of bankruptcy. **Hawkins'**

misconduct does, however, require the public reprimand we now issue, together with the admonition that there must be some changes in his attitude-blame for his misconduct cannot be laid at the feet of his clients. Neither can this disciplinary proceeding be characterized as persecution.

Respondent Patrick W. Hawkins is hereby publicly reprimanded for unprofessional conduct. He is ordered to pay costs and disbursements incurred in this proceeding in the amount of $250. Within two years after issuance of this opinion respondent shall successfully complete the following described CLE or other educational programs and shall report quarterly to the Director his progress in complying with these educational requirements:

(1) A program on bankruptcy rules, or if none is available, on the law of bankruptcy;

(2) A program of at least 10 hours in legal writing; and

(3) A program of at least 5 hours on law office management.

Public reprimand with conditions imposed.[3]

Note that the Minnesota Supreme Court, in addition to the public reprimand, ordered Mr. Hawkins to take a minimum of ten hours of legal writing instruction. Most state bar associations, and many commercial providers, offer continuing education programs that focus on the skills of legal writing. Such programs are not free; they are not even inexpensive. The expense involved in defending disciplinary proceedings, and then complying with any court-ordered discipline, provides yet another very practical reason to avoid disciplinary proceedings. Courts do not take these things lightly, and neither should anyone who wants to practice law in the United States.

C. THE RESPONSIBILITY TO RESEARCH

Poorly written court documents frequently mean the end of a client's case even if the documents are technically written properly. The rules of procedure for every court in the United States will invariably require that certain pleading[4] requirements be met. Learning the rules for writing effective pleadings requires years of studying the rules of procedure (civil, criminal, and appellate) and years of practice. A lawyer whose pleadings fall short of applicable rules is an unsuccessful lawyer, as demonstrated in

---

[3] *Id.* (emphasis added).

[4] A pleading is any written request to a court. Complaints, responses, motions—all documents filed with a court during the course of any legal proceeding, state or federal, civil or criminal, is referred to generically as a pleading. In any other context, U.S. English would not refer to "pleading" as a noun—only as a verb. But in legal writing it's common practice to refer to written court documents as pleadings.

the following case from a federal trial court. Paulette M. Owens, an experienced New York City lawyer, represented a plaintiff named Karen Duncan, who alleged that both her employer and her union representatives violated her employment rights.[5] The lack of specificity in her pleadings resulted in dismissal of the Ms. Duncan's claim. Read the excerpt below to see what happens when a lawyer's writing is inadequate for its purposes.

Inadequately pleaded factual allegations take at least two forms. **First, a complaint may be so poorly composed as to be functionally illegible.** This is not to say that a complaint need resemble a winning entry in an essay contest. "[A] short and plain statement of the claim," rather than clarity and precision for their own sake, is the benchmark of proper pleading. Rule 8(a), F.R.Civ.P.; *see Goldman v. Belden, supra,* 754 F.2d at 1065. However, **the court's responsibilities do not include cryptography, especially when the plaintiff is represented by counsel.** *See Heart Disease Research Foundation v. General Motors Corp.,* 463 F.2d 98, 100 (2d Cir.1972).

Second, **individual allegations, although grammatically intact, may be so baldly conclusory that they fail to give notice of the basic events and circumstances of which the plaintiff complains. Such allegations are meaningless as a practical matter and, as a matter of law, insufficient to state a claim.** *Barr v. Abrams,* 810 F.2d 358, 363 (2d Cir.1987); *McClure v. Esparza,* 556 F.Supp. 569, 571 (E.D.Mo.1983), *aff'd without opinion,* 732 F.2d 162 (8th Cir.1984), *cert. denied,* 471 U.S. 1052, 105 S.Ct. 2111, 85 L.Ed.2d 477 (1985).

Duncan's complaint, which was drafted by her counsel, is deficient in both respects. Grammatical and stylistic shortcomings aside, the complaint fails to state facts sufficient to apprise defendants or the court of plaintiff's claim. Moreover, certain factual allegations, which are grammatically unobjectionable and which would be legally significant if they were well-pleaded, are unacceptably groundless and conclusory. Although the complaint no doubt could be dismissed for these reasons alone, *see Heart Disease Research Foundation, supra,* 463 F.2d at 100; *Barr, supra,* 810 F.2d at 363, a review of its substantive deficiencies may prove useful to obviate subsequent, futile amendments.

---

[5] *Duncan v. AT&T Communications, Inc.,* 668 F. Supp. 232, 233 (S.D.N.Y. 1987) (internal footnotes omitted) (emphasis added). Note that this case was brought in federal, not state, court, because it invoked the plaintiff's rights under the federal laws that govern labor unions and employees' rights to organize. Unfortunately for the plaintiff, her lawyer's unclear writing derailed the lawsuit to the point that the court could not even reach the merits of her case. This was not an attorney discipline case, but it could certainly have led to one.

Duncan alleges race- and disability-based discrimination by AT & T, in violation of 42 U.S.C. § 1981, and breach of the duty of fair representation by the Union, presumably in violation of 29 U.S.C. § 185. In support of the § 1981 claim, she alleges that AT & T failed to offer her employment or employee benefits after she suffered an on-the-job injury; that it failed to provide her with complete information about employment opportunities and benefits; and that it failed to apply equitably its promulgated policies, specifically, those regarding employee disability benefits. Complaint ¶¶ 4–5, 8–10, 12, 14, 17, 42–44, 46–47. Similarly, in support of the claimed breach of the duty of fair representation, Duncan alleges that the Union failed to answer her inquiries concerning her inability to regain employment at AT & T; that it failed to counsel her adequately about employee benefits she might be due; that it failed to investigate why AT & T allegedly had not borne the cost of a medical test for Duncan; and that it failed to adhere to established guidelines, policies, and procedures. *Id.* ¶¶ 6–9, 17, 43–44, 46.

To state a claim for a § 1981 violation, the complaint must allege (i) that Duncan is a member of a racial minority group; (ii) that she applied and was qualified for reemployment in a position for which AT & T was seeking applicants; (iii) that despite her qualifications she was not offered the position; and (iv) that AT & T thereafter kept the position open and continued to seek applicants with Duncan's qualifications. *See McDonnell Douglas Corp. v. Green,* 411 U.S. 792, 802, 93 S.Ct. 1817, 1824, 36 L.Ed.2d 668 (1973).

Construing the complaint as liberally as possible, it alleges at best only the third of these four elements. Duncan's race is nowhere mentioned. The repeated references to a partial disability or handicap are of no help to her, since § 1981 prohibits only discrimination that is based at least in part on racial classifications. *Runyon v. McCrary,* 427 U.S. 160, 167, 96 S.Ct. 2586, 2592, 49 L.Ed.2d 415 (1976). The complaint fails to allege that Duncan applied or was qualified for reemployment in any particular position. Nor does it allege that AT & T ever made any position available, much less sought applicants for such a position. Rather, plaintiff complains in effect that defendants did not take adequate affirmative steps to assist her in finding a new job position. **These sorts of allegations, without any suggestion that plaintiff was treated differently from members of another race, fail to state a claim under § 1981.** *See Hudson v. International Business Machines Corp.,* 620 F.2d 351, 354 (2d Cir.), *cert. denied,* 449 U.S. 1066, 101 S.Ct. 794, 66 L.Ed.2d 611

(1980); *see also United States Postal Service Board of Governors v. Aikens,* 460 U.S. 711, 715, 103 S.Ct. 1478, 1482, 75 L.Ed.2d 403 (1983) (inquiry in Title VII case is whether employer is treating some people less favorably than others because of race).

* * *

These rules require dismissal of Duncan's fair representation claim on a number of grounds. The complaint does not state whether Duncan is a member of Local 1150. Thus, on its face it establishes no basis for holding the Union defendants to a duty of fair representation. Whether or not she is a member, however, the complaint also fails to allege either a violation by AT & T of any provision of a collective bargaining agreement or an attempt by Duncan to air a grievance. Instead, aside from conclusory statements—e.g., that the Union did not adhere to established guidelines, policies, and procedures—the complaint dwells on the Union's alleged refusal to assist her in matters independent of any colorable case of wrongdoing by AT & T. In short, the complaint fails to set forth circumstances which would trigger the Union's duty of fair representation.

Here, the plaintiff's state law claim was dismissed as well as her federal claim, because the federal claim was the basis of that court's jurisdiction. Without the federal claim, the state law claim had to be dismissed from the federal court. This plaintiff's rights were extinguished due to her lawyer's legal writing, which was inadequate both structurally and substantively.

YOUR ASSIGNMENT: PROFESSIONAL RESPONSIBILITIES

Assume that you have been retained to represent Karen Duncan in her effort to pursue a grievance against her attorney, Paulette Owens. (For the purposes of this assignment, assume a complaint filed today would be timely.) Apply the following rules of professional conduct by which all New York lawyers must abide:

[1] A lawyer, as a member of the legal profession, is a representative of clients and an officer of the legal system with special responsibility for the quality of justice. As a representative of clients, a lawyer assumes many roles, including advisor, advocate, negotiator, and evaluator. As an officer of the legal system, each lawyer has a duty to uphold the legal process; to demonstrate respect for the legal system; to seek improvement of the law; and to promote access to the legal system and the administration of justice. In addition, a lawyer should further the public's understanding of and confidence in the rule of law and the justice system because, in a

constitutional democracy, legal institutions depend on popular participation and support to maintain their authority.

[2] The touchstone of the client-lawyer relationship is the lawyer's obligation to assert the client's position under the rules of the adversary system, to maintain the client's confidential information except in limited circumstances, and to act with loyalty during the period of the representation.[6]

Below is the procedure according to which a letter of complaint against a lawyer in New York City should be written[7]; follow the description below and draft a complaint letter against Attorney Owens on behalf of Ms. Duncan:

If you believe a lawyer may have violated the Rules of Professional Conduct, you can write a letter to the appropriate Committee or fill out and submit a form available from their websites. The form or letter should be as clear, specific and detailed as possible when explaining your complaint. The materials in your complaint should include the names, phone numbers and addresses of you and your attorney as well as copies of any pertinent documents, papers, and other information connected to the complaint. After a complaint is filed, it may be updated with new evidence. If new evidence becomes available after a complaint is dismissed, the complainant may ask that the complaint be re-evaluated. If the lawyer's office is located in Manhattan or The Bronx, a complainant should contact:

Departmental Disciplinary Committee Supreme Court,
Appellate Division First Judicial Department
61 Broadway, 2nd Floor
New York, New York 10006

Students should recall the form for letters from earlier chapters' discussions of writing demand letters and advice letters. The purpose, audience, scope and stance may be new, but the structure and format should not be. Remember to write clearly, concisely, and correctly, and with enough specificity that the bar association might determine from the letter's content whether Attorney Owens may have violated any rules of professional conduct.

Going forward, every student must be cognizant of the serious consequences that will follow from unauthorized or incompetent legal representation. Poor writing alone is a violation of lawyers' professional responsibility. There will always be errors that are technical and errors that are substantive, and some errors will result from inattention while

---

6 N.Y. Rules of Prof. Con. [1] (McKinney 2915).

7 This procedure is provided to the public by the Bar Association of New York City, which would be the local bar association where Ms. Owens was practicing law at the time this case arose. Its website may be visited here: http://www.nycbar.org/for-the-public/about-lawyers-and-judges/complaints-about-lawyers-and-judges-how.

others stem from inexperience. But errors are violations of lawyers' obligations to their clients, the courts, and the public, regardless of their form or cause. The principles of professional responsibility cannot be emphasized too much for any lawyer or law student in the United States. This book cannot provide more than an overview and a warning; from now on, students are expected to be on notice of, and to abide by, all applicable rules of professional responsibility.

Most law schools utilize a code of student conduct, or an honor code. Such codes are the first experience students may have with notions of professional conduct. These codes provide ideal opportunities for students everywhere to begin measuring the professionalism of their own conduct. Again, with great privilege comes great responsibility. The time to begin adhering to professionalism expectations is now.

D. A FINAL NOTE TO STUDENTS

This book can never substitute for live instruction, but its goal is to facilitate that instruction. Students and their teachers are encouraged to ask each other questions, compare legal systems and professional experiences, and use this book as a practical guide to U.S. legal writing. Students should remember that in a U.S. law school, the best answer to most questions is, "It depends." Nobody is expected to memorize the law. We are, however, expected to recognize questions and pursue their answers. Every exercise in this book is designed to help you do exactly that. Don't guess; look it up. Work smarter, not harder, and your future will be brighter. Studying the law is a rare opportunity, and it is my sincere hope that every reader of this book will make the most of this opportunity and will go on to have brilliant and rewarding careers. Wherever your education may take you, may the journey be a good one.

APPENDIX A

OFFICE MEMORANDUM

■ ■ ■

MEMORANDUM

Privileged Attorney Work Product

TO: Ann Piccard

FROM: #127

DATE: November 23, 2014

RE: Professional responsibility; possession of cocaine

State of Florida v. Allen Bold, File No. 14-2323[1]

Issues

I.   Under the Rules Regulating the Florida Bar, is it necessary to correct the cocaine possession error in the arrest report when it is an immaterial fact?

II.   Under Florida law, can Allen Bold successfully satisfy the elements of a medical necessity defense when he illegally possessed cocaine?[2]

Brief Answers

I.   Yes. It is our duty as professional advocates of the law to correct any inaccuracies of fact present in a case. The arrest report stated that Mr. Bold was in possession of ten grams of cocaine powder when he was arrested, though it was in fact crack, a rock form of cocaine. Although the discrepancy will not make a difference in our client's case, we must correct it, since allowing the State to proceed with the inaccuracy can call into question the entire validity of the facts of the case and would be a violation of the Rules Regulating the Florida Bar on our part.

II.   Probably not. In order to do so, Mr. Bold would have to show that he did not intend the harsh working conditions that led him to his cocaine

---

[1]   The memo's heading, including the "confidential" designation, must accomplish multiple purposes.

[2]   It is easiest to write objective issues using an under/does/when format, bearing in mind that the "does" clause is flexible. This formula includes applicable binding law (subject); key fact; precise legal question.

usage, that he did not have a more viable option to accomplish his work, and that the possibility of losing his lone client, family, marriage and job was more egregious than his attempt to avoid it by using cocaine. Mr. Bold probably won't satisfy all three elements successfully. **[NOTE: Brief answers begin with a bottom-line predicted outcome, followed by an explanation that summarizes (without citing) the key points of fact and law.]**

Facts

Mr. Bold has contacted our office regarding his criminal possession of ten grams of cocaine. He has informed us that he was in possession of crack cocaine, whereas the arrest report categorized it as cocaine powder. Additionally, Mr. Bold would like to proceed using a medical necessity defense. **[NOTE: The first sentence of any Facts section in an objective office memo should identify the client, the parties, and the basic nature of the problem.]**

Mr. Bold is a thirty-seven-year old partner at the Tampa law firm of Lipskowitz, Bold and Reed. Over the past year, he had been responsible for the loss of three of the firm's clients, which caused injury to his reputation and labeled him as a liability to his employer. He has represented his now only client, Malibu Boats, for over a year and a half, and after the loss of his other clients, Malibu Boats became his only hope to hold onto his job with the firm.

Malibu Boats' intent has been to open a manufacturing plant in Hillsborough County, and Mr. Bold has represented them in their expansion interests, negotiations and government relations. Our client informed us that he greatly underestimated the work that would be required to bring such a large company into the area. The volume of the work had put an immense amount of pressure on Mr. Bold to the point that his family, marriage, and personal health began to deteriorate, resulting in high blood pressure, severe stress, and exceedingly long hours of work over the past six months.

In order to accomplish his work, Mr. Bold started using small amounts of cocaine six months ago, a practice that he says is standard procedure for many working in corporate law. He soon thereafter formed a dependency on the drug. After purchasing what he believed to be cocaine and later turned out to be crack, he became addicted. It is his genuine belief that he needed it to function, and that he would have lost all of his hard work had he stopped using it.

Mr. Bold had a hearing regarding Malibu Boats on Friday, October 17, 2014, at the Thirteenth Judicial Circuit Court in Tampa. The hearing was very important and was causing him even more stress, since it was to determine whether his client could acquire the property needed for its manufacturing plant. Before the hearing began, Mr. Bold went to use the men's restroom. When he went to wash his hands, an unexpectedly high water pressure soaked the front of his pants. To avoid embarrassment at the hearing, Mr. Bold emptied out his pockets, took off his pants, and began drying them under a hand dryer.

As Mr. Bold was drying his pants, the bailiff for the presiding judge, Officer Alex French, entered the restroom. After using the urinal and washing his hands, he noticed the contents of Mr. Bold's pants' pockets on the sink, which included an unmarked prescription bottle containing cocaine. Officer French asked our client if the items on the sink belonged to him. Mr. Bold confirmed that they were and was then placed under arrest for possession of ten grams of cocaine. **[NOTE: Facts sections should specify dates and locations to the extent possible, to show jurisdiction if nothing else.]**

Discussion

1.   By failing to correct known inaccuracies in evidence or testimony, a lawyer "makes it impossible for the scales of justice to balance." *Dodd v. The Florida Bar*, 118 So. 2d 17, 19 (Fla. 1960). An attorney has a professional responsibility to correct any falsities known to him in a case, regardless of their effects on the case and its respective parties. R. Regulating Fla. Bar 4–3.3(a)(1). An attorney may disclose confidential client information "to the extent the lawyer reasonably believes necessary . . . to comply with the Rules Regulating The Florida Bar." R. Regulating Fla. Bar 4–1.6(c)(5).

> The primary function of trial court proceedings is to find the truth . . . in order that the applicable law may be applied thereto so as to reach a just conclusion. . . . When an attorney adds or allows false testimony to be cast into the crucible from which the truth is to be refined and taken to be weighed on the scales of justice, he makes impure the product. . . . No breach of professional ethics, or the law, is more harmful to the administration of justice or more hurtful to the public appraisal of the legal profession. . . .

> *Dodd*, 118 So. 2d at 19.

A lawyer injures the court's ability to provide justice when he knowingly allows the inclusion of an inaccuracy or error in a case. *Id.* Cocaine and its derivatives are not separated in their respective drug schedules and do not carry separate convictions. *Godfrey v. State*, 947 So. 2d 565, 566 (Fla. 1st DCA 2006). Cocaine, along with any of its derivatives, is classified as a Schedule II controlled substance, carrying a "high potential for abuse," a strict restriction for medicinal use, and a possibility of causing a "severe psychological or physical dependence" when abused. Fla. Stat. § 893.03(2)(a)(4) (2014). Possession of a Schedule II controlled substance without a valid prescription is unlawful and is classified as a third degree felony carrying a penalty of no more than five years imprisonment. Fla.

Stat. §§ 775.082(3)(e), 893.13(6)(a) (2014). **[NOTE: These paragraphs cite the rule of law and explain its context. The following paragraph applies it: REA.]**

In this case, we do have a professional responsibility to inform the court of the error in the arrest report, where it states that our client was in possession of a cocaine powder when it was in fact crack cocaine. It is our duty to maintain the proper respect of the court by practicing with honor, honesty, and candor towards it. *Dodd*, 118 So. 2d at 20. While maintaining client confidentiality is an important aspect of our profession, our duty to the court trumps it. Whether the error is material or not, and though our client's confidentiality will be breached, it is still our primary duty to maintain candor before the court. Because such a responsibility belongs to all attorneys and is an inherent component of our ethical code, the State will not argue against the correction of the arrest report. Therefore, it is both reasonable and necessary for us to disclose the error, as it will show compliance with the Rules Regulating the Florida Bar.

II.   The medical necessity defense is a more specific use of the necessity defense. *Jenks v. State*, 582 So. 2d 676, 679 (Fla. 1st DCA 1991). To establish a medical necessity defense, a defendant must show that he did not "intentionally bring about circumstances which precipitated the unlawful act; that defendant could not accomplish same objective using less offensive alternative available to defendant; and that evil sought to be avoided was more heinous than unlawful act perpetrated to avoid it." *Id.* at 677.

> The pressure of natural physical forces sometimes confronts a person in an emergency with a choice of two evils: either he may violate the literal terms of the criminal law and thus produce a harmful result, or he may comply with those terms and thus produce a greater or equal or lesser amount of harm . . . if the harm which will result from compliance with the law is greater than that which will result from violation of it, he is by virtue of the defense of necessity justified in violating it.

Id. at 678.

In *Jenks*, the defendants appealed a criminal charge for cultivation and possession of marijuana. *Id.* at 676. One of the defendants, suffering from extreme nausea from recently contracted AIDS, tested numerous prescribed medications to help ease the virus's side effects, to no avail. *Id.* at 677. After learning that marijuana had worked for others with similar symptoms, the defendants tried it as well, and began cultivating it for personal use after realizing its efficacy. *Id.* Along with the testimony of a medical expert, the defendants had their previous judgment reversed by establishing a medical necessity defense for their possession of marijuana by satisfying the necessary elements: (1) they did not intentionally contract the virus; (2) their medical expert acknowledged that no other alternative existed to appease the defendants' nausea; and (3) with the medical expert's testimony for support, the defendants showed that "if their nausea was not controlled, their lives were in danger." *Id*. at 679–80. **[NOTE: Again, the preceding paragraphs articulate, cite, and explain the law, and the following paragraph applies that law.]**

For Mr. Bold to use a medical necessity defense for his possession of cocaine, he must satisfy all three elements of the defense. *Id*. at 679. It can be argued that Allen Bold did not intend to bring about the burdensome circumstances that accompanied his representation of Malibu Boats in their expansion interests into Hillsborough County, which caused him to turn to cocaine for help. *Id*. 677. Though he was labeled an embarrassment and a liability to his firm, his loss of three clients can be attributed to the crippling pressure he faced with Malibu Boats. We can further argue that our client had no other alternative than to continue using cocaine to help him in his representation of Malibu Boats, due to his dependency on the substance. *Id*. Mr. Bold's possible failure would not only result in his firing from his firm, but could also cost him his marriage, his career, and his family. For the last element of the defense, we can argue that our client's possibility of being fired was the "evil sought to be avoided," and was "more heinous" than his possession of cocaine. *Id*.

However, Mr. Bold does not have a convincing argument for a medical necessity defense for his possession of cocaine. Though we can manage to satisfy the elements, it can be argued against us, with respect to *Jenks*, that the illegal use of a controlled substance to salvage a career is not analogous to its use to lessen the side effects of a terminal virus. It can be further argued that our client could have sought other forms of help, such as a therapist, another coworker, or even a medical professional, rather than turning to cocaine at the outset. Lastly, it can be argued against us that the possibility of losing one's job does not permit the breaking of the law, even though the act perpetrated may be standard procedure in one's work environment. Therefore, though he has a feeble argument, Mr. Bold will most likely not be able to successfully satisfy the elements for a medical necessity defense for his possession of cocaine.

Conclusion

Due to the clear language in the Rules Regulating the Florida Bar, we will have correctly performed our professional duty as attorneys when we bring to the court's attention the inaccuracy in the arrest report. Even though the error is immaterial, our failure to correct the error from cocaine powder to crack cocaine would call into question the credibility of the remaining facts and could result in disciplinary action for failing to abide by the Rules Regulating the Florida Bar. Since it is our duty to disclose our knowledge of a falsity in the case, the court will make the correction in order to have the most clear, fair and honest judgment entered on Mr. Bold, and to maintain the balance of justice.

Because of the loosely applicable circumstances in our client's case, and the lack of solid supporting case law, Mr. Bold probably won't establish a medical necessity defense for his cocaine possession. Though we can provide a compelling argument, it is unlikely that someone seeking to save their career can justify the use of cocaine when the defense is most often granted to people who have sought to alleviate their debilitating health symptoms illegally as a last resort. The court will most likely deny our client the medical necessity defense. **[NOTE: One short paragraph per issue or element in dispute is enough for the Conclusion.]**

I certify that I have complied with the word limit for this assignment and have followed all collaboration and academic integrity requirements. [#127]

APPENDIX B

MEMORANDUM OF LAW

■ ■ ■

Trial Brief/Memorandum of Law
(Arguments for and Against a Motion to Dismiss
for Prosecutorial Misconduct)

Argument

I. THE COURT SHOULD GRANT THE DEFENDANT'S MOTION TO DISMISS THE INDICTMENT, AND ALL COUNTS THERIN.

"[A] district court may properly dismiss an indictment . . . if the prosecutorial misconduct (1) was flagrant, . . . and (2) caused substantial prejudice to the defendant." *U.S. v. Garrett,* 2009 WL 16888181 at *1 (D. Minn. 2009).

In this case, the United States Attorney made inappropriate comments to the media about the case at hand in order to prejudice the Defendant in the mind of all perspective jurors. *Id.* The United States Attorney implied that the Defendant was a guilty liar. *Id.* The United States District Court denied the Defendants' motion to dismiss for prosecutorial misconduct. *Id.* The court reasoned that because the misconduct was not flagrant enough, it did not reach the substantial prejudice needed for dismissal. *Id.* Flagrancy in this case is outrageous conduct on behalf of the government. *Id.* The court also said that because the United States Attorney was talking about "public policy" instead of directing it at the defendant directly it was not outrageous conduct. *Id* at *3.

Unlike in *Garrett,* in which the comments were merely suggestive and about public policy as a whole, Ms. Deegan's constitutional rights to due process of law, fair and impartial trial, and effective assistance of counsel, as guaranteed to her by the Fifth and Sixth Amendments of the United States Constitution have been violated. *Id.* Ms. Deegan was not implied to be guilty, rather, David X. Haggler wrote a letter saying "[a]ny mother who lets her baby die alone deserves to burn in Hell, and Dana Deegan's red skin is perfectly suited for the fires of Hell." Defs.' Mot. Dismiss, ¶ 1.

He continued by saying "I hope to see her go up in flames sooner rather than later" and "[o]nly an uneducated Indian could support such a terrible mother." Defs.' Mot. Dismiss, ¶ 2–3. By speaking specifically of this case and calling the defendant by name, this is substantially more prejudicial. *Id.* "To constitute a Fifth Amendment violation under *Russell,* the government conduct at issue must be fundamentally unfair and " 'shocking to the universal sense of justice,' mandated by the Due Process Clause of the Fifth Amendment." *U.S. v. Marshank*, 777 F. Supp. 1507, 1523 (N.D. Cal. 1991). "Whether outrageous government misconduct exists turns on the 'totality of the circumstances.' " *Marshank*, 777 F. Supp. at 1519, 1523. Mr. Haggler's frequent interviews, letters, and attacks, contributed to the prejudice that Ms. Deegan cannot overcome by prospective jurors. Aff. Paul Robertson ¶ 1–3.

Looking at the totality of the circumstances surrounding Ms. Deegan's case, qualifies as outrageous conduct and a violation of Ms. Deegan's Fifth Amendment due process. *Marshank*, 777 F. Supp. at 1519, 1523. The court should grant the motion to dismiss based on a Fifth Amendment Constitutional violation, based on the government engaging in outrageous conduct at the expense of Ms. Deegan's rights. *Id.* at 1519.

"The Ninth Circuit has distinguished between the government's "passive tolerance" of misconduct and "conscious direction" by government agents, suggesting that the former is less egregious and therefore tempers the outrageousness of any government misconduct." *Marshank*, 777 F. Supp. at 1522. As Mr. Haggler made a conscious decision to make these racial slurs on many different occasions, demonstrates that his conduct was more than passive tolerance, but outrageous conduct by the United States government. *Id.* Ms. Deegan's Fifth Amendment constitutional right was not only violated, but it was intentionally violated by the United States and should therefore grant the defendant's motion to dismiss her indictment.

"In all criminal prosecutions, the accused shall enjoy the right to a speedy and public trial, by an impartial jury of the state and district wherein the crime shall have been committed." *Marshank*, 777 F. Supp. at 1522. A defendant's Sixth Amendment rights are violated only when the government intrusion results in prejudice to the defendant. *Id.* at 1525. Prejudice may manifest itself in numerous ways. *Id.* Mr. Haggler, acting on behalf of the government, created an extreme prejudice to Ms. Deegan by negatively influencing the perspective jury pool on a national scale. *Id. at 1519.*

The Court has the authority to grant a change of venue, and should, prior to voir dire when the publicity is inherently prejudicial. *U.S. v. Mandel*, 415 F. Supp. 1033, 1066 (D. Md. 1976). Although the remedy for a prejudicial jury is change of venue in *Mandel*, a violation of the Sixth Amendment requires a remedy tailored to the injury suffered. *Marshank*, 777 F. Supp. at 1525; *Mandel,* 415 F. Supp. at 1059. When Mr. Haggler began making the racial statements and slurs against Ms. Deegan to national news outlets, there was no possible way to suppress the evidence to select an impartial jury elsewhere. *Marshank*, 777 F. Supp. at 1521. Unlike in *Mandel,* where the defendant failed to present a concrete basis for inferring that government officials were responsible for a substantial amount of the publicity, it is apparent that Mr. Haggler, the Assistant United States Attorney, in this case created the prejudice caused to Ms. Deegan. *Mandel,* 415 F. Supp. at 1064.

"[D]ismissal is appropriate when there is a demonstrable prejudice or substantial threat thereof. *Marshank*, 777 F. Supp. at 1521.Even if the publicity is inappropriate, "The Supreme Court, in addressing governmental misconduct, held '[a]bsent demonstrable prejudice, or substantial threat thereof, dismissal of the indictment is plainly inappropriate." *Marshank*, 777 F. Supp. at 1521; *Garrett,* 2009 WL at*1. In Ms. Deegan's case, the Court should look to the totality of the circumstances to determine the tailored remedy, which in this case would be dismissal. *Marshank*, 777 F. Supp. at 1523, 1525.

Also, as reiterated in *Marshank*, [a] court may dismiss an indictment for prosecutorial misconduct either on constitutional grounds or by exercising its supervisory power. *Id.* at 1528. Even though this is not a favored remedy by the courts, to set a precedent allowing the government officials to continue to deliberately prejudice defendants and strip them of their constitutional rights could not be the Court's goal either. *Mandel,* 415 F. Supp. at 1059, 1064. Dismissal is warranted whenever the misconduct is flagrant, but must also have prejudiced the defendant. *Marshank*, 777 F. Supp. at 1529. Mr. Haggler released allegations of Ms. Deegan's case, producing a biased potential jury pool and causing counsel to be ineffective at reaching justice. Aff. Paul Robertson ¶ 3.

Although dismissal has not been a favored remedy of the Court, when justice demands it, it should be given. *Mandel,* 415 F. Supp. at 1059. Mr. Haggler continues to use Dana Deegan's case as a stepping stool for his political platform in his race for Governor, regardless of the injustice served. Aff. Paul Robertson ¶ 3. When such injustice and prejudice is shown, the remedy must be tailored to the damage, which in this case is irreparable. *Marshank*, 777 F. Supp. at 1525. The Assistant United States Attorney has rendered it impossible for the defendant to obtain a fair and impartial jury. *Id.* at 1521. Therefore, this Court should grant the defendant's motion to dismiss the indictment, and all counts therein, on the basis of a violation of Ms. Deegan's Fifth and Sixth Constitutional rights and prosecutorial misconduct.

[END OF ARGUMENT IN FAVOR OF GRANTING MOTION TO DISMISS]

UNITED STATES DISTRICT COURT

FOR THE DISTRICT OF NORTH DAKOTA

NORTHEASTERN DIVISION

UNITED STATES OF AMERICA,   Case No.4:07-cr-000510DLH

       Plaintiff,

vs.   GOVERNMENT'S BRIEF IN

OPPOSITION TO

DEFENDANT'S MOTION TO

DISMISS INDICTMENT

DANA DEEGAN,

       Defendant.

The United States of America, by and through its undersigned attorney, submits this response to defendant's motion to dismiss. The Government asks the Court to deny the defendant's motion to dismiss the indictment. The pretrial publicity is not flagrant and it is not substantially prejudice.

Statement of Facts

On October 20, 1998 the defendant, Dana Deegan, allegedly, with malice aforethought, unlawfully murdered her newborn son, willfully, deliberately, maliciously, and with premeditation. See Ind., 18 U.S.C §§ 1111, 1153, Jun. 6, 2007, 4:07-cr-00051. During the investigation, it was also found that beginning in February 2007 and continuing until May 16, 2007, the defendant knowingly and willfully falsified, concealed, and covered up by trick and scheme, material facts by falsely representing to Special Agents of the Federal Bureau of Investigation the natural and stillborn death of her newborn son, where in fact the defendant knew her newborn son had been born alive and was abandoned at birth. See Ind., 18 U.S.C § 1001(a).

On June 6, 2007, after the Grand Jury's indictment of the defendant, Mr. Haggler, the prosecuting attorney, called a press conference on the steps of the United States Courthouse for the Northwestern Division of North Dakota, and proceeded to explain to the public the arrest and indictment of the defendant stemming from the 1997 death of the defendants newborn son. See Aff. Paul Robertson, ¶ 2, Oct. 27, 2007, 4:07-cr-000510. Mr. Haggler held press conferences on several other dates, June 27, July 17, and August 1, 2007, where he furthered described the first-degree murder charge against the defendant. See Def. Mot. Dismiss, ¶ 1, Oct. 20, 2007, 4:07-cr-000510.

On June 10, 2007, Mr. Haggler wrote a letter in response to an editorial published in the Indian Country Times discussing the fate of the defendant if she is to be found guilty of this first degree murder of her newborn son that she has been charged with. See Def. Mot. Dismiss, ¶ 2. Mr. Haggler also was responsive to the local and national media on this case, and used the defendant and the entire Native American community as an opportunity to push the stance he is using to run for Governor in 2008, "get tough on crime." See Aff. Paul Robertson, ¶ 8.

Issue

Whether the Court should deny the defendant's motion to dismiss when the pretrial publicity by the United States Government is permissible and did not cause substantial prejudice to the defendant.

Argument

THIS COURT SHOULD DENY THE DEFENDANT'S MOTION TO DISMISS BECAUSE THE PROSECUTOR'S PRETRIAL PUBLICITY CONDUCT WAS NOT FLAGRANT AND THE CONDUCT DID NOT CAUSE SUBSTANTIAL PREJUDICE TO THE DEFENDANT.

" 'Because the drastic step of dismissing an indictment is a disfavored remedy . . . a district court may properly dismiss an indictment only if the prosecutorial misconduct [1] was flagrant, . . . and [2] caused substantial prejudice to the defendant.' " *United States v. Garrett,* 2009 WL 1688181 1, 2 (E.D. Mo. June 17, 2009) (quoting *United States v. Manthei,* 979 F.2d 124, 126 (8th Cir.1992).

Dismissing an indictment based on prosecutorial misconduct is a power that the court frequently discusses, but rarely invokes. *United States v. Samango,* 607 F.2d 877, 881 (9th Cir. 1979). In determining whether prosecutorial misconduct occurred that would lead to dismissal of the indictment, the courts use a two-part test. *Garrett,* 2009 WL 1688181 1, 2. Under the first part of the test, the defendant has the burden of proving that the prosecutorial misconduct was flagrant. *Id.* Only if the defendant fulfills the burden of proving the prosecutorial misconduct was flagrant is the second part of the test applied. *Id. Garrett* defines flagrant prosecutorial misconduct as " . . . demonstrable prejudice, or substantial threat thereof." 2009 WL 1688181 1, 2 (quoting *United States v. Morrison,* 449 U.S. 361, 101 S. Ct. 665, 66 L.Ed.2d 564 (1992)). The defense cannot fulfill this part of the test because Mr. Haggler's comments during the pretrial publicity were not flagrant. Mr. Haggler discussed the defendant's case with the media, but only in response to the questions presented by the media. While Mr. Haggler's comments were offensive towards the defendant, they did not meet the standard of being demonstrably prejudice, or substantially threatening to be demonstrably prejudice. The comments made by Mr. Haggler do not cause demonstrable prejudice towards the defendant to invoke a rare instance of dismissing the indictment. Therefore, the pretrial publicity is not flagrant.

In *Morrison* the Court made clear that "absent demonstrable prejudice, or substantial threat thereof, dismissal of the indictment is plainly inappropriate, even though the violation may have been deliberate" 449 U.S. 361, 365 (1981). The Court may find that the statements Mr. Haggler made to the media concerning the defendant are flagrant, but applying the rule in *Mandel,* this does not require that the indictment should be dismissed. 415 F. Supp. 1033, 1068 (D. Md. 1976). If the media statements made by Mr. Haggler are flagrant, the second part of the test makes clear that the indictment will not be dismissed unless the publicity caused substantial prejudice to the defendant. *Garrett,* 2009 WL 1688181 1, 2. The test the court should follow to determine substantial prejudice is " . . . whether under all the circumstances of the particular case, as a practical matter, it is within the capacity of the jurors to follow the court's admonitory instructions and accordingly to collate and appraise the evidence against each defendant solely upon that defendant's own acts, statements, and conduct." *Mandel,* 415 F. Supp. 1033, 1051 (D. Md. 1976) (holding the defendant did not make a sufficient showing of substantial prejudice resulting from publicity to entitle him to severance). There is no evidence in our case that the comments made by Mr. Haggler would cause every potential juror to be biased against the defendant, and not be able to clearly look at the facts at the case to make their decision. Mr. Haggler has used the defendant's indictment as an example for his platform for Governor. While his comments may persuade some of the constituents of North Dakota, not everyone will be tainted by his remarks. Consequently, the pretrial publicity comments did not cause substantial prejudice to the defendant and the indictment should not be dismissed.

In order to decide whether other remedies or, in such an extreme case, dismissal of the indictment is suitable it must be determined if there is substantial prejudice. *Mandel*, 415 F. Supp. 1033, 1051. The determination of substantial prejudice of publicity on potential jurors must await voir dire. *Id.* at 1059. In *Mandel*, the court referred to *Abbott Laboratories* where that court held "even though the publicity was prejudicial and inflammatory, the court must resort to voir dire before dismissing the indictment." *Id.* at 1068. Thus far, nothing is indicative that Mr. Haggler's comments have swayed potential jurors to such an extent that dismissal of the indictment is the only fair remedy. Even if there is evidence that some potential jurors have been influenced by the comments Mr. Haggler has made, the process of voir dire is in place to ensure there is a fair trial and the unbiased potential jurors are selected. There is no evidence that the statements made by Mr. Haggler would taint all of the jurors to an irreparable state. That is the importance of the voir dire process, to find jurors who are not prejudiced by media and other outside influences. Thus, although the comments Mr. Haggler made to the media may be found to be flagrant, they are not so substantially prejudice towards the defendant as to cause the indictment to be dismissed.

Prayer for Relief

For the reasons set out above, the Government respectfully requests that the Court deny the defendant's motion to dismiss the indictment.

Dated this 2nd day of February, 2015.

Student
_____

Student
Assistant United States Attorney
(813) 220 9385

APPENDIX C

APPELLATE BRIEF

■ ■ ■

**Appellate Briefs on Behalf of an Appellant
and an Appellee**

NOTE: This assignment required students to suspend their disbelief. The underlying trial and Circuit Court decisions that formed the bases for this appeal are real; the Petition to the U.S. Supreme Court was not. The underlying cases that support the appellate assignment were also used as the record on appeal. For purposes of this assignment, some otherwise required sections of the appellate brief were omitted.

In The

Supreme Court of the United States

DANA DEEGAN,

Petitioner,

v.

UNITED STATES,

Respondent.

**On Petition For A Writ of Certiorari
To The United States Court Of Appeals
For the Eighth Circuit**

PETITION FOR A WRIT OF CERTIORARI

767	###
FIRST ASST. FEDERAL PUBLIC DEFENDER	UNITED STATES DEPARTMENT OF JUSTICE
1401 61ST ST. S.	1401 61ST ST. S.
GULFPORT, FL 33707	GULFPORT, FL 33707
(727) 555-0000	(727) 000-5555

TABLE OF CONTENTS

TABLE OF AUTHORITIES

TABLE OF AUTHORITIES, continued

OTHER AUTHORITIES

STATEMENT OF JURISDICTION

The United States Court of Appeals for the Eighth Circuit issued its judgment on May 25, 2010, notice of appeal was timely filed. The jurisdiction of this Court is appealed according to 28 U.S.C. § 1254(1) (2014) and Rule 10(c) of the Supreme Court Rules.

STATEMENT OF THE QUESTIONS PRESENTED

I.   Whether the Eighth Circuit erred in finding that neonaticide is the same crime as a "run-of-the-mine" second-degree murder when Ms. Deegan suffered from depression and dissociation at the time of delivery and acted impulsively in leaving her baby alone.

II.   Whether the Eighth Circuit erred in disregarding historical and intergenerational trauma as a mitigating circumstance that should be considered when sentencing Native American women who suffered the consequences of the historical abuse of Native Americans.

STATEMENT OF THE CASE

I.   Statement of the Facts

Ms. Deegan, a member of the Three Affiliated Tribes, lived in poverty and isolation on Fort Berthold Indian Reservation with her three young children and her abusive husband. *United States v. Deegan*, 605 F.3d 625, 627 (8th Cir. 2010). She suffered from a history of physical and sexual abuse from her alcoholic father and his friends throughout her childhood. *Id.* at 639 (Bright, J., dissenting). Her common law husband continued the physical and sexual abuse, and he spent the little money that they had on drugs. *Id.* at 640.

Ms. Deegan suffered from depression and dissociation at the time of the offense. *Id.* at 629 (majority opinion). In 1998 she secretly delivered a healthy male infant in the bathroom of her trailer. *Id.* at 642 (Bright, J., dissenting). Ms. Deegan cleaned him, clothed him, and wrapped him in a blanket. *Id.* Then she placed him in a basket before impulsively leaving him alone in the trailer for approximately two weeks. *Id.* The baby was dead when she returned home. *Id.* She wrapped him in a blanket, placed him in a suitcase, and deposited the suitcase in a ditch close to her trailer. *Id.*

In 1999 a worker found the suitcase with the baby's remains near Ms. Deegan's trailer. *Id.* The FBI conducted an investigation, and DNA analysis confirmed that Ms. Deegan was the baby's mother. *Id.* When the FBI initially interviewed Ms. Deegan, she falsely claimed that the baby was a stillborn. *Id.* at 627–28. She eventually admitted that he was born alive, and she impulsively left him alone because she was unable to care for a fourth child by herself. *Id.*

Ms. Deegan was charged by a grand jury with first-degree murder and charged with making false statements to the FBI. *Id.* She entered a plea agreement for second-degree murder. *Id.* She submitted a report prepared by Dr. Resnick, an expert in neonaticide, arguing for leniency based on her psychological and emotional condition at the time of the offense, her history as a victim of abuse, and the impulsive nature of her act. *Id.* At the sentencing hearing the district court adopted the sentencing guideline in the presentence investigation report and sentenced Ms. Deegan to 121 months imprisonment. *Id.* at 629.

Ms. Deegan appealed her sentence of 121 months' imprisonment to the Eighth Circuit. *Id.* The Eighth Circuit affirmed the judgment of the district court. *Id.* at 636.

II.   Standard of Review

This Court should apply the de novo standard of review. Questions of law "must be resolved de novo on appeal." *Elder v. Holloway*, 510 U.S. 510, 516 (1994). Determining whether the Eighth Circuit erred in finding that neonaticide is the same crime as second-degree murder, and erred in disregarding historical and intergenerational trauma as a mitigating circumstance that should be considered when sentencing Native American women are questions of law. This Court should review the questions de novo because they are questions of law. *Id.*

ARGUMENTS

I.   **MS. DEEGAN'S CRIME OF NEONATICIDE DOES NOT FALL WITHIN THE "RUN-OF-THE-MINE" SECOND-DEGREE MURDER BECAUSE THE CIRUCMSTANCES THAT LEAD TO THIS CRIME ARE DISTINCT FROM OTHER HOMICIDES.**

The circumstances of this homicide are horrific, however the crime Ms. Deegan committed does not "come within the 'run-of-the-mine' guidelines for second-degree murder." *Deegan*, 605 F.3d at 637 (Bright, J., dissenting). Federal courts have not defined or described neonaticide. Dr. Resnick defined it as "the killing of an infant within the first twenty-four hours following birth." *Id.* at 627 (majority opinion) (quoting Resnick).

Experts portray neonaticide as distinct from other homicides that occur. Joanna Woolman & Sarah Deer, *Protecting Native Mothers and Their Children: A Feminist Lawyering Approach,* 40 Wm. Mitchell L. Rev. 943, 965 (2014). This crime usually involves a mother who is faced with an "overwhelming state of desperation at the time of the infant's birth and lacks adequate resources to mentally handle the situation of delivering a child." *Deegan*, 605 F.3d at 643 (Bright, J., dissenting) (quoting Resnick). The mother will often "conceal[ ] and den[y] her pregnancy." *Id.* The mother endures a significant amount of pain in order to conceal her pregnancy and delivery. *Id.* at 643–44.

Ms. Deegan was in an overwhelming state of desperation when the homicide occurred, which is demonstrated by her depression that hindered her from taking care of her three children, and her impulsive action of leaving the baby where he could be easily discovered. *Deegan*, 605 F. at 641, 644 (Bright, J., dissenting) (quoting Resnick). She lacked adequate resources to mentally handle a fourth child because she did not have a support system, no one knew she was pregnant, and she was alone during delivery. *Deegan*, 605 F. at 641 (Bright, J., dissenting). Ms. Deegan concealed and denied her pregnancy because she suffered three miscarriages and experienced menstrual spotting throughout her previous pregnancies. *Id.* She was able to dissociate herself from the pain that pregnancy and delivery brought because of the abuse she suffered throughout her life. *Id.* at 629 (majority opinion). Therefore, this Court should review the question de novo, and reverse and remand for resentencing because Ms. Deegan's crime of neonaticide does not fall within the "run-of-the-mine" second-degree murder.

A.   **Ms. Deegan did not form the requisite malice aforethought for second-degree murder because she did not have an awareness of a "serious risk of death" and her conduct was not a "reckless and wanton and a gross deviation from a reasonable standard of care".**

Any murder by a defendant with the requisite malice aforethought that is not first-degree murder is second-degree murder. 18 U.S.C. § 1111(a) (2014). Malice aforethought exists in a defendant when, looking at all the surrounding circumstances, he or she has an awareness of a "serious risk of death" when his or her conduct is a "reckless and wanton and a gross deviation from a reasonable standard of care." *United States v. Williams*, 342 F.3d 350, 356 (4th Cir. 2003) (concluding "[he] was aware of the risk of death or serious bodily harm as he 'actively participated' in the robbery").

Ms. Deegan did not recklessly deviate from a reasonable standard of care because she did not believe she was pregnant, she put it out of her mind and she concealed it, and she neither planned for the killing of the infant nor for the caring of the infant. *Deegan*, 605 F.3d at 641, 644 (Bright, J., dissenting). The surrounding circumstances are evidence that she did not recklessly deviate from a reasonable standard of care because she was alone while giving birth and her three children were in the trailer but unaware of the delivery. *Id.* at 627 (majority opinion). She did not act recklessly when she assisted the baby with breathing, fed him, cleaned him and dressed him, and then wrapped him in a blanket before putting him in a suitcase in a ditch near the trailer. *Id.* at 642 (Bright, J., dissenting). Ms. Deegan was not an "active participant" because she acted impulsively when she left him alone with no food, water or caretaker, and then kept him close to home because of her emotional attachment. *Id.* at 627 (majority opinion). Ms. Deegan did not have the awareness of a serious risk of death because she was suffering from major depressive disorder, post-traumatic stress disorder, dysthymic disorder, and dissociation that overwhelmed her judgment and strained her psychological

3

resources to care for her children. *Id.* at 643 (Bright, J., dissenting) (quoting Resnick). Therefore, this Court should review the question de novo, and reverse and remand for resentencing because Ms. Deegan did not form the requisite malice aforethought for second-degree murder.

B.   Sentencing for neonaticide cases should be consistent and lenient throughout the courts in order to avoid sentencing disparities and promote respect for the law.

There are federal sentencing guidelines enacted to create consistency in federal criminal cases for people that commit the same type of crime with the same type of criminal history as the defendant. BJ Jones & Christopher J. Ironroad, *Addressing Sentencing Disparities for Tribal Citizens in the Dakotas: A Tribal Sovereignty Approach*, 89 N.D.L. Rev. 53, 55 (2013). Neonaticide is a crime of domestic concern, which federal courts typically do not handle. Margaret Ryznar, *A Crime of Its Own? A Proposal for Achieving Greater Sentencing Consistency in Neonaticide and Infanticide Cases*, 47 U.S.F. L. Rev. 459, 469 (2013). Currently in federal and state courts there are no statutes that make neonaticide a separate offense with consistent sentencing. *Id.* State court convictions of neonaticide range from murder to manslaughter. *Id.* "A sentence [should] promote[ ] respect for the law and consider the need to avoid unwarranted disparity among defendants who have been found guilty of similar conduct." *Deegan*, 605 F.3d at 656 (Bright, J., dissenting). Harsh sentences are imposed "to afford adequate deterrence to criminal conduct," and "to protect the public from further crimes of the defendant." 18 U.S.C. § 3553(a)(2)(B)-(C) (2014).

Only one other neonaticide case is recorded in federal courts, and it also occurred on an Indian Reservation. *United States v. Tom*, 494 F.3d 1277, 1279 (10th Cir. 2007). The defendant was charged and convicted of second-degree murder, and sentenced to seventy months imprisonment and three years of supervised release, which the court found to be adequate to deter him from reoffending. *Id.* Ms. Deegan was sentenced to almost double that defendant's sentence for the same type of crime and with the same type of criminal history. *Deegan*, 605 F.3d at 656 (Bright, J., dissenting). Both the sentence in *Tom* and the sentence imposed upon Ms. Deegan are harsher penalties than those imposed upon defendants who commit similar crimes but are prosecuted in a state forum. *Deegan*, 605 F.3d at 656 (Bright, J., dissenting); *Tom*, 494 F.3d at 1279.

The court in *Tom* found the defendant's sentence was harsh enough "to afford adequate deterrence to criminal conduct," and "to protect the public from further crimes of the defendant." 18 U.S.C. § 3553(a)(2)(B)-(C) (2014); *Tom*, 494 F.3d at 1279. Ms. Deegan "ha[d] [ ] in the nine years between the act and being brought to trial" "gotten her life together, been a good mother, and not been a risk to the community." *Deegan*, 605 F.3d at 654 (Bright, J., dissenting) (quoting Resnick). "[I]ncarcerating Ms. Deegan would not likely deter other individuals from committing neonaticide," "[she] presents an extremely low risk that she would commit any further conduct which was criminal in nature." *Id.* at 656.

The Eighth Circuit Court says that "the need to avoid unwarranted sentencing disparities among defendants . . . refers only to disparities among federal defendants." *Id.* at 635 (majority opinion). However, the federal sentencing commission can locate no other neonaticide cases. *Id.* at 656 (Bright, J., dissenting). Therefore, federal cases that involve a defendant who committed the same type of crime with the same type of criminal history do not exist for the purpose of sentencing comparisons. *Id.* Thus, in order to avoid disparities it is necessary to consider sentencing of neonaticide defendants in state court. *Id.*

Sentencing disparities also exist throughout state courts. However, sentences imposed for neonaticide cases are more lenient in state courts. *See State v. Buffin*, 511 So. 2d 1255, 1256 (La. App. 2d Cir. 1987) (convicted of negligent homicide, sentenced to two years hard labor). Although there are neonaticide convictions for first-degree murder in state court, this harsh of a charge is rarely brought upon neonaticide defendants, and they are often convicted of a lesser charge ultimately. *Holt v. State*, 117 N.W.2d 626, 628 (Wis. 1962) (convicted of first-degree murder); *Compare State v. Osmus*, 276 P.2d 469, 470 (Wyo. 1954) (charged with first-degree murder, convicted of manslaughter).

The sentencing record reveals a neonaticide crime committed off the Indian Reservation by a college student at North Dakota State University "who gave birth to a child, wrapped the baby up, stuck the child under a bed, and then ultimately disposed of the child. . . ." *Deegan*, 605 F.3d at 656 (Bright, J., dissenting). The NDSU student was charged under the state laws of North Dakota and sentenced to three years' probation. *Id.*

Ms. Deegan's sentence promotes disrespect for the law and judicial system "when compared to the lenient [three year probation] sentence [given to] a woman off the reservation for this special crime of neonaticide." *Id.* at 657. The NDSU case and Ms. Deegan's case involved "very similar kinds of situations." *Id.* at 656. Similar to the student, Ms. Deegan gave birth to the baby, wrapped him up in a blanket, put him in a suitcase, and ultimately disposed of the child in a ditch near her home. *Id.* "On this record, there is no just reason for the sentencing disparity between these two women." *Id.* at 662. This inconsistency occurred because Ms. Deegan's crime arose on the reservation and was heard in federal court. *Id.* Therefore, this Court should review the question de novo, and reverse and remand for resentencing because sentencing for neonaticide cases should be consistent and lenient throughout the courts to promote respect for the law.

II. A DEPARTURE FROM THE SENTENCING GUIDELINES AND CONSIDERATION OF NON-STATUTORY MITIGATING CIRCUMSTANCES IS WARRANTED BECAUSE MS. DEEGAN'S CONDUCT FELL OUTSIDE THE "HEARTLAND" OF TYPICAL CASES.

The sentencing guidelines were established by Congress for "sentencing similarly situated offenders in order to provide for greater certainty and uniformity in sentencing." *Id.* at 645. The sentencing guidelines create a "heartland" of typical cases. *Koon v. United States,* 518 U.S. 81, 116 (1996). The "heartland" of typical cases receives a sentence "within the range of applicable guidelines," "but when the court finds an atypical case, one to which a particular guideline linguistically applies but where conduct significantly differs from the norm, the court may consider whether a departure is warranted" by considering non-statutory mitigating circumstances. *Id.* at 92.

A letter from the Sentencing Commission "reflects that [they] were unable to locate another case of neonaticide besides the present case," and "*Rita* established that no neonaticide case was considered in developing the guidelines." *Deegan,* 605 F.3d at 649 (Bright, J., dissenting); *Rita v. United States,* 551 U.S. 338, 348 (2007). Ms. Deegan's crime of neonaticide "falls outside the 'heartland' for second-degree murder sentences," and non-statutory mitigating circumstances may be considered to determine if a departure is warranted. *Deegan,* 605 F.3d at 648, 649 (Bright, J., dissenting).

This Court has concluded that "the Eighth and Fourteenth Amendments require that the sentence . . . not be precluded from considering, as a mitigating circumstance, any aspect of a defendant's character or record and any of the circumstances of the offense. . . ." *Lockett v. Ohio*, 438 U.S. 586, 604 (1978); *See also United States v. Oldani,* CRIM.A. 3:09-00010, 2009 WL 1770116, at *6 (S.D.W. Va. June 16, 2009) (considering military service); *See also Eddings v. Oklahoma*, 455 U.S. 104, 115 (1982) (considering evidence of a difficult family history). Non-statutory mitigating circumstances can be anything related to the defendant's background, character, or experiences. *Koon,* 518 U.S. at 92; Sharon Turlington, *Completely Unguided Discretion: Admitting Non-Statutory Aggravating and Non-Statutory Mitigating Evidence in Capital Sentencing Trials,* 6 Pierce L. Rev. 469, 480 (2008). The Eighth Circuit has previously considered the cultural difference of Native Americans as a non-statutory mitigating circumstance in federal sentencing decisions. *United States v. Decora,* 177 F.3d 676, 677 (8th Cir. 1999) (departing based on the adversity the defendant faces on the reservation); *See also United States v. One Star,* 9 F.3d 60, 61 (8th Cir. 1993) (departing based on the unusual life on an Indian reservation). Therefore, this Court should review the question de novo, and reverse and remand for resentencing because departure from the sentencing guidelines and consideration of non-statutory mitigating circumstances is warranted for neonaticide cases. *Deegan,* 605 F.3d at 649 (Bright, J., dissenting).

6

A. Historical and intergenerational trauma is a non-statutory mitigating circumstance that should be taken into consideration when sentencing Native American women.

Dr. Maria Yellow Horse Brave Heart defined historical and intergenerational trauma as "the traumatic effect of certain events in Native American history [that] is internalized and passed on to later generations through epigenetic transfer, among other means." *United States. v. Woody,* CR-13-08093-001-PCT, 2015 WL 1530552, at *6 (D. Ariz. Apr. 6, 2015). "The cumulative psychological wounding resulting from colonization, relocation, and other historical traumas can create a sense of hopelessness or lack of control that permeates Native American culture." *Id.* "These types of traumas increase individuals' risks of experiencing traumatic stressors while also decreasing their opportunities to draw on the strengths of their culture, family, or community for social and emotional support." Delores Subia BigFoot, Janie Braden, *Adapting Evidence-Based Treatments for Use with American Indian and Native Alaskan Children and Youth,* 28 Child. L. Prac. 76 (2009). Native Americans experienced a disparate amount of events that created risk for trauma reactions. *Id.* Historical and intergenerational trauma should be considered as a mitigating circumstance because of "the evolving standards of decency that mark the progress of a maturing society." *Trop v. Dulles,* 356 U.S. 86, 101 (1958). "The standard itself remains the same, but its applicability must change as the basic mores of society change." *Graham v. Florida,* 560 U.S. 48, 58 (2010).

The U.S. government has failed to provide Native Americans equal legal protection. *Deegan,* 605 F.3d at 662 (Bright, J., dissenting) (quoting the appendix to the dissent). During the 1790s "Indians possessed the land, and whites wanted the land," thus "policies, treaties, courts, and other federal agencies embarked upon an array of attempts to address the 'problem' " by "strip[ping] [the Indians] of their sovereignty, their lands, and their cultures." Ann Piccard, *Death by Boarding School: "The Last Acceptable Racism" and the United States' Genocide of Native Americans,* 49 Gonz. L. Rev. 137, 151–52 (2014) (quoting Dr. Brave Heart). "In 1879 the federal government undertook to destroy all Native American culture by sending Indian children, forcibly when necessary, to day or boarding school," and it "forbade the speaking of Indian languages, prohibited the conduct of traditional religious activities, outlawed traditional government, and made Indian people ashamed of who they were." *Id.* "The trauma of shame, fear and anger has passed from one generation to the next, and manifests itself in the rampant alcoholism, drug abuse, and domestic violence that plague Indian country." *Id.* These events led to female inferiority, which slowly decreased the power of Native American women and began the abuse of them and their children. Woolman & Deer, *supra,* at 951. Violence against Native American women is a pervasive problem. *Deegan,* 605 F.3d at 663 (Bright, J., dissenting) (quoting the appendix to the dissent). They are more likely to be subject to sexual violence and physical violence than other women in the U.S. *Id.* The basic mores of society have progressed to recognize the unjust treatment that Native Americans received throughout history. *Graham*, 560 U.S. at 58; *See generally* Piccard, *supra,* 151. The evolving standards of decency support the recognition of historical and intergenerational trauma as a mitigating circumstance when sentencing Native American defendants. *Id.*

"The cultural deprivations and discriminations of American Indian people merely because of [their] heritage has contributed to the psychological deficits that [Ms. Deegan] was unable to overcome." *Deegan,* 605 F.3d at 662 (Bright, J., dissenting) (quoting sisters letter). Ms. Deegan's sister described the penetrating effects as "depression, anxiety, and post-traumatic stress disorder" that historical and intergenerational trauma created for their family. *Id.* She depicted their childhood home as a warzone: there were "some good times of laughter and love, but one never knew when an attack of rage and violence was about to happen." *Id.* "If the violence against Ms. Deegan had been stopped . . . if she had been given moral and societal assistance in raising the three children in her family, this crime of neonaticide might never have occurred." *Id.* at 664 (Bright, J., dissenting) (quoting the appendix to the dissent). Therefore, this Court should review the question de novo, and reverse and remand for resentencing because the non-statutory mitigating circumstance of historical and intergenerational trauma should be taken into consideration when sentencing Native American women.

CONCLUSION

For the foregoing reasons, it is respectfully requested that the judgment of the United States Court of Appeals for the Eighth Circuit be reversed and remanded for resentencing.

Dated: APRIL 12th, 2015 6:00 PM

Respectfully Submitted,

_____

767
FIRST ASST. FEDERAL
PUBLIC DEFENDER
1401 61ST ST. S.
GULFPORT, FL 33707
(727) 555-0000
Counsel for Petitioner

CERTIFICATE OF SERVICE

I certify that a true copy of this document will be delivered via email to opposing counsel on April 12th, 2015 at 8:00 PM.

_____

767

INTEGRITY CERTIFICATION

I certify that I have complied with the word count restriction on this brief and have followed the collaboration and academic integrity requirements for this brief.

_____

767

No. 15-1234

IN THE
UNITED STATES SUPREME COURT

DANA DEEGAN,

Petitioner

v.

UNITED STATES OF AMERICA,

Respondent

On Appeal From The United States Court of Appeals

For The Eighth Circuit

#762, Esq.,

Counsel for Respondent

SUCOL

1401 61st St. S.

Gulfport, FL 33707

(727) 562-7883

TABLE OF CONTENTS

TABLE OF AUTHORITIES

CASES

STATUTES

OTHER AUTHORITIES

STATEMENT OF JURISDICTION

The United States Court of Appeals for the Eighth Circuit affirmed the United States District Court for the District of North Dakota's sentence of Dana Deegan on May 25, 2010. The jurisdiction of this Court is invoked pursuant to

28 U.S.C.A. § 1254(1) (West 2014).

STATEMENT OF THE QUESTIONS PRESENTED

I.

Whether neonaticide is second-degree murder

II.

Whether the Eight Circuit correctly declined to consider historical trauma as a mitigating factor in Dana Deegan's sentencing

STATEMENT OF THE CASE

A. Statement of the Facts

Dana Deegan, a member of the Three Affiliated Tribes in North Dakota, secretly gave birth to her fourth child in the bathroom of her mobile home on the Fort Berthold Indian Reservation on October 20, 1998. *United States* v. *Deegan*, 605 F.3d 625, 627 (8th Cir. 2010). Ms. Deegan cleaned, dressed, fed her newborn child, placed him in a basket and left the house, to which she returned two weeks later. *Id.* Upon her return to finding the baby in the basket dead, she put its body in a suitcase and placed it in a ditch near her home. On May 18, 2008, after entering a plea agreement with the government, Ms. Deegan was sentenced to 121 months imprisonment for the second-degree murder of her infant child by the United States District Court for the District of North Dakota. *Id.* at 628. Ms. Deegan acknowledged that she "unlawfully and with malice aforethought caused his death by leaving him alone in the house for approximately two weeks." *Id.* On appeal, Ms. Deegan argued that her sentence for second-degree murder was unreasonable and that the trial court "committed both procedural and substantive errors when imposing sentence," by failing to take into account her historical trauma as a mitigating factor in her sentencing. *Id.* at 629. The United States Court of Appeals for the Eighth Circuit affirmed the trial court's judgment, finding that it "adequately explained its chosen sentence of 121 months' imprisonment" in consideration of the valid mitigating factors and that the sentence was reasonable. *Id.* at 625. This appeal soon followed to challenge the judgment of the Eighth Circuit.

B. Standard of Review

When reviewing both issues, the Court should apply the *de novo* standard. The *de novo* standard should be applied because the issues presented involve the construction and application of federal statutes, making them questions of law, and "Questions of law are reviewed *de novo* . . . [the] standard applies to any legal decision reviewed on appeal." Fed. Ct. App. Manual § 31:3 (6th ed. 2014). Indeed, other courts considering issues of federal statutory construction and interpretation have applied the *de novo* standard. *United States* v. *McVeigh*, 153 F.3d 1166, 1193 (10th Cir. 1998) (identifying questions of statutory elements as questions of law reviewed *de novo*). In light of the *de novo* standard, this Court should give some deference to the lower court and should thus affirm the judgment of the Eighth Circuit.

ARGUMENT

> THIS COURT SHOULD AFFIRM THE EIGHTH CIRCUIT'S DECISION AFFIRMING DANA DEEGAN'S SENTENCE BECAUSE NEONATICIDE IS SECOND-DEGREE MURDER AND THE EIGHTH CIRCUIT CORRECTLY DECLINED TO CONSIDER HISTORICAL TRAUMA AS A MITIGATING FACTOR IN HER SENTENCING.

The unlawful killing of a human being with malice aforethought, while lacking premeditation, is second-degree murder. 18 U.S.C.A. § 1111 (West 2014). Neonaticide is "the killing of a newborn infant on the first day of life," Dr. Phillip Resnick, who is considered the leading expert on neonaticide, explained at Ms. Deegan's sentencing hearing. *Deegan*, 605 F.3d at 642. Ms. Deegan, after delivering her fourth child alone in the bathtub of her mobile home, placed her child in a basket, abandoned it for two weeks, and returned to find the body, which she then placed in a suitcase and deposited in a nearby ditch. *Id.* at 627. Dr. Resnick further explained "as is common in cases of neonaticide, Ms. Deegan neither planned for the killing of the infant or for the caring of the infant." *Id.* at 644. Dr. Resnick's testimony shows that Ms. Deegan lacked premeditation in the killing of her infant child. In stating that she had no intention to care for her newborn child, Dr. Resnick showed that Ms. Deegan acted with malice aforethought.

"[M]alice aforethought may be established by evidence of conduct which is reckless and wanton and a gross deviation from a reasonable standard of care, of such a nature that a jury is warranted in inferring that [the] defendant was aware of a serious risk of death or serious bodily harm." *United States* v. *Williams*, 342 F.3d 350, 356 (4th Cir. 2003). Ms. Deegan's act of leaving her newborn infant unattended for two weeks was a reckless and wanton deviation from the reasonable standard of care expected of a mother, and she was well aware of the serious risk of death to the infant if abandoned. According to Dr. Resnick, the aversion to both caring for a newborn and killing it is common behavior in neonaticide cases, not just in Ms. Deegan's case. In *State* v. *Hopfer*, 112 Ohio App. 3d 521, 558 (Ohio Ct. App. 1996), the defendant delivered her infant daughter in her bathroom, after which she disposed of it in plastic bags, bundled it in blankets, and deposited it in a nearby garbage truck, where it was found four days later. The discarding of the body close to home relates to Ms. Deegan's act of placing the suitcase containing the dead child in a nearby ditch, conduct that "is not what one would expect from someone who is planning to take another's life." *Deegan*, 605 F.3d at 644 (Bright, J., dissenting). Due to the common lack of premeditation, along with the presence of malice aforethought in neonaticide cases, neonaticide is second-degree murder, and this Court should affirm the judgment of the Eighth Circuit.

In imposing a sentence, the court need consider "the nature and circumstances of the offense and the history and characteristics of the defendant" along with making allowances for the judgment to "reflect the seriousness of the offense . . . promote respect for the law . . . provide just punishment for the offense . . . afford adequate deterrence to criminal conduct . . . [and] protect the public from further crimes of the defendant." 18 U.S.C.A. § 3553(a) (West 2014). Ms. Deegan argued in the Eighth Circuit that the trial court "failed on the record to engage in any meaningful discussion whatsoever of the § 3553(a) factors," due to its refusal to consider her historical trauma as a mitigating factor. *Deegan*, 605 F.3d at 629.-Historical trauma can be defined as "cumulative emotional and psychological wounding across generations." Ann Piccard, *Death By Boarding School: "The Last Acceptable Racism" and the United States' Genocide of Native Americans*, 49 Gonz. L. Rev. 137, 162 (2013). No federal court has thus far mentioned or incorporated historical trauma into law. Though the federal statute for imposing a sentence states that trial courts should consider the "history and characteristics" of the defendant, historical trauma itself is not a mitigating factor. § 3553(a). As a Native American woman and a child of physical and sexual abuse, Ms. Deegan is arguing that the Eighth Circuit failed to consider her historical trauma, aside from her agonizing life since childhood, as a mitigating factor in the imposition of her sentence. Though this Court reviews this case *de novo,* it should give deference to the Eighth Circuit's judgment for correctly declining to consider historical trauma as a mitigating factor. The correct interpretation and reasonable consideration of the § 3553(a) mitigating factors, along with the fact that there is no mention or incorporation of historical trauma as a valid factor in federal law, shows that the Eighth Circuit was correct in declining to consider historical trauma as a mitigating factor and that this Court should affirm its judgment.

A. Ms. Deegan's Conviction Should Be Upheld Because Neonaticide Is Comprised Of The Requisite Malice Aforethought, General Intent And Lack Of Premeditation To Constitute Second-Degree Murder.

Upon consideration of all valid mitigating factors, including neonaticide, a charge for second-degree murder is appropriate in the killing of a newborn infant. *State* v. *Heiges*, 779 N.W.2d 904, 915 (Minn. Ct. App. 2010) (defendant convicted of second-degree murder for neonaticide and sentenced to 299 months in prison.) "A charge of first-degree murder requires proof of premeditation, while second-degree murder requires malice aforethought." *United States v. Tom*, 494 F.3d 1277, 1281 n.2 (10th Cir. 2007) (clarifying why defendant should not receive first-degree murder charge for crime within Indian country). Neonaticide is murder that lacks premeditation yet contains the malice aforethought required to be categorized as second-degree murder. Ms. Deegan's mental state surrounding the birth and death of her fourth child provides for both the requisite malice aforethought and lack of premeditation to constitute second-degree murder. "[S]econd-degree murder requires only a general intent, meaning the defendant 'is aware that the result is practically certain to follow from his conduct, whatever his desire may be as to that result.'" *United States* v. *Serawop*, 410 F.3d 656, 663 (10th Cir. 2005) (distinguishing specific from general intent in order to separate first and second-degree murder requirements). Dr. Resnick himself stated that Ms. Deegan's mental state is common in neonaticide cases, where the mother neither plans to kill the child nor to care for it following its birth. *Deegan*, 605 F.3d at 644. The lack of a want to care for the child following its birth shows that Ms. Deegan had the requisite malice aforethought and general intent to amount to second-degree murder. She knew that she had no intention of caring for the child, and she was fully aware that it would die if she left it unattended for two weeks. Ms. Deegan's response to the questioning of why she abandoned her child, that she "didn't want to be there anymore . . . as a mother," shows the presence of general intent, that she left her newborn infant alone in a basket for two weeks and was aware that by doing so, the baby would die. *Id.* at 642 (Bright, J., dissenting).

VII

Furthermore, Ms. Deegan's disagreement with her sentence for second-degree murder is unwarranted, due to the fact that she references non-federal cases for support. *Deegan*, 605 F.3d at 635. Even if such case comparison had been permitted, both *State* v. *Heiges* and *State* v. *Hopfer* provide for much harsher sentences, 299 months and fifteen years respectively. Additionally, *Lewis* v. *United States*, 118 S. Ct. 1135, 1135 (U.S. 1998), provides a defendant who was originally charged of first-degree murder of a child under state law, then was later convicted of second-degree murder on appeal due to the crime occurring on an Army base, which is also under federal jurisdiction. In spite of the fact that this Court reviews this issue *de novo*, it should give deference to the Eighth Circuit for correctly determining neonaticide as second-degree murder. Because she possessed malice aforethought, general intent and lacked premeditation in the killing of her newborn child, characteristics that are common in neonaticide cases, Ms. Deegan was correctly convicted of second-degree murder, and this Court should thus affirm the Eighth Circuit's judgment.

B. Ms. Deegan's Conviction Should Be Upheld Because Historical Trauma Is An Inapplicable And Invalid Factor In The Imposition Of A Sentence.

"Accordingly, after giving both parties an opportunity to argue for whatever sentence they deem appropriate, the district judge should then consider all of the § 3553(a) factors ... he must adequately explain the chosen sentence to allow for meaningful appellate review and to promote the perception of fair sentencing." *Gall* v. *United States*, 128 S. Ct. 586, 596–597 (U.S. 2007) (identifying the need for consideration of § 3553(a) factors upon calculating Guidelines range). Ms. Deegan is arguing that her historical trauma should have been considered as a mitigating factor under § 3553(a). Though the factors include "the history and characteristics of the defendant," § 3553(a)(1), the accumulation of emotional and psychological torment throughout generations is not a factor, nor should it be, as it has never been incorporated in the imposition of a sentence. Piccard, *supra*, at 137. The mere speculation of the "emotional and psychological wounding" having passed down to Ms. Deegan from her ancestors is unwarranted. Her argument that historical trauma should have been considered by the lower courts is an attempt to embellish her harrowing life thus far in order to alleviate her sentence. The oppression experienced by Ms. Deegan's Native American ancestors is not an attributable part of her own "history and characteristics," nor should it serve to diminish the severity of her crime.

As for the valid mitigating factors, the Eighth Circuit took into consideration Ms. Deegan's personal history of physical and sexual abuse. "Deegan also presented evidence of her troubled personal history and family

VIII

circumstances. . . . Deegan's mitigating evidence convinced the district court that a sentence of more than ten years . . . was greater than necessary to satisfy the statutory purposes of sentencing." *Deegan*, 605 F.3d at 634. The furthest extent that this Court should consider Ms. Deegan's "history and characteristics" is to take into account the events that may have contributed to the death of her infant child, namely, her history of physical and sexual abuse. An appellate court does not "require a district court to provide a mechanical recitation of the § 3553(a) factors when determining a sentence . . . it simply must be clear from the record that the court actually considered the § 3553(a) factors in determining the sentence." *United States* v. *Feemster*, 572 F.3d 455, 461 (8th Cir. 2009) (identifying the importance of actual consideration of § 3553(a) factors over simple recital). Though a mechanical recitation of the mitigating factors was not required, the Eighth Circuit thoroughly reviewed the applicable mitigating factors in Ms. Deegan's history, recognizing the trial court's acknowledgment that "Deegan's life had not been 'easy,' . . . plagued with physical abuse and sexual abuse," and that "it had 'real compassion for her and her family and what she had gone through.'" *Deegan*, 605 F.3d at 630. However, the Eighth Circuit was correct in not considering Ms. Deegan's historical trauma, as it does not apply as a mitigating factor in the terms of her "history and characteristics" nor as attributable to the murder of her infant child. It is clear from the Eighth Circuit's majority opinion that all of the valid mitigating factors in Ms. Deegan's case were considered and correctly applied.

It is important to reflect on how the Eighth Circuit examined Ms. Deegan's personal history in comparison to how other courts have when discussing mitigating factors. A sentencing court may give little consideration to a defendant's personal history and characteristics when examining the mitigating factors and applying them against the aggravating circumstances of their crime. *Eddings* v. *Oklahoma*, 102 S. Ct. 869, 882–883 (U.S. 1982) (allowing little consideration of defendant's personal history when applied evenly against aggravating circumstances). Seeing as historical trauma is separate from personal history and not a valid mitigating factor, the Eighth Circuit was correct in not considering it. However, Ms. Deegan's personal history of physical and sexual abuse was thoroughly considered and correctly applied against the aggravating circumstances of her crime, affirming a reasonable sentence. In *State* v. *Hopfer*, the defendant's "excellent academic record, lack of criminal history, clean disciplinary record, and previously stable family life" was considered, and previously stable family life" was considered, and her sentence to fifteen years imprisonment for the neonaticide of her daughter was found reasonable. *Hopfer*, 112 Ohio App. 3d at 536. In *State* v. *Heiges*, the defendant's 299-month sentence for the second-degree murder of her newborn child was also found reasonable, in light of the domestic abuse she endured, her "mental condition at the time of the offense, and her amenability to probation." *Heiges*, 779 N.W.2d at 915. In this case, Ms. Deegan "has been a law-abiding citizen her entire life, has no juvenile offenses, no adult offenses, [is] not an alcohol or drug abuser . . . [and] has shown considerable remorse for what she has done." *Deegan*, 605 F.3d at 654 (Bright, J., dissenting). In comparing these similar neonaticide cases to Ms. Deegan's case, it is clear that her personal history has been considered and she has received a more reasonable sentence than others have. "[T]he state courts must consider all relevant mitigating evidence and weigh it against the evidence of the aggravating circumstances. We [the Supreme Court] do not weigh the evidence for them." *Eddings,* 102 S. Ct. at 878. As this issue is reviewed *de novo,* this Court should give deference to the Eighth Circuit for correctly declining to consider historical trauma as a mitigating factor. The sentencing court clearly considered Ms. Deegan's traumatic upbringing and applied it against the aggravating circumstances of her crime much more reasonably than other courts have. The determination of valid mitigating factors is a responsibility given to the courts below, and they were correct in not considering Ms. Deegan's historical trauma. This Court should affirm the Eighth Circuit's judgment, since it correctly declined to consider Ms. Deegan's historical trauma as a valid mitigating factor in her sentencing.

CONCLUSION

The judgment of the Eighth Circuit should be affirmed, since neonaticide is second-degree murder and historical trauma was correctly not considered as a mitigating factor in Ms. Deegan's sentencing.

Dated: April 12, 2015.

Respectfully Submitted,

<u># 762, Esq.</u>
Counsel for Petitioner, United States of America
SUCOL
1401 61st St. S.
Gulfport, FL 33707
(727) 562-7883

X

CERTIFICATE OF SERVICE

I certify that a copy of this document was emailed to the person listed below on April 12, 2015.

Respectfully Submitted,

#***, Esq.

Counsel for Petitioner, United States of America

SUCOL

1401 61st St. S.

Gulfport, FL 33707

(727) 562-7883

I certify that I have complied with the word count restriction on this brief and have followed the collaboration and academic integrity requirements for this brief.

#762

INDEX

References are to Pages